AUTHOR HUNTING

BY THE SAME AUTHOR

Fiction

CAVIARE
VALENTINE
BITTERSWEET
DOUBLE LIFE
EVERY WIFE
FAIR EXCHANGE
HASTY MARRIAGE
VAIN PURSUIT

———

THE COAST OF PLEASURE:
   An Unconventional Guide
   to the French Riviera

———

MEMORIES OF A MISSPENT YOUTH,
   1872-1896. With an Introduction
   by Max Beerbohm

MEMORIES OF YEARS SPENT
MAINLY IN PUBLISHING
1897–1925

AUTHOR
HUNTING
BY
AN
OLD
LITERARY
SPORTS
MAN
GRANT
RICHARDS

ILLUSTRATED

PUBLISHED IN NEW YORK
BY COWARD-McCANN, INC.
1934

Text Composition in Janson by S. A. Jacobs, New York
Printed and made in the United States
of America

To Harry Clifford, to J. D. Hughes, to Fred Richardson, to David Roy and to J. G. Wilson, five good booksellers who love literature and are my friends, I dedicate these memories of happy and unhappy years.

*". . . You should call your book The Tragedy of a
Publisher who Allowed Himself to Fall in Love with
Literature. The publisher who does that, like the picture
dealer who likes pictures or the schoolmistress who gets
fond of her pupils, is foredoomed. A certain connoisseurship
in the public taste is indispensable; but the slightest uncom-
mercial bias in choosing between, say, Bridges' 'Testament
of Beauty' and a telephone directory, is fatal . . ."*
BERNARD SHAW, in a letter to the Author,
23rd May 1934.

CONTENTS

CONTENTS

LIST OF ILLUSTRATIONS

PREFACE

MY first thanks are due to Bernard Shaw. He has not only given me permission to make use of the many letters which appear in my narrative but he has also read some of my proofs and, by correction and occasional addition, has saved me from many errors. He has also allowed the use of the brief note which appears on a preceding page. To Theodore Dreiser also I am grateful for permission to quote as fully as I have done from his letters to me and from his writings. I could hardly have written of him at all without that permission. Max Beerbohm has allowed me to use two of his early caricatures; William Nicholson and Mrs. Kinnell (to whom it belongs) have permitted the reproduction of the Nicholson portrait of "Max"; Henry Lamb has allowed the reproduction of the drawing of me which he made at Cadgwith in 1909—by the way, I was actually his first patron, which is in itself something to be proud of! To H. G. Wells also I owe thanks for permissions; to the Executors of Sir William Orpen; to E. S. P. Haynes, who has helped by reading some of my proofs and from his Beerbohm collection; to E. V. Lucas; to Alvin Langdon Coburn; to Thomas Burke; to Ernest Bramah; to William Heinemann Limited for a Swinburne passage; to A. R. Orage for waiving his copyright in the John Bull "Max" caricature; to F. H. Evans; to Miss Hester Frood; and to Ilbery Lynch. In fact, this book about my friends could never have been written without my friends' assistance. And I must thank John Wiles for his index.

I am very conscious of the error of scale in this book. I started off gaily enough in the hope that I should be able within its covers to deal with the years from 1896 to 1925 in the same way that I dealt with the years 1872 to 1896 in *Memories of a Misspent Youth*. But the thing couldn't be done—by me at any rate. There were so many men and affairs I wished to write about. Take G. B. S., for instance. The story of the publication of the first books ran away with me. I had, I felt, too valuable a mass of material to use only a little of it or to compress it. I had published A. E. Housman's *A Shropshire Lad* and his *Last Poems*. I did not wish to confine myself to a bare statement of that fact. The Dreiser episode, too. It has significance in the history of American letters. Certain figures had to stand out and to occupy what may seem to some a disproportionate amount of space. I couldn't help it. To have done otherwise than I have done would have been to produce a publisher's catalogue. Of course, I have a mass of unused material in my head—some day, if I am encouraged, I may try again. The Tragedy of a Publisher who Fell in Love with Literature is not fully told.

GRANT RICHARDS.

AUTHOR HUNTING

I

THE EASY THRESHOLD

M<small>R.</small> GRANT RICHARDS begs to announce that he will <small>COMMENCE BUSINESS as a PUB-LISHER</small> on January 1, 1897, at No. 9, H<small>ENRIETTA-STREET</small>, Covent-garden, W.C. (*Athenœum*, Dec. 5, 1896).

H<small>ENRIETTA</small> STREET, Covent Garden, is a street largely given over to the sale of vegetables and of books and periodicals. In my mind it is a dull street, a street without interesting history except that Chapman and Hall occupy Number 11, the staircase of which must often have creaked under the footsteps of Charles Dickens, Anthony Trollope, George Meredith, John Morley and Frank Harris, and that at Number 14 Williams and Norgate, the publishers of the *Synthetic Philosophy*, used to receive what must have been the frightening visits of Herbert Spencer. It is a street which has always given me the impression of being correct and conventional, save for that brief space of time when Robert Standish Sievier edited the *Winning Post*, that flower of pre-War journalism, at Number 30 (now occupied by Mr. Peter Davies) and by his occasional presence lent it a certain naughtiness, a slight flavour of worldliness. Yes—and as I pass these proofs for press I recollect that Frank Harris, in his decline, edited one of his "society" weeklies somewhere in the street. That fact must often have given rise to a certain liveliness. . . .

It was in Henrietta Street at midnight on December 31, 1896, that the passer-by might have heard, and been surprised at hearing, the strains of music, the noise of a hired piano to be exact, and of young voices raised in song, proceeding from Number 9, a house whose façade certainly did not suggest that it could in any way be dedicated to revelry. The passer-by no doubt wondered. And he was right to wonder. I have often wondered myself. How could I have brought myself to greet that momentous New Year in my brand-new office with a party, my virgin office, my office which was to be devoted to serious affairs? How could I have been both so high-spirited and so youthful as to be entertaining my friends with the strains of the aforesaid piano, the opportunity of dancing, much indifferent drink—rum punch and the like—and even more indifferent food, when, according to the Victorian tradition—and the Good Queen was alive in those days—I should have been darting nervously about the premises with a duster, measuring racks and shelves and hanging up pictures, generally preparing for the arrival of my staff at nine o'clock and tuning my soul against that eventful moment when, figuratively, we should take down the shutters and the business of Grant Richards: Publisher would be open to the world, and I myself, aged twenty-four years, two months and ten days, would be at the receipt of custom, all eager for authors and manuscripts?

That, no doubt, is the way in which the thing ought to have been done. That it was not, was, I fear, due to the fact that I was not grown up. And my staff was not grown up either. It consisted of my cousin, Jerrard Grant Allen, not long out of Charterhouse and younger than I by six years, and one errand-boy who was, I fancy, about as youthful as you could catch a working boy in those days.

It was not a bad party. That I do well remember. I hope that those who both survive and remember look back on it with kindness. No one became even a little intoxicated; by modern standards it would have been considered dullness itself; it was all very proper and conventional. The only person who had any cause for excitement was a commissionaire who arrived by what seemed to be a happy chance at the exact stroke of midnight and found, instead of a sleepy caretaker, a gathering in which youth and beauty were unusually conspicuous, for it included two of W. J. Stillman's beautiful daughters, and Dr. George Bird's grand-daughter, Elsie York, who, later, became the mother of Eve Kirk, the talented painter whose work helps, with that of Mary Cassatt, Berthe Morisot, Mrs. Swynnerton, Ethel Walker and Miss Hudson, to prove that it is not necessary to be a man to be a painter.

To return to the commissionaire: he brought with him a telegram from Rome, a telegram from the lady who had three or four times refused me in the year that was passing, but who had never, so to speak, administered the final blow with sufficient dexterity. In consequence I had continued to hope. In that telegram she wished me all success in my great adventure. It wanted only these few words to crown my joy. . . . Surely she would not have telegraphed if she were not relenting, thinking better of her oft-expressed decision. Now, thirty-seven years later, I had better set it down that that telegram of hers meant exactly what it said and nothing more. All the same, I do think that when young women return to sanity and construct a fresh code of morals and manners for their own governance they should be very definite about such things. To a young man aged twenty-four one girl is much the same as another, as long, of course, as she possesses the kind of good looks that appeals to him, is the right colour, shape, height and so on. The sooner therefore it is hammered into his head that he may sigh and sigh after one particular fair year after year and yet never win her hand, the better it will be for him and the sooner he will be able to devote his energies to his proper business and his hours of dalliance to other and kinder damsels. Anthony Trollope thought the same: "A lady must be very decisive—very, if she means to have her 'no' taken at its full meaning".

Well, we danced, or, I should say, as I am not a dancing man, my guests danced the New Year in and I and my cousin were certainly none the worse for it when, punctually at nine o'clock, in spite of the late hour at which our party had

3

dispersed, we unlocked the door, welcomed our errand-boy and disposed ourselves for business.

Of course a good deal of spade-work had already been done.

I had conceived this idea of "commencing publisher" early in the previous summer. Having had experience in the wholesale bookselling house of Hamilton, Adams and Company,[1] a firm that a little before I left it had amalgamated with Simpkin, Marshall and Company—and having, in the seven years that I had served W. T. Stead in all sorts of capacities in the office of his *Review of Reviews*, examined practically every book that issued from the ordinary publishers, and having, too, largely through Grant Allen, my uncle by marriage, met half the literary men of the period, it almost seemed that, loving books as I did, it would be squandering my mercies if I did not go into publishing. I was satisfied that I should never myself be an author, and publishing, introducing authors to the world, seemed the next best thing to writing. There was however the money difficulty to overcome. Capital is not generally at the disposal of the son of a retired Oxford don. However, Grant Allen believed in me and promised that, other things being equal, I should have all his books to publish. That weighed with my father. After some persuasion he was induced to arrange with his bank to lend me five hundred pounds on his guarantee; another uncle, T. W. Jerrard, a successful warehouseman in Wood Street and a man on whose kindness and encouragement I could always depend, promised me two hundred pounds; and Grant Allen himself was prepared to put up seven hundred and fifty pounds—he would have found more but, not long before, John Lane, who had published his *The British Barbarians* and *The Woman Who Did*, had borrowed a thousand of him. Lane's business was not old and he was beginning to find that a nest of singing birds, like a racing stable, required keeping up. One day,

[1] As had my cousin.

4

therefore, he telegraphed to my uncle that he must see him at once. Grant Allen, always ready to help, went up to town at once, had Lane's difficulties explained to him and, although he was very far indeed from being a rich man, went to his bank, arranged the loan and handed over the sum required to the founder of The Bodley Head. He had no cause to regret it.

So fourteen hundred pounds was the capital on which I could rely; it was not a great deal of money, but to my sanguine mind it was enough to begin with. No one warned me, as I should have been warned, that almost certainly I should find it insufficient. I was sanguine; Grant Allen was sanguine; he had the liveliest belief in my nose for a good book or a coming author (had I not introduced him to the work of H. G. Wells and Richard Le Gallienne?); my other friends extended to me a very cordial blessing. Even the wise Edward Clodd, secretary to the London Joint Stock Bank as well as a writer of repute, thought my venture might succeed. The nervous J. S. Cotton, who had been for so many years editor of the *Academy*, saw no reason why I should not turn my taste and enthusiasm into money. Another uncle by marriage, John Leman Whelen, the manager of the National Bank, the banker of my father and of Grant Allen, was all for the venture, although he knew nothing about books and had been one of the founders of the Young Men's Christian Association. He was a dear, upright fellow, but he was too much of an optimist for those whom he liked and who had won his confidence.

So much having been arranged, I departed for my yearly fortnight's holiday, choosing Bohemia under the impression, not that it had a sea-coast, but that it was a romantic, rugged and mountainous land, spotted with mediaeval castles, and that it was eminently suited for a walking tour. As for the last, so I dare say it was. Anyhow, I went off by myself, realised when I reached Eger from Nuremburg that the country might be romantic but that it was manufacturing rather than mountainous, and that a solitary walker would have the devil's own job to make himself understood in a language the very letters of which were unreadable. However, as in the course of my peregrination I reached Pilsen and drank the best lager beer at its source, I had every cause for self-congratulation.

After Pilsen, Prague. I do not know what Prague is like to-day, thirty-eight years later, but in those days it was a city comparable for its beauty to Oxford, Edinburgh, to any city in the world indeed. Even in the company of Hungarians I cannot but place it higher than Budapest—at least the Budapest of pre-War years—in the scale of attraction. Its hotels were verminous, but its streets and buildings, to the rather inexperienced English eye, were of a dream-like, fantastical quality, and with the shallow Moldau, on whose farther side rose the calm dignity of the Hradschin, spread like a slow-moving carpet 'twixt town and town, it had a spirit, an atmosphere, all its own. I spent a week or more in its narrow by-ways, speaking to no soul except the servants of my hotel and, on one occasion, to a young Jew, of whom, when searching for the Jewish cemetery, I asked the way. He was willing to show me, but my question surprised him. He would take me to the burial-ground, he said, and would give me ten minutes to see it, and then—well, then he would take me to a really worth-while "Salon de Damy". At the time I had not the slightest idea what he meant and, realising my ignorance, he left me to my tombs. The incident was hardly romantic, but a kind of comic-opera atmosphere *had* previously offered itself at Eger. Chance took me in the town of Wallenstein's assassination to an hotel in which the son of the house had worked at the Café Royal in London. He claimed to recognize me and dedicated a day to showing me the town and its neighbourhood. He was an efficient guide, but he was not really content until he had driven me down the river and had introduced me to half a dozen damsels whom he described as his cousins and who were making a small island musical with their songs and gay in the manner of *Lilac Time* and *Congress Dances* with their dancing, their

6

flitting hither and thither in the sunshine and their happy laughter. Heavens! How dense, how unforthcoming, I proved myself! But then I had so little silver in my pocket! And my lack of either German or Czech was an obstacle to serious flirtation. All the same I implore young men who want to spend a holiday abroad to be in no way deterred by not knowing the language. One soon learns something. In Bohemia I had to show that I wanted a lodging or a meal by making use of the most elementary signs, but in the long run I always made myself understood. It all added to the fun.

On the way home I walked about Saxon Switzerland— and that alone was worth all the money—taking myself down the Elbe by steamer to Herrnskretchen, where my room cost me a mark and a half and my dinner—a partridge and so on, taken in the open air at the side of a torrent—about the same sum. Such a bird it was, cooked by the innkeeper himself, an old man; I am dismayed to think that he is not still in this world. He *was* a cook; he was even cook enough to make a freshly-killed partridge a thing of joy. As I ate that partridge I read the only book in my knapsack, *Evan Harrington.* Is there a better book for a young man to read as he sits in dappled sunshine at the side of a torrent and demolishes a partridge—especially if he is on the threshold of adventure?

From Herrnskretchen I went on to Dresden and discovered in myself a dislike of Raphael which has, I am glad to say, persisted to the present day.

II

FIRST CONTACTS: G. B. S., E. V. L. AND OTHERS

THE holiday came to an end. I returned to London and
to my duties with W. T. Stead. He knew that I was
to leave him at the end of the year—and was quite cheerful about it! He was, during the months that remained,
very understanding when, to some extent, I must have
seemed to neglect my proper work while I made arrangements for the new business which I was to inaugurate.
For without delay I began to commission books, to hunt
authors.

I ought of course to have laid my foundations with greater
care. I ought to have considered in detail the sort of programme on which I should be justified in embarking with so
small a capital as fourteen hundred pounds. I ought to have
worked out a "budget". I did not. I was, even in those early
days, inclined to take undue risks. In this case I had, I believe, a subconscious feeling that if I allowed myself to be
even reasonably careful I should be doomed to early failure.
In my case success would be achieved by audacity. After
all, too, as I felt sure that I could tell a good manuscript
from a bad and as I had never had any difficulty in recog-
nising the young author who was going to do something
really worth while, it would be a weakness to pin myself
to a schedule. I had already in my head a long list of men
and women whose books I had, so to speak, reviewed, and
after whom I intended to go. It all promised to be so
simple.

There were among my acquaintances one or two who
knew that I had a harder row to hoe than I suspected.

8

Lewis Hind, for instance.[1] Hind had succeeded to Cotton's chair in the *Academy* office. Villiers, who could never have made any money out of the paper, had one day sold it without much ado to John Morgan Richards, a wholesale vendor of patent medicines with an office in Holborn. He was a handsome old man with a castle in the Isle of Wight, John Oliver Hobbes as a daughter and some interest in the literary art. Indeed the author of *Some Emotions and a Moral* succeeded in turning him into a patron of letters, a little Mæcenas. Hind abandoned the more scholarly traditions of the *Academy* and turned it into something a great deal more lively and, I confess, much more readable. He could afford to do so. His proprietor had money and was willing to spend it. E. V. Lucas, Arnold Bennett and Francis Thompson were among the young men who worked for him. It became a very lively affair, as indeed was to be expected, for Lewis Hind was himself lively. Something of a squire of dames. He was in my memory, after Arthur Roberts, the first man to wear a Captain Coddington topper.[2] (An enterprising hatter should put that silk hat on the market again: he might make money out of it.) I remember sitting with Hind and John Lane one May day in the old Hogarth Club.

[1] His assistant editor, Wilfred Whitten, wrote a welcoming interview with me for the *Academy* of January 16, 1897. Apparently I told him that I "regarded fiction as highly speculative". I did—and do. By the way, that number has a special interest to-day: it contains a four-column review of *John Gabriel Borkman* by G. B. S. and a note on Walter Pater by Lionel Johnson. And it has yet another interest in that H. G. Wells declares in a symposium that the books which most pleased and interested him in 1896 were Conrad's *Outcast of the Islands*, Crane's *George's Mother* and *Maggie*, Barrie's *Margaret Ogilvy*, Sullivan's *Flame Flower*, Stevenson's *Weir of Hermiston* and Steevens's *Monologues of the Dead*—"heaven alone knows which impressed me most". "No book", he added, "made such a distinctive effect on me as *Jude the Obscure* in '95." Three readers as diverse as A. B. Walkley, Harry H. Marks, M. P., and Zangwill give first place to Harold Frederic's *Illumination*. One might have asked what Harry H. Marks, M. P., did in so literary a galley, but Lewis Hind's net was wide: it took in John Porter of Kingsclere, who voted for Seton Merriman's *The Sowers* and Conan Doyle's *Rodney Stone*.

[2] We who are old enough are not likely to have forgotten Arthur Roberts as Captain Coddington in *In Town* at the Prince of Wales's.

Hind was wearing his new hat for the first time and Lane was wearing *his* hat which was by no means new. They were both perturbed. It was a Saturday and Lane was unusually anxious to find the address of an author, a poet, in whom he thought he could see possibilities. The author was Owen Seaman! Could I help? ... Would I make some excuse for going into the Savile Club and inducing the porter, if, as Lane thought, Seaman was a member, to send a letter to him by special messenger? That interest in the man who was to be editor of *Punch* was to be profitable to Lane. Indeed Owen Seaman had possibilities!

To return to Hind. I was to be a publisher; I was an acquaintance; moreover, I was a fellow-frequenter of the Meynell household; we used to meet at the Steevenses'; he would help me if he could. He caused it to be known that he had ideas which, if I liked, he would impart. I did like, and I asked him to lunch at Romano's. Hind could see no future for a new publisher—unless he did something revolutionary. Otherwise there were so many publishers that a new one would never be noticed. No use carrying on like all the rest; no use repeating the programmes and methods of Heinemann and Lane. Something entirely fresh was necessary. And he had the necessary something in his head. It was that I should start boldly with a widely advertised announcement that all my books, whatever they were, whether they were long or short, flippant or scholarly, popular or recondite, should be published at the same price—say, half a crown. Looking back I am much inclined to think that there was more than a little in this idea. But I had not enough money for so revolutionary an experiment—I could see that it would want a great deal of money—and besides, I had, however vaguely, other plans with which the Hind programme would clash.

The first book for which I actually signed a contract was Edward Clodd's *Pioneers of Evolution from Thales to Huxley*. I had wanted him to write a history of the evolutionary theory but he preferred the more piecemeal way of attacking the subject. I bought the copyright for the odd sum of one hundred and seventy-one pounds, sixteen shillings and sixpence, and, knowing little or nothing about the value of American rights, made no stipulation with regard to America. However, I did sell those rights, as my friend's agent, to Dr. Sheldon, of Appleton's of New York, for another hundred, and the only cloud that ever threatened to mar my relations with the book's author resulted from my deducting ten per cent as my commission! I made a gross profit on the book of a little over a hundred pounds.

When I was a very young boy I used in the Grant Allen household to hear a great deal of the Darwinian Theory. The theory was, of course, just the sort of thing to appeal to a schoolboy's idea of humour. And in that connection I seemed to hear often of Samuel Butler, the author of *Erewhon*, and of some controversy in connection with Darwin in which he was a protagonist and in which my uncle and his friends were involved. But I had forgotten all about that by the time I gave Edward Clodd his commission and so, when his manuscript arrived, I did not look to see whether he had anything to say about Butler and his *Life and Habit*. I have now looked and cannot help feeling regret that Butler's name is not in the index, although Clodd gives a certain .amount of space to Buffon. I should explain that the reason for my re-awakened interest is that since I wrote this page I have been reading Clara Stillman's *Samuel Butler: A Mid-Victorian Modern*, in which what may be called the case of Butler *v*. Darwin gets so much attention that for a while it pushed other things out of my mind.

I came across a stray but pertinent reference to Grant Allen in one of Butler's books. He is writing about holidays. "I grant that when in his office a man should be exact and precise, but our holidays are our garden and too much precision here is a mistake. Surely truces, without even an *arrière pensée* of difference of opinion, between those who are compelled to take widely different sides during the greater part of their lives, must be of infinite service to those who can enter on them. There are few merely spiritual pleasures comparable to that derived from the temporary laying down of a quarrel, even though we know that it must be renewed shortly. It is a great grief to me that there is no place where I can go among Mr. Darwin, Professors Huxley, Tyndal and Ray Lankester, Miss Buckley, Mr. Allen, Mr. Romanes and others whom I cannot call to mind at this moment, as I can go among the Italian priests. . . ." Yes, Grant Allen and Butler would have got on very well together had they met, say, in Monsieur Sella's garden at the Cap d'Antibes.

My next venture was to arrange with Grant Allen for a series, his Historical Guides. I was to pay him eighty pounds in advance of royalties for each volume. We were to begin with Paris.

And having secured these books I went after G. B. S.

I had been in the habit of seeing G. B. S. at first nights; I had even corresponded with him.[1] Now I had to make an opportunity of talking to him. It was not so very easy. He had the reputation of inaccessibility—not from vanity or whim, but because he was so concerned with his jobs, so preoccupied with his own and current affairs, with his political work, with music, with the theory and practice of socialism. . . . I suppose that I wrote to him and begged an appointment, said that I would meet him anywhere, at any time, and that I told him that my dearest wish was to be his publisher, to produce his plays, to produce all his books, to be publisher in ordinary and publisher extraordinary to Bernard Shaw. That really and truly was the way in which I looked at the affair. Where Shaw was concerned I was very prescient. . . . He answered me. We must have exchanged a letter or two. Here is his first response to my suggestion:

29 FITZROY SQUARE, W.
8th November, 1896

DEAR SIR,

As far as I have been able to ascertain—and I found my opinion on what I have been told by Heinemann, Lane

[1] See *Memories of a Misspent Youth,* by Grant Richards, 1932.

and Walter Scott of their experience with dramatic works by Pinero, Wilde, George Moore, etc.—the public does not read plays, or at least did not a very few years ago. Have you any reason to suppose that it has changed its habits?

I have by me three realistic plays, including the one published by Messrs. Henry, as to which there need be no difficulty, as it is as dead as a doornail. One of them is a frightful play; but it ought to be given to the world somehow: indeed it may perhaps be performed by the Independent Theatre to an invited audience. At least they are always hankering after this.

I have also three plays which are works of dramatic art purely, and which include *Arms and the Man*. But the other two have not yet been performed; and it would be better to wait until after their production before printing them.

Another little play, which is to be performed at the Lyceum, I will probably publish through the theatre; but there is no reason why its sale should be restricted to the inside of the house after the first run.

One quite indispensable condition is simultaneous publication in America. Indeed there is much more to be made out of my name there than here at present.

Yours faithfully

G. BERNARD SHAW

Later he said that I might meet him after the next theatrical first night and walk with him as far as his home in Fitzroy Square, a course that I had had myself the temerity to suggest. There is nothing like showing consideration for one's intended victims. It only wants a little imagination. In this case I pulled it off. As I was to be allowed to talk to G. B. S. I had little fear of the result.

The chief things Shaw had to say to me as we strode into Tottenham Court Road and proceeded rapidly past Bartholomew and Fletcher's, Heal's and all the other furniture shops, was that I was crazy to think of printing his plays, that to do so would ruin me in no time, that there was no sufficient public for them yet; and so on and so on. It seemed to me more than doubtful whether he was even attempting to hear what I had to say. We were walking too fast. Shaw was wearing his large, shovel, felt-hat and his baggy brown Jaeger suit and his poultice tie; I was in dress-clothes. We must have looked more than a little odd. He would hardly allow me to get an oar in. However, whenever I did have a chance I chipped in with a fresh appeal to what I considered common horse-sense. G. B. S., however, would have none of it, and continued to impress his views on me until, after a time relenting, he left me at his own door in the spirit of on your own head be it if you insist; do not expect me to speak up for you in the Bankruptcy Court. What did all this pessimism matter to me? In theory at least George Bernard Shaw had agreed that I should produce the Plays. The fact that J. T. Grein as Henry and Co. had already produced *Widowers' Houses* without attracting many buyers, counted for very little in my mind, did not in any way reduce the elasticity of my steps, as I walked home to Flood Street, Chelsea, from Fitzroy Square. Having the promise of Bernard Shaw on my first list of announcements, I had indeed made sure that I should succeed in putting myself on the map.

Who came next? Edward Verrall Lucas, I fancy—E. V. Lucas. In one of its Autumn numbers that year the *Fortnightly Review* printed an article by Lucas, then an almost unknown writer. It was on the Ideal Anthology for Children. Would he come to see me at Mowbray House, at the office of the *Review of Reviews*? He would, and did. We sat on the couch and discussed the possibility of his making a book out of his dream. He was working on the *Globe*, he told me, and would enjoy the task. I think we arranged there and then that he should be paid fifty pounds for the work. The bargain was a fair one. Neither of us at that time had any name.

I fancy that neither he nor I would to-day give fifty pounds to an anthologist who had no following to boast of. It suited both of us; he was almost unknown as a critic; I was quite unknown as a publisher.

And then Leonard Merrick came to sit on the same couch. A dark, Semitic, sensitive type, Merrick. I had recently read a novel that Chatto and Windus had published and I thought it was time that its author made a greater stir. Yes, he would write a novel for me, a short novel. We arranged terms—a hundred pounds for the copyright—and *One Man's View* was the result, the first novel for which I had given a commission. It did not prove to be a commercial success, but I was, nevertheless, very pleased with it. When it was ready for the printer I sent it to Herbert Aris, who then, thirty-five years ago, represented Butler and Tanner, the Frome printers, and does so still. We had been old associates in Paternoster Row and in the art of working our way into the pits of theatres on first-nights. I remember that I insisted on discussing with him, when I handed over the Merrick manuscript, the possibility of decorating the book's title-page with some other second ink than scarlet. Wouldn't green look well? Or blue? His firm experimented, but the result was not satisfactory.

I have said that *One Man's View* was not a commercial success. In fact, in spite of placing the American rights and then disposing of the serial rights to one Reichardt for thirty-five pounds, I lost about a hundred pounds on it. That made no immediate difference to my plans. I have always insisted on going after my money when the sale of a book has not come up to expectation through what I have been convinced was the fault of the public rather than that of the author. I have had many successes as a result. (Ernest Oldmeadow's *Susan*, following *The North Sea Bubble*—such an amusing book!—is a shining example.) I published two or three other novels by Merrick—*The Actor-Manager* (of which I supplied the plot), *The Quaint Companions* and *Conrad in Quest of his Youth* were among them—but we never suc-

15

ceeded in ringing the bell. I wonder why. The appearance of *The Actor-Manager* was against it. Old Thomas Leighton, of the firm of Leighton, Son and Hodge, bookbinders, came to me and said he was convinced that the day of the sober, quiet cloth cover to a novel was over. Cloth covers must be as clamant, as strident, as bad wall-paper if they were to attract purchasers. I gave him his head with *The Actor-Manager*. The result was pretty bad. That Thomas Leighton was a great man at teaching his customers. He taught me the use of the bill of exchange! But he was old-fashioned, secretive. I asked him once whether I couldn't go over his binding works. He was outraged by the idea. His other customers would object to a rival publisher seeing their books in process of manufacture. But to go back to Merrick. Years later, W. Robertson Nicoll took him up. He began to be talked of as the one novelist whom other novelists liked to read. I believe it to have been all bunkum. His books were good. He did not need the praises of more successful practitioners in the same art—except as an advertisement. And I suppose it was as an advertisement for Merrick that the series was invented. Anyhow, Nicoll rounded up Merrick's books and reprinted them, each with an introduction by some other eminent man of letters. I do not think there was any considerable Merrick boom as a result. His stories are still mildly sought after by collectors of nineteenth-century stuff, but it never went much further than that.

And then I hatched all out of my own inside—unless Frederick Whelen had a hand in its creation, which I hope for the sake of his own repose he had not—a very bad egg indeed. Every publisher likes to have an Annual. Mine was to deal with Politics year after year, each side being dealt with by an expert. *Politics in 1896* was the name I gave the first and only issue; it was a retrospect of what had happened in 1896. I put my cousin, Frederick Whelen, in as editor, discussed with him whom we wanted as contributors, and sat back and waited for success. Surely Bernard Shaw on Socialism, H. W. Massingham on Liberalism, G. W. Steevens

on Foreign Affairs, H. W. Wilson on the Navy, and Robert
Donald on London—to say nothing of the others—would
compel many thousands of five shillingses out of the pockets
of the public. Not at all. The thing was a ghastly frost. I
lost two hundred and fifty pounds on it. My copy is auto-
graphed by G. B. S. at the end of his own article, and this no
doubt makes it valuable, but as a whole it is only interesting
for such declarations as G. B. S.'s that "any of the Great
Powers could (if the others would allow it) swallow up the
Transvaal as a whale swallows a herring"[1]; and that of
G. W. Steevens, the "Balliol Prodigy", who announced that
"we can do no better than cultivate the best relations with
the one power on earth" [the United States] "which it would
be folly to beslaver and madness to provoke", and that
"readiness for war is the best guarantee, not only of peace,
but of the peaceful enforcement of our national will". From
the book-publisher's point of view it is a horrid error to attempt to dish up last year's events except in a very well arranged and indexed work of pure reference. I did not repeat
that mistake. By the way, it appears that Shaw thought
poorly of the book's scheme and even less of his own contribution. In sending me on January 4, 1897, from 29 Fitzroy
Square,[2] the second part of what he describes as his "beastly
article" and telling me "to set the printers on to it at once
to save time", he adds, "unless you take my advice and burn
it". But that, even if I had agreed with him, I could not do,
as I had paid him thirty pounds—or thirty guineas—for it!
Shaw used to sign "G. Bernard Shaw" in those days.

Elsewhere[3] I have written of Hubert Crackanthorpe's
endeavour in the autumn of 1896 to get me to purchase the
apparently moribund *Savoy*. I have since found the letter in

---

[1] See p. 150.
[2] William Archer's address, many years later, became 27 Fitzroy Square.
[3] See *Memories of a Misspent Youth*, by Grant Richards, 1932.

which, writing on October 30 from 18 Avenue Kléber, Paris, he raised the matter:

MY DEAR GRANT RICHARDS,

I have just heard from Arthur Symons that the *Savoy* is to cease in December. Would you be disposed to consider the idea of taking it over then with me as editor? I do not know under what conditions Smithers would be willing to cede the title: but I imagine that an advantageous arrangement might easily be arrived at. The sum you mentioned that you might be prepared to risk (£250) would, I expect, be sufficient to continue a monthly magazine which already has secured a certain *clientèle* and had a certain *succès d'estime*. I believe without vanity that my name (for certain reasons which I need not specify) would be more valuable than Symons', and certainly yours would be an improvement on that of Smithers. You are a new firm [I didn't exist at that time as a firm]: we should make a fresh start; break away from the "Beardsley tradition" and have, I think, a very fair chance of success . . .

We continued to discuss the matter by correspondence, but it came to nothing. I saw that I could not afford the venture. Soon afterwards, Crackanthorpe's life came to a violent end.

And as for the *Savoy*, I do not think it could have been saved. The reaction had not spent itself. The magazine had made a brave start. Its prospectus, dated November 1895, promised good things: ". . . the logic of our belief that good writers and artists will care to see their work in the company with the work of good writers and artists. Readers who look . . . for only very well-known or only very obscure names must permit themselves to be disappointed. We have no objection to a celebrity who deserves to be celebrated, or to an unknown person who has not been seen often enough to be recognised in passing. . . . We have no formulas, and we desire no false unity of form or matter. We have not invented a new point of view. We are not Realists, or Romanticists, or Decadents. For us, all art is good which is good art." The Beardsley design or picture for the front of the prospectus was not attractive, but it may, in another sense of the word, have attracted. Anyhow it had to be withdrawn in favour of another more seemly, but even less attractive.[1]

The prospectus undertook to provide us with Bernard Shaw, George Moore, Ernest Dowson, Havelock Ellis, W. B. Yeats and Arthur Symons side by side. We were promised Thomas Hardy in "an early number". Unlike its prototype, the *Yellow Book*, the editors did not provide a leaven of conventionalism. Of course, if Lane had not been frightened into parting with Beardsley the *Savoy* would never have been born. That Lane *was* frightened D. S. MacColl made sufficiently clear in a letter to the *Week End Review* of February 28, 1931: "My recollection is that John Lane took fright when Beardsley was mentioned at the Wilde trial as a friend of Wilde's. He . . . asked me to save the situation by taking on the *Yellow Book*. . . . I of course told him that, apart from other reasons, it was impossible for a friend of Beardsley to supplant him, and sent him away with a flea in his ear for running away at a threat of trouble. I do not remember what he did in the matter of the editorship, but his motive for the change seems clear enough." What Lane actually did was to replace Beardsley by Patten Wilson, already one of the artists attached to his establishment, not as art editor but as cover designer and general purveyor of art to the magazine.

---

[1] G.B.S., on reading the typescript of this chapter, provided me with an interesting different version of this incident: "It was not the *cover* of the *Savoy* that made the trouble, but the preliminary pictorial circular. Beardsley made a charming design of a Pierrot stepping out on to the stage to announce the paper. Smithers foolishly objected that it suggested flippancy and that John Bull would like something serious. Beardsley revenged himself by substituting a monumental John Bull for the Pierrot. Eighty thousand of this were circulated before George Moore's scrutiny detected that John had been represented in a condition of strained sexual excitement. All the contributors thereafter met and informed Smithers that he must 'withdraw' the circular. Not having any of the 80,000 left he agreed; and peace was restored." Edgar Jepson in his book *Memoirs of a Victorian* tells yet another story. I have both circulars but there is nothing to show which is the earlier.

Robert Ross, writing in the *Academy* in January, 1906, says that he does not know that the *Savoy* "exactly healed the breach between Beardsley and the public, but it gave the artist another opportunity; and Mr. Arthur Symons an occasion for song and prose".

And Smithers? I never saw Smithers, but his friends and authors have described him as an engaging if unusual personality. He surprised one of my friends by taking him for a long, long walk through London streets. Neither of them had noticed where they were going and as night closed in they found themselves, say, in Dalston. *"Tiens!"* said Smithers, if he had any French, or "Don't worry!" if he had only English—"I have a mistress here. We'll go and have tea with her—no, we'll take some beer with us. . . ." On enquiry my friend discovered that Smithers had mistresses all over London. He chose them for the neighbourhoods in which they lived, that, wherever he was, he might always find company—in much the same spirit as that in which the Postmaster-General sprinkles post offices throughout the length and breadth of London. . . .

Robert Ross was solid for Smithers. "Why is the name of Mr. Leonard Smithers—here simply called *a* publisher—omitted . . . ?" he asks in reviewing a revision of an essay on Beardsley which Arthur Symons first published in 1897 and which Messrs. Dent reissued in 1906. "Mr. Smithers was the most delightful and irresponsible publisher I ever knew. Who remembers without a kindly feeling the little shop in the Royal Arcade (*et in Arcadia ego*) with its tempting shelves; its limited editions of 5,000 copies; the shy, infrequent purchaser; the upstairs room where the roar of respectable Bond Street came faintly through the tightly closed windows; the genial proprietor?" In the same article, Ross deals with what he describes as "Beardsley's expulsion" from the *Yellow Book*. It took place, it seems, on April 10, 1895. "A number of poets and writers blackmailed Mr. Lane by threatening to withdraw their own publications unless the Beardsley Body was severed from The Bodley Head. . . . Mr.

Lane could hardly be expected to wreck a valuable business in the cause of unpopular art." And again, I should add, since the Ross article is, I fear, unlikely to be reprinted, another of its passages: "Quite wrongly Beardsley's art had come to be regarded as the pictorial and sympathetic expression of an unfortunate tendency in English literature. But, if there was any relation thereto, it was that of Juvenal towards Roman society. Never was mordant satire more evident. If Beardsley is carried away in spite of himself by the superb invention of *Salome,* he never forgets his hatred of its author. It is characteristic that he hammered beauty from the gold he would have battered into caricature." Was Ross really convinced of the literal truth of all this? No, of course he wasn't: he was, so to say, talking through his hat in the engaging way that he had. He was in fact writing in a rhodomontadish manner. However, I knew Beardsley well, and assuredly there were sides of the Oscar Wilde gospel with which he had no sympathy.

Yes, Smithers did have courage. It was he who produced, clandestinely, Beardsley's *Lysistrata.* I bought a copy once for an American friend—not from Smithers but from one of the two most respectable booksellers in London. It cost me ten guineas. That was in 1899. The bookseller trusted me not to give him away.

III

FAMILY INTERLUDE: A FRIEND OF KEATS
—ROBINSON ELLIS

THE kindly souls who are reading this book will, I hope, forgive me if I interpolate here a few lines about those years through which I lived before I pulled down the shutters on January 1, 1897. In spite of the fact that Max Beerbohm introduced it to the world, few of them may have read *Memories of a Misspent Youth, 1872-1896*, the book of reminiscences that I published in 1932. They were the record of a boy, the son of an Oxford don who was not wealthy and who certainly was not very much interested in his son's interests and ambitions. Nor were those interests and ambitions very interesting. I was educated at the City of London School, went of my own accord as soon as possible into the business of wholesale bookselling, spent a great deal of my time with Grant Allen, my uncle by marriage, became unintelligently interested in the theatre and, at eighteen, entered W. T. Stead's office, only quitting it to embark on the adventure of which this book tells.

And there is one passage in the history of my family to which I should like to return. I wrote in the earlier book of "some solid connection between the family of Richards and that of John Keats". The point interested Mr. Maurice Buxton Forman, who had helped me to the facts as far as he was then able; and I in turn put him into touch with my father's younger and sole surviving brother, the Rev. John Richards. For a while I heard nothing more about the matter, but to my surprise on opening the *Times Literary Supplement* of April 26, 1934, I discovered a longish article by Mr. Forman, *Keats and the Richards Family*, in which the subject is dealt with as of some importance, and, since it enables me to add to the record, I will make use of it. Mr. Forman writes at some length of "the social relations between John Keats and the brothers Thomas and Charles Richards". Sidney Colvin, he says, in his *Life of John Keats* was "practically silent about these two men; while Miss Amy Lowell in her *John Keats* contented herself with devoting a page to the discussion of the possibility of Thomas Richards being the author of a sonnet written in a copy of Keats's *Poems*[1] inscribed 'From the author to his Friend, Thos. Richards'". Certainly Colvin is silent except that he quotes the same Keats letter that I quoted myself. As for Miss Lowell, the interest of her page from my point of view is her saying that "nothing is known about this Richards. A certain C. Richards was the printer of the book, therefore Thomas Richards may have been his son, or his brother, more likely the former." Miss Lowell's "more likely" was wrong. Thomas was the printer's brother and my great-grandfather.

A further question which until recently vexed the Keats authorities was to which of the brothers, Thomas or Charles Richards, Keats was referring in his journal letter from which Mr. Buxton Forman's care now enables me to quote correctly and more fully. (The original holograph is in the Stark Collection in the library of the University of Texas):

"I know three witty people all distinct in their excellence—Rice, Reynolds and Richards. Rice is the wisest, Reynolds the playfullest, Richards the out o' the wayest. The first makes you laugh and think, the second makes you laugh and not think, the third puzzles your head—I admire the first, I enjoy the second, I stare at the third. The first is Claret, the second Ginger beer, the third Crême de Bzrapqmdrag. The first is inspired by Minerva, the second by Mercury, the third by Harlequin Epigram

[1] Now in the William M. Elkins collection at Philadelphia.

Esqre. The first is neat in his dress, the second slovenly, the third uncomfortable—The first speaks adagio, the second allegretto, the third both together. The first is swiftean, the second Tom cribean, the third Shandean—and yet these three Eans are not three Eans but one Ean."

"Mr. Grant Richards in his *Memories of a Misspent Youth* (1932)," says Mr. Forman, "claims for his great-grandfather, Thomas Richards, the distinction of being the poet's friend, apparently basing his claim on rather vague family tradition; and family tradition is now confirmed by documentary evidence. 'Richards', with no Christian name, occurs five times in Keats's published letters. On December 17, 1816, he wrote to Cowden Clarke:—'I believe you I went to Richards's—it was so whoreson a Night that I stopped there all the next day—His Remembrances to you.' In February, 1818, he wrote to his brothers who were then staying at Teignmouth:—'Richards tells me that my Poems are known in the west country, and that he saw a very clever copy of verses, headed with a Motto from my Sonnet to George.' A year later he told George and Georgiana that 'he had not seen Richards for this half year . . .' and in the same journal letter, in April, he said:—'I was unfortunate to miss Richards the only time I have been for many months to see him.' The passage in which the three R's are described occurs in the letter to Georgiana begun on January 13, 1820, and finished hurriedly on the 28th in order to catch George at Liverpool before he sailed on his return journey to America."

The curious thing is that, years before I wrote my *Memories*, the "documentary evidence" of which Mr. Forman writes came under my eye. My uncle had shown it to me; I had read it carefully and had told him it was very valuable, had given him "some good advice about keeping the Keats letter unfolded, to preserve the paper", and had then forgotten all about it! Now, therefore, to Mr. Forman, who owes the sight of it to the accident of my introduction, belongs all the credit of its discovery. Here it is:

MY DEAR RICHARDS,

    I think the fortnight has passed in which I promised to call on you—I have not been able to come—My Brother Tom gets weaker every day and I am not able to leave him for more than a few hours. As I know you will be anxious about us, if I cannot come I will send you now and then a note of this nature that you may see how we are. Remeber (*sic*) me to Mrs R—— and to Vincent.[1]

Yours most sincerely
JOHN KEATS

"Keats did not date his letter and it bears no post-mark," says Mr. Forman, "but Richards had had fourteen years' training in the Government service and he folded it carefully down the middle and endorsed it on the back, '1818/J. Keats/9 Octr'."

"The Keats letter", its owner, my uncle, the Rev. John Richards, tells me in a letter on April 30, 1934, "was given me in a most casual way by my father's sister, Mrs. Staples". That was "more than sixty years ago". It was sold at Sotheby's on May 28, 1934, for three hundred pounds. Most gifts, "casual" or calculated, are less valuable!

Mr. Buxton Forman says definitely that this Thomas Richards, my great-grandfather, was "a civil servant. He was appointed a junior clerk of the first class in the Storekeeper's Office of the Tower on July 1, 1804, promoted in 1827 and died in 1831". Mr. Buxton Forman's article has sent me also to Charles and Mary Cowden Clarke's *Recollections of Writers* (1878): "Tom Richards—a right good comrade, a capital reader, a capital listener, a capital appreciator of talent and of genius." Cowden Clarke was my grandfather's godfather. In an unpublished letter of 1810

---

[1] Charles Cowden Clarke's father-in-law.

from Cowden Clarke to my great-grandfather he refers to the child: "I cannot help thinking that my little godson will at a future period rise considerably above mediocrity." And in 1818, in a letter also unpublished and now, with the other, in the possession of Mr. M. Buxton Forman, while saying to the father "Tom, you are very nearly the oldest friend I have . . . you by your precept as well as by your example laid the foundation of all my love of literature", he writes of the child as "old gravity my Godson".

A further batch of letters to my great-grandfather, also recovered from my uncle's muniment room by Mr. Buxton Forman, is from Charles Armitage Brown. From it it appears that my ancestor was intimate with the Charles Wentworth Dilkes and that there had been some rivalry as to whether the older Thomas Richards or the Dilkes should have charge of Brown's son. "Let him [that son] be like Tom [my grand-father] and I am satisfied," Brown writes in 1822, the year in which Peacock's *Maid Marian* was published, to old Thomas Richards, who then lived at "9 Providence Place near Vauxhall Gardens". An amusing reference to my great-grandfather's job in life in the Ordnance Department in the Tower occurs in a later letter of the same year: ". . . for what are you but a knave to the Duke of Wellington?—heavens preserve me! It never struck me before that my friend Richards was such low company!"

"Old gravity", my grandfather, preserved to his end the characteristic that had earned his nickname from Cowden Clarke—I say his "nickname", but I do not think that it persisted; I have heard no reference to it in the family. He had, as had his son, Franklin Richards, my father, a grave, a thoughtful face; I remember that across it there would flit, as across a sombre landscape on a cloud-laden February day, a flash of sunshine, a smile that irradiated all his being. I have but one letter of my grandfather's and it is so charac-teristic of the "old gravity" side of the man, and of his time and his class, that I will give it in full. It must have been written in 1890 or 1891, and the *Review* to which it refers was W. T. Stead's *Review of Reviews*. The name of Stead was distasteful to him. No doubt he had been shocked by Stead's *Maiden Tribute* in 1885 and generally by the habits of the new journalism which Stead had fathered. The fact, too, that I was making a living under Stead's auspices was not pleasing in his eyes; nor did he, I fancy, think very highly of the society of gentlemen of the press for his grandson! Here is the letter:

HOLLAND ROAD

May 14

MY DEAR GRANT,

I must write and thank you very much for *Review*, and for thinking of me. At same time add that I do not want you to go on adding to my liabilities on that score, as I feel that my interest in the periodical ceases with your share in it. Therefore, please take my name off the free list, and accept thanks for past favours.

I hope you have kept well? You must not omit your old custom of giving me an hour occasionally. I daresay, as time goes on, the old thief (*Time*, I mean) makes himself the more tiresome in his demands.

Yours affectionately

THOMAS RICHARDS

My grandfather died in 1896 at Oxford, where he had gone to live in order to be near his two sons: my father and Herbert Richards, my father's younger and bachelor brother, who had for many years occupied at Wadham the same position that my father held at Trinity. And in this connection I may quote a further letter, from the *Times Literary Supplement* (of May 17, 1934):

KEATS, RICHARDS AND ELLIS

SIR,—The connection having been established by Mr. Maurice Buxton Forman between Keats and the two brothers Richards, one of whom was the great-grandfather of Mr. Grant Richards, it may perhaps be permissible to recall that Mr. Grant Richards's father, the late Franklin Thomas Richards, for many years Fellow and Tutor of Trinity College, Oxford, was in that capacity a close friend and colleague of the late Robinson Ellis (Corpus Professor of Latin) whose mother was, according to the present President of Trinity's article in the last volume of the D.N.B., 'a Miss Robinson, who is described (disparagingly) by Keats in his first letter about Fanny Brawne'.

E. COLL. TRIN.

I had something to say of Robinson Ellis in my other book and of his wish that my mother or I would find him a suitable wife. He was a dear old man, an original. He would write his letters on scraps of paper. In November 1892 he writes to thank me for the gift of Grant Allen's *Attis* of Catullus; in March of the following year to say how much pleasure the reading of my father's *The Eve of Christianity* had given him, and he adds that the umbrella he had left in my rooms "arrived safely and I was able to take a walk in security"; and in December of the same year he writes a very characteristic letter on rather less than a quarter of a sheet of paper:

TRIN. COLL. OXON
Dec. 25, 1893

DEAR GRANT RICHARDS,

I do not think of being in London this vacation, but hope to be there at Easter. Then I will fly to see you, and we will go to a spectacle together.

The professorship though long delayed was all the more satisfactory at last. I was elected, I hear, unanimously. A. Sedgwick said it was an instantaneous thing. I am now no longer a fellow of Trinity, but am a fellow of C.C.C. Still I remain in my rooms here.

The salary is 900 £ a year. This is good and a nice thought for Xmas! A lady has given me an enormous Tea-Cosy.

Yours very truly
ROBINSON ELLIS

ROBINSON ELLIS

Later I was to hear of Robinson Ellis, his umbrella, and another election—the election at Cambridge to which he sallied forth from Oxford in the early morning, the election for the Professorship of Latin, in connection with which Herbert Richards had told me with regret that A. E. Housman, the author of *A Shropshire Lad*, hadn't the ghost of a chance for several reasons, but for one in particular—that Robinson Ellis, resentful, would certainly vote against him. . . . But Robinson Ellis placed scholarship before any personal feeling that he might have; I have every reason to believe that he voted for the successful candidate.

IV

PRODUCTION–THE KELMSCOTT PRESS–THE *DAILY*
CHRONICLE–W. B. BLAIKIE AND OTHER
EDINBURGH PRINTERS

I HAVE described some of the books for which I arranged
before we took down our shutters in Henrietta Street.
When the first of January, 1897, had dawned I soon discovered that to arrange for books was one thing, but to produce them was another. What did I know about production?
In effect, nothing. True, I knew as an amateur as much as
for the present I need know about the appearance of books,
but I had never paused to consider how what was attractive
in that appearance had been arrived at. I had now to argue
the thing out for myself, and inevitably I had to proceed by
imitation rather than by invention. The output of three firms
had attracted me: the books that bore the imprint of the Macmillans, those of William Heinemann, and those of John
Lane. I had not been much attracted by the books for which
William Morris was responsible, rather disliked them in fact,
and could allow them few virtues other than that which
came to them from his persistence that when one opened a
book one should see the two printed pages as one whole and
not as two, that the inner margins should hardly be greater
than was rendered necessary by the requirements of the
binder, and that the outer and bottom margins should much
exceed those at the top. The thing was often overdone, but
the principle was right, and the Kelmscott convention profoundly influenced the printers who were not too hide-bound
to cast off a bad habit. In fact, with the 'nineties the vicious
practice of putting a slab of type as nearly as possible in the
centre of the page and ignoring entirely its relation to the

type on the opposite page came almost to an end. Printers went back to the balance and proportion of the old manuscript books and to the books of the artist-craftsmen who had followed the birth of printing. As I shall show, the Morris practice was to have a great effect on the format of the most important new books of my publishing life, the books of Bernard Shaw.

It must not be thought that William Morris and his admirers had it all their own way. They had their critics. Thus in 1893 the *Daily Chronicle*—always to the fore where matters of interest to book-lovers were concerned[1]—had a lengthy article, "The Kelmscott Press: A Master Critic on the Master Printer", in which Morris gets some shrewd knocks. "His books, like his wall-papers, are specially intended, not for the proletariat he loves, but for the capitalist he hates" is a point the "Master Critic" makes before passing to technical details. "When it comes to the actual printing, his books are filled with blemishes which would be ascribed to carelessness even in printers of lesser pretensions. There is a weakness, a faintness in many of his impressions, which is unpardonable when the standards he sets up and the prices he asks are borne in mind. . . . I cannot understand how such slovenly work is

---

[1] The *Daily Chronicle* under Massingham was a marvel of a paper. It should have made, and no doubt to a considerable extent did make, young England art-conscious. A few columns about the arts were not thrown in as a make-weight, but books, pictures, buildings and the technical processes connected therewith, were all of them treated as vitally important to human life, as important, let us say, as horse-racing or the activities of Sir Augustus Harris. As an example, in 1896 the *Chronicle* had a series of articles on the New London and, instead of sticking them into the paper in such a manner that no one not already interested in his civic responsibilities would care to read them, they appeared illustrated in a manner so imaginatively connected with the theme as to compel attention. Most of the drawings were made for the purpose and they were, in the main, made by men who understood the limitations of their newspaper medium. Alfred Parsons, Joseph Pennell, Raven Hill, A. S. Hartrick, T. B. Wirgman, W. W. Russell, Fred Pegram, E. J. Sullivan, F. H. Townsend, Herbert Railton, W. B. Wollen, Edgar Wilson—where is the newspaper that will employ men of the same standing to-day? On one occasion Whistler's etching *Black Lion Wharf* is given a half-page to itself. The pages I have before me have aged very little in thirty years.

allowed to be issued from the Kelmscott Press." These so-
cialists who are also artists in decoration have sometimes been
known to bear an excessive admiration for one another, and
Walter Crane hurried to the defence of "Mr. Morris and his
splendid work". Particularly does he "wonder when editors
of influential papers will see the palpable injustice of allowing the weight of their journals to support immature or mere
ill-natured and ill-considered personal opinions, especially
on art"—an unfortunate sentence, when one reflects that if
Walter Crane had been equipped with ordinary knowledge
of the literary and artistic worlds he would have realised at
once that the article could have been the work of only one
man, Joseph Pennell, whom no one could accuse of imma-
turity or of ill-considered personal opinions. Joseph Pennell
had the best of the correspondence.

I clearly remember one instance of Morris's willingness to
compromise. In his own house in Hammersmith was a hand-
rail in one of the ground-floor rooms: it had an odd appearance and I examined it. I found that where it was in full
view it was of fine rich wood, oak or something of the kind,
but that when it turned a corner and was in some obscurity
the fine wood gave place to an inferior and cheaper kind!

Let me hasten to add that I am a great admirer of the
Doves Press, which had all the virtues and none of the
weaknesses of the Kelmscott Press which it succeeded. Its
books had a noble sincerity and simplicity. Would that I had
still a set of its Bible! By the way, the sale-room value of the
Morris books has dropped considerably since the slump set
in. One cannot however argue from that, for the same thing
has happened to nearly all books!

In those late years of the last century the best commercial
printing was being done by T. and A. Constable, by R. and
R. Clark and by Ballantyne, Hanson and Company, all of
Edinburgh, and by C. T. Jacobi at the Chiswick Press in
London. There were others, but these were the firms who
had the highest consistent level. Clark did most of the

Macmillan work and to Clark I turned first, for I had decided that my books, even though they did cost more to produce than they would if I went elsewhere and satisfied myself with a lower standard, were to look at least as well as those of my competitors.[1] Of course I had plenty of silly ideas. I must do something original with my title-pages and with such decorations as were allowable in the text. The choice of a new colour for the title-page of Leonard Merrick's novel was one of them. I did plenty of books with cock-eyed title-pages. I remember the motive at the back of my endeavour was my wish to do something as attractive and as just as Heinemann had done in Whistler's *Gentle Art*. I never attained so great a success. The Whistler was, from the point of view of "lay out", one of the supreme achievements of the decade. Ornaments and decorations are sad pitfalls for the man who does not really know his job. How many books otherwise quite decent in appearance were ruined in the 'nineties by their decorated title-pages, their fidgety end-papers, the adornments which were supposed to help the page-heading? Often I carried my own silly ideas into practice, assuring myself that I knew more about it than my printer-counsellors; sometimes I achieved results which were not too bad. Witness the use of the little typographical decorations on the pages of E. V. Lucas's *A Book of Verses for Children*, decorations that were used again in *The Open Road*. The worst of it was that in those days the reviewers ladled out praise for the appearance of a book whether conception and execution were good or bad. They had only to feel sure that the publisher was trying. Poor fellows, in those days they knew no better. The men who were competent judges were hard to find. Clark did both the Lucas books for me, and Hugh Clifford's *In Court and Kampong*. This last indeed

[1] I must have achieved some success, for thirty years later Gerard T. Meynell wrote on October 20, 1927, in *The Times Literary Supplement* about its "Printing Supplement": "You mention who have done something to make their books look better, but as far as I am able to see you do not mention Grant Richards, who was one of the first publishers to produce decent-looking books."

was one of the first books they sent me, and I was chagrined when, turning over the first set of printed sheets, I discovered that they had omitted to add their own imprint in one or other of the accustomed places. I remonstrated, asking them to realise that one not only wanted to employ good printers but that one also wanted in such days of ignorance to have evidence that one had done so. I wished, so to speak, to have my book "signed". The omission was accidental.

There was another Edinburgh firm which was doing more even than Clark to change the appearance of the printed book—the firm of T. and A. Constable. W. B. Blaikie, the head of the house, was a scholar, a recluse, a gentleman of the old school, a man nearly always in indifferent health, an artist, an astronomer, a furious smoker of pipes, a friend of Stevenson and of Henley, and one of the chief financial supports of the *Scots Observer* and its successor. To listen to the talk of Walter Biggar Blaikie was an education not only in printing but in the gentler, happier ways of life. To be his friend was to know that one had the ribbon of a Scottish legion of honour. He was never too busy to help. It was he who planned out typographically the magnificent Edinburgh Stevenson; he designed the format of Henley's papers; he designed, though he did not print, the *New Review* when Henley stepped into its editorial chair. He was a master.

Blaikie printed many books for me: Alice Meynell's anthology *The Flower of the Mind*, W. E. Henley's Edinburgh Shakespeare—a folio that was a failure in everything but appearance—the Winchester Jane Austen, and many others. He aimed at a more solid, a blacker, page of type than did most printers at the time he came into the field; he used a heavier headline and set it much closer to the body of the type; in fact in many ways he reverted to the old tradition. To see his work at its best look at the first edition of George Moore's *Impressions and Opinions* and at Henley's *Views and Reviews*, both the publications of a scholar-bookseller, David Nutt, whose place of business stood where Bush House stands now, and who found a brave death by drowning in an attempt to save another from the river at Melun. W. B. Blaikie's influence for good in printing cannot be exaggerated.[1]

I have written the name of Ballantyne, Hanson and Company. They were, I suppose one would say, a Scottish house with a London branch. In Edinburgh "old" Hanson ruled, Edward Hanson, who was not really old at all. He was a gentleman by tradition and performance and the work his firm did was something for a publisher to be proud of. In London Charles McCall was his lieutenant. They did, I think, the best of the Heinemann books. Nowadays their Edinburgh premises are occupied by worthy successors, Neill and Company, and those in London by *Country Life*.

In London there were many good commercial printers. They had an advantage over Edinburgh in that they were nearer; one could step round and talk. But they were dearer. Edinburgh might be, was indeed, the metropolis of the printing trade, and it actually did most of the best work, but in spite of the cheapness of sea-transport, distance did tell and helped to off-set the fact that compositors, machine-hands and so on drew a lower wage and thereby enabled their masters to present a considerably lower estimate. I have mentioned C. T. Jacobi of the Chiswick Press. He was an artist too, and he had publishing ideas; indeed The Chiswick Press Editions of English Classical Works is hardly to be surpassed. I remember that its issue, with its modest but comely volumes edited by Gosse, Dobson, Richard Garnett, Saintsbury and others, raised John Lane's anger. Up to that time Lane had had much of his work done at the Chiswick Press, but when one day I asked him if he did not think well of the printing of *The Journal of a Voyage to Lisbon* he replied

[1] In the *Catalogue of the Collection of Printed Books and Music* formed under the direction of the Publishers' Association for the Royal British Commission at the Paris Exhibition, 1900, four books published by me appear: one, Constable's work, a volume of the Winchester Edition of Jane Austen; three from the R. and R. Clark presses, E. V. Lucas's *A Book of Verses for Children*, Wilfred Whitten's anthology *London in Song*, and E. V. Lucas's *The Open Road*. I did not go to look at them in their glory. I was too busy with the Manet paintings.

impatiently that it was no doubt excellent but that as "these people" were setting up as publishers he would see that they had no more of his printing. ... C. T. Jacobi printed for me Walter Leaf's *Versions from Hafiz*.[1] By the way, to refresh my memory I have just examined a copy of the Chiswick Press *Hydriotaphia* and I notice that, elegant as is the page of type, the actual machining is a little grey. Perhaps the paper has swallowed too much of the ink in these forty years. Such things happen. Moreover, however beautiful a page may be when it leaves the hand of its compositor, it may go wrong when it comes to be printed off. Too little ink may be used, or the ink may not go well with the paper. To borrow a phrase from the wine trade, paper and ink may not marry satisfactorily. Something of the sort happened with the Edinburgh Shakespeare. Blaikie produced a perfect folio page, a model of gracious dignity, but when the book came to be delivered some constituent in the ink or in the paper had given the page a slightly yellow and greasy appearance. I pointed this out to John Ayling, Blaikie's partner, a man less sensitive to criticism, but he and I could never get to the bottom of it. I hadn't the heart to take my complaint to Blaikie himself.

Printing is only the first stage in the making of a book after it has been written and delivered to the publisher who is to give it to the world. The printer sets up the type of the book and prints it off, but he very seldom provides the paper. That is the publisher's job. He knows the kind of paper he wants and has to look for it at the paper-merchant's. Heaven has to help him when he starts business if he knows as little about paper as I did when I began. There are enough mysteries about paper and enough difficult technicalities to take a month of Sundays to master. Some publishers keep delicate paper-weighing machines hard by their desks. Mostly swank, I suspect! Personally, I was fortunate enough to make the acquaintance of Harold Bayley of the firm of Spalding and

[1] Jacobi died in 1933 at the age of eighty. His *Notes on Books and Printing* is a work of great value.

Hodge, who carried on their trade at that time in an ancient warehouse in Drury Lane, near to the house in which my paternal grandfather had had a printing business, which, however, came to an end before my time.[1] Realising Bayley's qualities, I put myself in his hands. Perhaps he had not in those early days developed his Shakespearean heresies, but, whether he had or not, I had not reason to suspect their existence, and I grew to rest tranquil in the knowledge that his people had, or could get, the best paper, and that he had a ready understanding, an intuition almost, of what I wanted. In Arthur Waugh's book of publishing reminiscences there is a tribute to Harold Bayley. He deserves it. In a drawer of my desk I have now a folder of papers cut to the various sizes. He made and gave it to me in the spring of 1897. Throughout the whole of my publishing life I have relied on his advice.

After the paper has been delivered to the printer and the book has been printed off, its sheets have generally to go elsewhere to be bound. I had to find a binder—an easy job in my case, for I knew already A. S. Thomson of the Straker firm, who in those days when land in the neighbourhood had not been made so valuable by newspaper competition (and competitions!) did their binding just east of the Temple. They bound the *Review of Reviews*, and it was natural for me to go to them. Later I invoked the assistance of Leighton, Son and Hodge, who did such admirable work for John Lane and who were said to have helped him financially. I do not know what truth there was in that story, but they certainly worked admirably together. Old Thomas Leighton, a gentleman of the old school, whom I have already mentioned, was an odd cove. I liked him.

Publishers, who as a rule seldom have compunction about copying one another's ideas, are also always looking out for improvements in the format of books. Their rivals invent and they copy. Heinemann suffered a great deal from such flattery. I recall that, on my first visit to him as a callow youth

---

[1] See *Memories of a Misspent Youth*, by Grant Richards, 1932.

interested in books, he complained bitterly of the action of one of his rivals, a bearded gent. Heinemann had suddenly bethought himself of reversing the cloth used for binding and making the back do the work that had hitherto been done by the face. One could in this way get an entirely different range of effects. The book so bound looked very unlike its fellows on the counter of a bookshop, challenged notice, was effective in a new way. Straightway his older rival came out with a range of bindings in which the same device was employed. Heinemann, always liable to go off the handle, went right off it on that occasion and sat down and wrote a letter in which he made a mountain of his complaint, but he ended on a softer note by suggesting that if in future his rival would refrain from such flagrant imitation, he in his turn would gladly and secretly help him with his counsel and knowledge, so that the offender might have the credit of occasionally evolving an original idea of his own. Since that time reverse cloths have been in general use.

V

"THE DWARF OF BLOOD" AND HUGH CLIFFORD—*PINK-'UN*
PEOPLE—VAN LOON AND MALAY CURRIES—NATHANIEL
GUBBINS AND JOHN CORLETT—MY FIRST LIST

THE stage was now properly set. I was a publisher. I had an office in a region studded with other publishers. Manuscripts had been sent to me to consider. I had already books to publish. I had confidence.

Actually the first book to appear with my imprint was Edward Clodd's *Pioneers of Evolution*, and at its end are two pages of announcements, announcements not printed, as common firms affect, on the back of pages which carry the proper type of the book itself, but on pages which are given up to similar advertisement. (Never surrender yourself to a publisher who is careless in this respect.) Announcements of promise. Nine books altogether. All of them were justified in the event by success, although in the case of the one novel the success was, for the moment, of esteem rather than of sale. First, the *Paris* and the *Florence* in the series of Grant Allen's Historical Guides. They and their successors had a warm welcome, but my aunt could never understand why it was that, in spite of what would nowadays be called a consider-able fan mail, the series did not make our fortunes. I of course knew how many had been sold, but the comparative smallness of the number was strangely discrepant with the agreeable stories of returned travellers who declared that half the English and American visitors to the Louvre, and the Uffizi were carrying the little green books. But that is one of the things one soon learns as a publisher—never to trust estimates of sale, not even the estimates of important book-

39

sellers. Apart altogether from the fact that it is in the nature of things for a bookseller to make the best of affairs when he is asked by a customer how some particular book in which clearly that customer is interested is selling, there is the inevitable tendency to exaggerate in one's own mind the number of times a gratifying occurrence has happened. The bookseller and his assistant for one reason or another always say to the enquiring customer that such and such a book is doing splendidly. Moreover, in the case of those Guides there was the lending habit to be taken into account. The average unintelligent person always borrows a guide-book when he can. And again, the ordinary traveller in foreign parts had —and has now more than ever—to think of his shillings.

Next to the Grant Allen guides came another of his books, *The Evolution of God: Researches into the Origin of Religion.* The book did not come out under that title. It was published as *The Evolution of the Idea of God,* it being urged on my uncle by a far-seeing friend that the interpolation of the three words "of the Idea" would turn the edge of much prejudice. He was right. I am reminded by the many appearances of Grant Allen in this list of one of the horrid *gaffes* of my life. Running through my first catalogue with my uncle I casually remarked that I must look for a book by an Ablett or an Acland so that his name might not stand so prominently in the very forefront of my list. Yes, I said that, thoughtlessly and heedlessly, to the man whose kindness, appreciation, confidence and money had put me where I was! . . . Grant Allen did not protest. He had too understanding a heart.

Sir Hugh Clifford's *In Court and Kampong* came next. I look on the securing of Hugh Clifford for my list as an instance of the way in which the born publisher finds his books. Many months before there had come for review to the *Review of Reviews,* all the way from the Straits Settlements, where it was published at the office of a local newspaper, a paper-covered volume. It was a good book, a collection of Eastern essay-stories. I remembered it, and, holding that publication so far off was hardly publication at all, I wrote to its author, the Resident at Pahang, and, in the sequel, published several of his books. After two or three years he came home and "The Dwarf of Blood" of the old *Sporting Times* (Lt.-Col. N. Newnham Davis), attracted by the descriptions of a life he had known in his early soldiering days, asked me to bring him to dinner at the Naval and Military Club. "The Dwarf" gave us a true Malay curry.

I was not to have so authentic a curry until, some ten years later, I happened to arrive in New York harbour on the very day on which a Dutch East-Indiaman came in laden with the spices and condiments of the Orient. I was surprised to find Hendrik Van Loon waiting for me at the pier. He declared that we had corresponded much, that it was necessary that we should actually meet without loss of time, that as it was Saturday he was sure I could have no appointment for that night, and that, the Dutch boat having just come in with the necessary material, I was to dine with him at the Dutch Club and give him a pleasant opportunity of proving that there were other cuisines than that of France. I, who had already a reputation for caring unusually for the things of the table, eagerly accepted. Van Loon had other guests—journalists, men of letters. The soup was new to me, and good. Then came the curry. The Malay servant came round with a tray of small saucers, each containing a condiment that one added to the chief dish according to taste and habit. He omitted however to tell the ignorant stranger—and we were all, save our host, ignorant—anything of their strength and quality. Knowing no one in the party, I was looking at my new acquaintances rather than at what I was taking on my plate. Suddenly the man across the table startled me by shedding tears. I could see no reason for this emotion. The man next to him became in a moment victim to the same malady; and then, almost before I knew, I was myself attacked by such agony as I had never known. . . . I had helped myself too freely of this condiment and that, and had carried them to my mouth without caution. I drank. I drank water; I drank whisky and water. The more I drank the greater became my suffering. I always say that I ran out into Gramercy Park and applied my tongue to the cold metal of a lamp-post. I could get no relief. My pangs continued for hours. . . .

After Hugh Clifford on that first list of mine came Leonard Merrick with his *One Man's View*, which did not sell, and then fiction of a different kind, W. T. Stead's *Real Ghost Stories*, which did. Followed the first announcement of E. V. Lucas's anthology for children of which the title was not then fixed, and after it a book *Meat and Drink: Chapters on English Cookery* (to appear under the better title of *Cakes and Ale*), by Edward Spencer, "Nathaniel Gubbins" of John Corlett's *Sporting Times*, a man who was the constant enemy of what he described as the *à la* school of cookery, who had been an officer in a crack regiment, whose real name was Mott and who was a good fellow and not such a hard drinker. It was with Edward Spencer that, following a suggestion of mine, George Steevens and I went to Newmarket to see the Cesarewitch run, an excursion that led to one of the best pieces of writing in the early *Daily Mail* and which helped to make Steevens's name. "Nathaniel Gubbins" also took me to the Derby. I was to arrive very early at his Epsom cottage. John Corlett would be there. We were all to breakfast together. I was jubilant. Surely I should have the kind of breakfast that the *Pink-'Un* people were always boasting about. Actually we did have tea and toast and bacon and eggs and marmalade! A disillusion indeed. As we drove off in a four-wheel cab to the course, Corlett asked me what I knew about racing. I disclaimed any knowledge, so, according to custom, he handed me his race-card to mark. A novice in such event is supposed to have unusual luck. I did mark the card—one horse for every race. They all won. But we none of us backed them. On another occasion when Gubbins took us to Epsom and to the Press Stand he came back from a foraging expedition to tell Corlett and me that Kempton Cannon, the jockey and no unworthy brother of the better-known Mornington Cannon, had been complaining that his uncle, old Joe Cannon, the trainer, never put him up on a good horse. "I told him so straight," said Kempton. "Well, you shall have a winning ride to-day," the old man had answered, and, sure enough, in a later race Brechin, who started at five to one, duly obliged, as the sporting writers say. If I wanted to recapture the sounds and sights of one day nearly forty years ago I should only have to go to Gloucester Road and regard the street which may or may not have been called after the race-horse. It seemed easy in those days for those in the charmed circle to find winners! I do not suppose it was.

To go back to Gubbins's book. I had the brilliant idea that Phil May, a familiar of the *Pink-'Un* staff, should do a design for the cover. He said I should have it next day. It would not take long. There should be none of the usual delays to which he had accustomed editors. Ultimately I had to go down—a month later, having been patient for thirty separate days and having struggled to get my design on each of those days—to Holland Park Road and hang about outside Herbert Schmalz's studio till Phil May emerged from his lair. I waited several hours. Phil, when he did come out, saw me without turning a hair. He remarked casually that he had been thinking of my drawing and that if I would come in to his studio he would do it while I waited. And he did—in half an hour. It assured the success of the book.

Yes, there were nine books on that list of announcements and, with Clodd's book itself, there were ten. A pretty good list. And I still had Bernard Shaw up my sleeve!

That first office of mine was very well suited to be the home of a publisher. Medical publishers had it after me. I wonder whether they were ever tempted to make use of the trap-door that came at the threshold of my own room. It might be of greater use to a medical publisher than it proved to me for, through his clients, a medical publisher would, like Burke and Hare, be able to dispose of the bodies! It was a very practical trap-door giving immediately and without steps into a stone-paved cellar. A Sweeny Todd trap-door. It would have been easy to fit it with a mechanical device operated by a lever at the side of my desk. But why should a publisher want to do away with an author? The other way round, yes —occasionally. A publisher may stand in an author's way, but for a publisher actually to put an end to an author would be like killing a goose who might one day lay a golden egg. Many would-be authors are mad of course, mad as March Hares, and many of a publisher's visitors are capable of boring their hosts to distraction, but to be mad or a bore is not to deserve sudden extinction. Besides, your publisher may well be content when he has managed to get his visitor back into the outer office and on the way to the street. The real trouble is when the visitor won't get up and go and, although he has nothing to say, will insist on saying it again and again at inordinate length. I have glanced at my clock a dozen times and yet have had no real effect on him. It is his day out and he is going to make the most of it. He is bent on having as much time devoted to him as he can manage. Much too often, if he has already achieved the dignity of being the author of a book published elsewhere, he spends the first quarter of an hour of his first visit in explaining why he cannot possibly continue publishing his books with the firm which published his last. The firm is old-fashioned, or it doesn't advertise, or its reader has had the impertinence to suggest an alteration or an omission. He must tell you all about it, and not seldom does he reflect, without shadow of reason, on the solvency and honesty of the house which has spent time and money on his work.

Even in my first month's work I had quite enough of that kind of thing. There isn't any satisfactory way of stopping it. One precaution I did not have the strength of mind to practice: one should never remain standing after one's visitor has taken his seat; if one does one has surrendered the initiative; one has lost the power of rising and of so suggesting that the interview is at an end. Personally I start by intending to remain seated like a doctor or a solicitor or a bank-manager, but restlessness drives me from my chair; before I know what I am doing I have risen and have taken a place with my back to the fire and to the clock—and then I know that I have as good as wasted the next half-hour!

On the other hand, the man who brings a manuscript to a publisher need not think that that publisher is conferring a great honour and service if he consents to retain the manuscript and have it read. How, in the name of wonder, does your author suppose the publisher will find new blood if he has not an ever-open door? Many of the most successful manuscripts come from the hands of the dullest visitors and are the least attractive in appearance. Yes, whether your caller be a working man who has written a book, or what he thinks will make a book, or whether he be a duke, the publisher who has intelligence and a feeling for his trade will see him and talk to him and be patient for a while. How was *The Ragged-Trousered Philanthropists* found? I will tell that story later on.

Finally, and on the whole, I think a publisher wastes the time of his author quite as much as an author wastes the time of his publisher—but there are, even now, more authors

Besides, authors who are not mad—and even some of those who are—make good company.

VI

E. V. LUCAS AND RICHARD WHITEING—W. H. SMITH AND
SON AND *ESTHER WATERS*—A GLIMPSE OF
ALFRED HARMSWORTH

I OWED much in those first days to the then Alfred
Harmsworth. He dropped in to see and encourage me
and caused George Steevens to write a "*Daily Mail* Special"
on my appearance. Some of its sentences are amusing to-
day: "In this fine, early, open season" [it was January] "new
publishers are coming up in the neighbourhood of Covent
Garden like crocuses. A representative of the *Daily Mail*
went down to Henrietta Street yesterday to inspect the interesting phenomenon. There he found Mr. Grant Richards, who had come through during the night. For a plant of
such tender youth he looked remarkably robust.

" 'You too, Mr. Richards,' he began, with native courtesy.

" 'Me too,' he replied in the undefiled English of your true
publisher. 'Why not?'

" 'Aren't there too many of you?'

" 'Can't be too many,' he cried cheerfully. 'There are
plenty of people to write good books and plenty of people to
read them. I am here to bring these kindred souls together.' "

I told Steevens about *Politics in 1896*: " 'More than one
member of the *Daily Mail* staff contributes.' " (True:
Steevens himself and H. W. Wilson.)

" 'Put me down for ten, then,' began our representative
with enthusiasm. 'But your terms?'

" 'Strictly net,' said Mr. Richards. 'I invite the public to
buy a three-and-sixpenny book for three-and-sixpence, instead of a five-shilling book for three-and-ninepence. Why
shouldn't they?'

46

" 'They will," said our representative with conviction.

"He departed with the further conviction that Mr. Richards is young, energetic, and knows his way about the business. Two years in the great wholesale house of Simpkin, Marshall and Co., and seven more at the right hand of Mr. Stead in the *Review of Reviews* office, have taught him as much about publishing as is worth knowing. The only feature of the business that will take him by surprise is the fabulous profits. It is a comfort to find a nice, clean, empty publishing office without any piles of dusty books to tumble over, and spoil your clothes with. But those who wish to transact business with Mr. Richards before his office is choked with tenth editions of masterpieces had better hasten to 9 Henrietta Street, to-day or to-morrow."

E. V. Lucas commented in the "By the Way" column in the *Globe* on this interview and its reference to the "Me too" solecism: "We may add that a well-known firm of publishers are about to issue a novel called *Under the Circumstances*, a phrase which is anathema to all literary purists."

Looking back now in 1934 on those first months of 1897 I cannot but believe that they were the only months during which as a publisher I have enjoyed any protracted peace of mind. To repeat myself: I *was* a publisher: I had an office; I was being kindly spoken of in other papers than the *Mail;* the books I produced were having their fair share of notice; the literary world of London was aware of my existence; authors were bringing me their manuscripts to consider; I was able to commission books; I could summon young painters to me and ask them to execute this and that piece of work; I could rejoice in seeing Bernard Shaw on one day and E. V. Lucas or Richard Le Gallienne on another. Lucas indeed had become my "reader", my literary adviser. He would come in from the *Globe* office, round the corner in the Strand, when his daily column of work was done, and would tell me what he thought of the last manuscripts that had gone to him, and we would exchange ideas. . . . One day I told him that I had arranged that Le Gallienne should produce a new *Rubaiyat*. I meant that I had arranged that he should, with the aid of such translations as already existed, produce a new version. A rather half-baked and ill-educated idea, that. Lucas misunderstood. Thinking that I meant that Le Gallienne had consented to write a *Rubaiyat* of the last years of the nineteenth century, an adaptation of the Omarian philosophy and the FitzGerald method to the life, the ideal and practice of the years we were living through, he became enthusiastic and declared his envy of the skill which was mine in inventing such ideas and the power that I had borrowed of carrying them out. Quickly he discovered his error—and, more slowly, I confessed to mine, for I saw that it was indeed an error to employ Le Gallienne's gifts on so unnecessary a task. FitzGerald had rendered Omar into imperishable verse; Heron Allen and others had translated him in more literal fashion. Why should Le Gallienne be set to work all over again? Felicities his little book had—was ever a book signed by his name which had not felicities? —but how much better it would have been if I had listened to Lucas's implied counsel, had had the courage to ask the author of *English Poems* to cancel our agreement and to consider giving us a new poem in the Omar manner. Perhaps even in those days Le Gallienne had such a thing in his mind, for in 1908, eleven years later, I published for him his *Omar Repentant*, in which, however, he did not adapt the Omarian philosophy, but forswore it utterly. Here are two stanzas in which it must be understood that the poet is addressing a young companion in a Broadway saloon:

What is the book I saw you with but now?
"The book of verses underneath the bough"!
So that old poison-pot still catches flies!
"The jug of wine, the loaf of bread, and Thou"!

Boy, do you know that since the world began
No man hath writ a deadlier book for man?
You smile—O yes, I know—how old are you?
Twenty—well, I just measure twice your span.

It was on one of his early visits to Henrietta Street that Lucas told me of Richard Whiteing and of a novel which that middle-aged, but most capable, journalist had written, but which had not yet found a publisher. Would I like to see it? Would I like to meet its author? Of course I would like to do both, and since, as I recall the matter, Lucas was a friend of Whiteing's and was not, in consequence, willing to act as the book's sponsor, it was made clear to me that I must take or reject it on my own responsibility, or that of some other adviser whom I might elect to consult. This indeed was the more necessary in that the book had already been several times rejected. Well, I read the manuscript, was greatly attracted by it, became convinced that it would prove a success, and published it. *No. 5 John Street* was my first considerable commercial success. In the *Who's Who* for 1925 that I have just consulted I see that the date of its publication is given as 1899, and I am surprised. I should have put it as early as 1898. But *Who's Who* is right. In the meantime I had met the author—in Lucas's company at a dinner he gave for the purpose in his flat in Great James Street.[1] Whiteing was a white-bearded man who talked about rowing; he had an attractive son. How it could have happened that any publisher could have read the manuscript of his one famous book without wishing to bring it out, I cannot think. But such things happen. And of course directly the book had appeared and had been hailed as a considerable achievement then other publishers flocked round its author. Would he promise his next book? He described to me afterwards in detail how one such interview had gone:

"We should very much like your next novel, Mr. Whiteing. I hope you will be free to bring it to us."

---

[1] Lucas invented entertaining dinners in those early days at 5 Great James Street. I have the menu of one of them, on December 2, 1898. It was a good dinner and the menu was amusing: "*Mélange de plusieurs choses*" was his description of the *hors d'œuvre*; "*pétoncle a l'écaille*" figured as the fish; the roast was "*le taureau, innocent et péremptoire*"; "*pour ivresse*" were provided a good claret and *Ecossais*, while "*pour l'autre chose*" came "*eau*". Alas, thirty-six years ago!

"That's odd, Mr.——. You had the chance of publishing *No. 5 John Street* and you refused it without apparent hesitation."

Mr. —— smiled: "We all make mistakes. That was my damned reader. I can't read everything myself. If I did I should never have allowed your book to go back to you.... How many have you sold?"

"I don't know: I haven't had any statement yet. Ten thousand—fifteen—I can't say."

"Well, it doesn't matter. We should have sold twice—thrice—as many. We should have advertised it more; we should have pushed it more . . ."

"Grant Richards seems to have been pretty energetic. Anyhow he did read it and did accept it; you didn't and wouldn't."

"Yes, and I suppose he's made a pile out of it, so he's had his reward. Of course his is a new firm. Has no travellers. Does all his travelling through Simpkins; he's no travellers of his own. We have—several."

That kind of talk had its almost inevitable effect. Whiteing believed that ingenious touch about the travellers. When he told me that the successor to *No. 5 John Street* was to go elsewhere he said frankly that he couldn't afford to sell through me two copies of a book when someone else, having travellers, could sell three or four or five, but, he added, he was leaving me with regret. The "fact" that I had no travellers had induced him to accept an offer from another house; it had stuck in his mind when it had been told to him and, later, it had borne seed.

The fellow who had told Richard Whiteing the story about my having no travellers was really rather a dastard. Nor was it a true story. Mine was a new house; it had been in existence less than three years; but I knew the value of travellers and I had two of my very own. And a pretty penny they cost me. One travelled as a whole-time job London and its suburbs; the other spent all his time trying to sell the books that I published in the provinces. "If I had known the truth", Whiteing went on, "I'd never have gone elsewhere. But it's too late now. I was deceived, but there it is: the agreement's signed."

Since those days sneaking away other publishers' authors has become the practice of the trade. In 1899 it was looked down upon. Most publishers then had a way of considering their business as bound by the considerations and conventions that bind lawyers and doctors. You do not hear of a lawyer attempting to sneak away the clients of one of his rivals, nor does a medical man allow himself to woo another's patient by specious offers of lower fees or more intelligent treatment. . . .

I must not, however, say that I had travellers from the very first days of my business. It was better that I should not have them when my list was so small that I could handle it myself without undue difficulty. It was worth a great deal to me to get to know personally as many booksellers as I could, to win, if possible, their good-will, to learn their views, to listen to their suggestions. They knew more about the public taste and the caprices of book buyers than I could do. I learned for instance a great deal from old William Faux, who decided what orders should be given by W. H. Smith and Son's library, and from Frederick Evans of Jones and Evans in the City. In those days Evans, who was a friend of Bernard Shaw's, one of his first adherents indeed, occupied East of Temple Bar much the same position as J. G. Wilson of Bumpus's occupies now in the "West End". Incidentally he was an uncommonly good photographer and it was one of his portraits of the author that was used as frontispiece to the first edition of *Plays Pleasant and Unpleasant*. In the issues of those books he took a lively and active interest and much of the small success of sale that came to them in those first days was through the little Queen Street shop over which Evans presided.

Faux, of "Smith's", was a much older man than Evans, not forward-looking at all. He would not have been an adherent of G. B. S. in the days of *Plays Pleasant and Unpleas-*

51

ant. When I knew him he was ripe for retirement. In his anecdotage he loved to tell, or even to hear, a good story, and, if a publisher or his representative did dare to submit to him a novel which was not from the conventional point of view as suitable for a young lady subscriber as the powers in those days thought essential, Faux would like to savour the impropriety before he declined the book. In fact, he was pleasantly human.

Poor Faux! Very much did he bring a swarm of hornets about his ears when he refused to circulate George Moore's *Esther Waters* among his subscribers, whereas Mudie's, the other big library in those days—the spring of 1894—made no overt objection to it. The *Daily Chronicle's* literary editor could see no reason for Faux's action and devoted a deal of room to the subject, announcing that the Society of Authors "contemplated action". The Society's founder, Walter Besant, however, was non-committal, saying that he had not read the book. In fact, no action was taken. Sir Frederick Pollock, the Chairman of the Committee, while agreeing that the Smith censorship was illogical, explained: "Mr. George Moore has himself desired us not to proceed with it. In any event, the Committee could at most have only made a formal protest, for it seems clear that there is not any legal remedy." He then calls on the firm to "vindicate their consistency by promptly withdrawing from their library and bookstalls such improper and indelicate works as *Clarissa Harlowe*, *The Heart of Midlothian* and *Adam Bede*"; and he adds a few words about the work of Tennyson and John Milton!

It is unlikely that W. H. Smith and Son would have been intimidated even if action had been taken. They were not like that! But eminent literary hands wrote letters on the subject to the *Chronicle*, Conan Doyle opening the campaign with the statement that George Moore's novel was "a great and very serious book . . . on the very highest plane of fiction" and that "exclusion from Smith's stalls and library means that the work is cut off at the meter as far as the country consumer goes. . . . If the book is objectionable there are recognised means for suppressing it. . . . If *Esther Waters* is to be placed outside the pale of legitimate fiction, it is difficult to say how any true and serious work is to be done within it." (Doyle was to have his own troubles with would-be censors a little later on when he wrote and published through me his novel, *A Duet*, a book of which, oddly enough, Smith's sold more copies than anyone else. But that was after Faux had passed on.)

The next day Faux is interviewed. First, patting Conan Doyle on the back, he gives his reasons for the book's rejection. No, he had no objection to the Moore output *en bloc* —"I know Mr. Moore personally, and he is an excellently clever fellow, which nobody can deny"—but Smith's had taken *A Modern Lover* on trust and had then seen cause for investigating each Moore novel as it came along. His firm's quarrel with *Esther Waters* was owing to "treatment". Hardy's *Tess* was a book they did circulate. An exact parallel? No. *Tess* is "delicately inferential; *Esther Waters* is precisely positive. What is merely delicately inferred in the one, is bluntly told in the other." And then Mr. Faux advances the unanswerable argument that out of fifteen thousand subscribers only one subscriber had complained of their decision. After all, he claims, those myriad subscribers wanted "books to carry into their home—books they ought to read". Well it was that Mr. Faux had gone before the present-day novelist could shock the old librarian with the modern "precision"!

The battle continued. George Moore, interviewed, admitted that his book was probably getting "a splendid advertisement", but thought that he was "well enough considered in the literary world to have been able to do without it". (I doubt that myself—from the commercial point of view at least; the advertisement as far as 1894 was concerned made Mr. Moore.) He said he was willing to submit the book "to any competent tribunal; a tribunal of bishops, of lawyers, of literary men pure and simple, of officers of the two services —as you like" and that he would abide by the result. Then

Conan Doyle returns to the charge, and Madame Sarah Grand and Hugh Chisholm back him up. The next day George Moore himself writes a letter in which he challenges Faux "to name a single person who thinks as he does—prelate, politician, man of letters" and declares that "the facts force him to the conclusion that personal prejudice plays a large part in the general boycott of my books at Smith's Library". Follows a piece of hard Scotch argument in an indictment of W. H. Smith and Son from William Archer, who finds it one of "life's little ironies" that Mr. Moore should be boycotted while Mr. Thomas Hardy circulates unquestioned "since the author of *Tess* has introduced into English fiction a note of sensuality from which *Esther Waters* at any rate is entirely free.... I neither suggest nor believe that Mr. Hardy's work is 'immoral'. It possesses the only morality for which anyone need care a jot—the morality of delicate and nobly-inspired art. But if Mr. Faux's 15,000 are of the opinion that morality consists of the discouragement of sexual impulse, or even of its unalloyed manifestations, I think they should clamour for *Esther Waters* and demand the suppression of *Life's Little Ironies*."

Then a new clash is to be discerned in the conflict: Edward Clodd, shocked at the implied attack on his "supreme artist" Thomas Hardy, rushes into the battle to say that the passages I have quoted "show entire misapprehension of the lofty and earnest spirit which informs" the writings of his master. It really begins to be great fun, this battle, especially when L. F. Austin brings up ammunition with a story that, years before, Smith's, on the complaint of one reader, had withdrawn from their stalls the Christmas number of James Barr's *Detroit Free Press* containing Rudyard Kipling's *Badalia Herodsfoot* "because Badalia like Esther had her 'blemishes' ". On that occasion the firm was induced to withdraw its boycott.

As far as I know the *Chronicle* correspondence ended when a very sensible man, George C. Carley, remarked that in less than six months Mr. Moore had made "extraordinary progress towards the acceptance of the main thesis of Mr. Ruskin's art criticism—the inter-dependence of art and morals". For it seemed that in the *Speaker* of March 25, 1893, Mr. Moore had written as follows: "I plead guilty to the grave offence of having played to the gallery. The picture is a work of art, and therefore void of all ethical significance. In writing the abominable phrase, 'but it is a lesson', I admitted as a truth the ridiculous contention that a work of art may influence a man's moral conduct; I admitted as a truth the grotesque contention that to read *Mlle de Maupin* may cause a man to desert his wife, whereas to read *Paradise Lost* may induce him to return to her." So Mr. Moore in March, 1893, but in May, 1894, he says to the *Chronicle's* interviewer (and does not afterwards repudiate) that "I wrote *Esther Waters* in sincere love of humanity, out of a sincere wish to serve humanity". Small wonder if the editor felt that there was no need for more. On a later occasion, I remember, Mr. Moore delivered himself of the apothegm that "a masterpiece is always, as it were, an assault on the moral conscience". By the way, Mrs. Atherton—Gertrude Atherton— in her *Adventures of a Novelist* holds up Captain Oswald Ames, a friend of King Edward's—the tallest man in the British Army, and who led in consequence the Diamond Jubilee procession—as having been guilty of the perfect snobbery when he disposed of George Moore's novel in one phrase— "I am not interested in reading about servants". "Ozzie" Ames was no more a snob than we all are, and the phrase "not overburdened with brains" does his memory far less than justice. He was a clever and amiable fellow and there seems after all no particular reason why a man should not be at liberty to proclaim that a servant's life and psychology do not interest him without being written down a snob. There are men who don't like reading about novelists, and there are others who refuse to read about financiers, people like Sister Carrie and Ivanhoe, Chinamen, visitors to Capri, undergraduates and Jane Eyre. One should be allowed one's tastes. "Ozzie" Ames read books and talked about them with more than usual intelligence.

I had begun to interest myself in George Moore years before the publication of *Esther Waters*. His *Speaker* art-criticisms opened my eyes and prepared me to see something in modern French painting; and his *Impressions and Opinions* was one of the books that influenced me most—as they used to say in the 'nineties. Indeed in June, 1891, I reviewed it in the Catholic *Lamp*. I summed up with "Mr. Moore's ideas are fresh and original, although perhaps not clothed in the most beautiful English, Mr. Moore being no stylist"! Perhaps he wasn't in those days. He taught himself to write. But oh, the sublime impertinence of nineteen-year-old youth!

In those 'nineties, I should add, books were refused by the libraries for other reasons than that they were "improper". The inclusion in the title of the name of the Diety was enough in itself to cause a book to be put on the black list. One T. Mullet Ellis wrote a novel with some such title. It was refused by Smith's and the heart of its creator was outraged. Failing to overcome the firm's prejudices, he determined to bring the matter before his fellow-citizens—by appealing to their suffrages at a general election which was about to be held! He stood as candidate in opposition to that member of the Smith family who was at the time the sitting member for the Strand Division! It required some courage to appeal to the public from such a platform! He found, as I told him he would find, that the ordinary elector cares little for questions of literary censorship. And I fancy that, if truth were told, the novel was declined as much for other reasons as because of its name.

I began this chapter with a reference to what I owed to Alfred Harmsworth and it has made me search among my letters. Elsewhere I have said that it was I who introduced George Steevens to "Alfred" as a result of his asking me who did the "Occ. Pars." in the *Pall Mall Gazette*, and the proprietor of the young *Daily Mail* never failed to appreciate the work that "the Oxford prodigy" did for him. Thus in September, 1896, he is annoyed that Stead, writing about the

McKinley-Bryan fight, has said that "not one single London paper has taken the trouble to send even a third-class correspondent to the scene of the great conflict". The *Mail* had sent George Steevens: "Mr. Steevens is certainly one of the best", Alfred Harmsworth writes to me from the Burlington Hotel; and he adds: "Mr. H. W. Wilson told me yesterday of your contemplated venture. May I wish you a great share of Fortune's favours". To this I naturally replied, thanking him for his good wishes and promising to get my Editor to correct his error, for on September 29 he writes again, from Elmwood: "Do not worry Mr. Stead, he has plenty to do and I do not care for 'pars' particularly. I only thought it might look like a reflection on Steevens who is, in my opinion, a most able writer and the best man I could have chosen in England. I shall watch your progress with great interest and if I can put anything in your way I will." A couple of months later Stead was wanting some information about the (? *Daily Mail*) company and "Alfred" writes to me: "I must apologise for the delay in replying to your letter, but I have only been allowed to do a little work each day for some time. What information does Mr. Stead want? Anything he wishes to know is at his disposal, though I would much prefer that, instead of referring to our money-mongering, he mentioned my efforts to carry on the work he started of teaching the millions something about the Empire. We have despatched travelling correspondents to nearly all the Colonies and their reports will be published in our London and provincial daily papers." I cannot prove it, but I am under the impression that Stead was offered the editorship of the *Daily Mail*.

VII

MY FIRST "JOURNEY" TO THE PROVINCES
–A VISIT TO PARIS

IN the autumn of 1897 I started out, with such books as I
had ready, to "travel" the North of England and Scotland.
It was from the trade point of view rather late to begin such
a journey; most booksellers were of the opinion that they
should be shown no more books until after Christmas, and,
in consequence, it was not all fun. Some of them were very
bleak in their reception of this new publisher. Indeed one
would have thought that a publisher was their foreordained
enemy. Here's a new publisher; let's heave half a brick at
him! That was the note. It was a period of acute dissatis-
faction and depression in the trade. To give to the public a
discount of twenty-five per cent on the "published price" of
a book was, if not the rule, at least a very general thing.
Some booksellers stood out against it, but they suffered in
consequence. Indeed there was a tendency to give even a
larger discount. (I remember how I myself when at school
would go to the Civil Service Stores in Queen Victoria Street
for the sake of paying one-and-fivepence-halfpenny instead
of eighteen pence for one of the old two-shilling yellow-
backs. I had at that time the ambition of buying and reading
every one of Miss Braddon's novels, a sufficiently ambitious
undertaking, from the point of view both of time and money,
for a boy of fifteen!) Naturally, as a result, bookselling was
not a healthy business—and it was becoming the habit for
booksellers to look to the publishers to make things healthy
again. In the circumstances it was perhaps not so very surprising that when a new publisher appeared in a bookshop
he should be treated as if he represented in his own person the

slowness to act of all the other men of his trade or profession. In very fact, of course, the publishers were in no way responsible. The trade terms they gave to the booksellers allowed a fair margin of profit; it was no fault of theirs if some booksellers, doing a cash trade in London, where expenses of carriage and so on did not eat into profit, came to the conclusion that it would pay them to give away the greater part of their discount to the customer. How big a cash trade could be done the shops of Messrs. Denny—then at the corner of Wych Street hard by St. Mary-le-Strand—and of the Dunns and Glaishers and Stonehams proved. The practice of giving these discounts spread to the provinces, and did even more harm there than it did in London.

Something had to be done to stop the rot. The publishers were not to blame, but it was certain that unless a stand was made, and quickly, the bookseller's trade would suffer. The good bookseller who paid his experienced assistants a fair wage would be crowded out—especially in the country —and then the publisher would be in a fix, and so would the author! Characteristically a compromise was arrived at. More and more books were published at a net price, which meant that they were only supplied to the bookseller on condition that he upheld that price and passed none of his discount on to his customer. At first only the "serious" books were so treated, but it became increasingly the practice to make books net. John Lane made his whole list net, and I remember that when I began as a publisher he paid me a visit for no other reason than to try to induce me to do the same. But it was a long time before the trade as a whole took to publishing fiction in this way.

When at length that was achieved it was a great day for the bookseller. Still, nowadays he has an equally serious problem: What is he to do with his bad stock, his stock of books which have missed their market? . . . But publishers have that problem too. It is the result of books appearing at a greater rate than they can be absorbed by the public. Bad stock in recent years has not only eaten into profits; it has done more: it has in several cases eaten them up. A book that no one seems to want is one of the most unsaleable articles in the world. The shopkeeper whose capital is invested in bottles of wine or blankets or armchairs can always have a bargain sale or job off his stock at a sacrifice to one of his rivals. His actual loss on his outlay need not be great. But if a bookseller has to-day a stock of the much heralded, ridiculously advertised, and greatly boomed novels of a few months ago, what can he get for it? Wine increases its value with keeping; so does soap. Do novels? Some, yes. Perhaps one in ten thousand. A "mint copy" (i.e. a thoroughly clean uncut copy in its original wrapper) of the novel that was being run after in the circulating libraries two years ago will to-day be difficult for the bookseller to sell at a fifth of what he paid for it. And what is the publisher to do with his unsold fiction stock? He can pulp it or he can sell it for what he can get. In the autumn of 1898 my cousin, young Grant Allen, was travelling the provinces for me. On October 26, 1898, he wrote to me from Bournemouth. After praising the shops and the personnel of two Winchester book-is by far the best man. I think his is the finest shop I've ever sellers, Wells' and Gilbert's, he proceeded: "Commin here seen—a sort of Hatchard's. . . ." I break off here for I find I am quoting from the wrong letter, for it does not contain the passage I wanted. Here it is, the date being July 21, 1900: "Bournemouth and Southampton both seem to like your scheme [a cheap-book plan] immensely, but I could not get big orders as ——'s have recently jobbed off 27,000 copies of their six-shilling novels[1] to —— of Southampton, and —— of Bournemouth are helping to sell them. . . . Of course the 27,000 represent practically *all* ——'s stock." I wonder how many seven-and-sixpenny novels that particular firm would have to job off to-day if they wanted to clear their stock! I quote this passage to show that the evil of over-production is not a new one. If nowadays a publisher

---

[1] In those days—and till after the War started—novels were ordinarily priced at 6s., which meant 4s. 6d. to the customer.

can get from the dealer sixpence a copy for his "heavy" seven-and-sixpenny novels he is fairly fortunate! And other books are difficult to dispose of in much the same way. Take biographies and books of travel for instance—no, do not let us take them now: the subject is too depressing for discussion at the outset of a publisher's career!

To return to my first provincial "journey": it was not a great success commercially, but I learned so much from it that I never regretted the expenditure of time or of money. I travelled light and I travelled very cheap. At Derby I remember my visit coincided with the November race-meeting. It was a good thing that it did coincide with something, for it certainly did not find the booksellers in a buying mood. Moreover, one of the days I spent there was an early-closing day and, having nothing else to do, I went to the races and lost a pound. I backed a horse, Bowline I think it was called, in a long-distance race at five to one. When the distance was half covered and my horse was obviously tailed off, my bookmaker beckoned to me and said that he was altering my bet to ten to one! I held him in regard for the rest of the afternoon, but I made no more ventures, and later on it occurred to me that he would have made even more certain of my future custom if he had gone further still and had handed my golden sovereign back to me! That evening I saw enough golden sovereigns. Having taken a room at an unpretentious inn, I found after dinner that I was sharing the only sitting-room with a typical bookmaker and his equally typical clerk. Figures from a Tom Webster caricature, they were. The old red-faced man took a look at me and, satisfied that I was harmless, nodded to his junior, who then produced a satchel and a wallet and poured their contents, bank-notes, gold and silver, on the table. I had never seen so much money. No doubt it looked more than it was, but I went to bed wondering whether of the two kinds of book-making I had chosen the better!

Most booksellers in the North were particularly un-encouraging to me on that trip. They were a hard lot, some of them, hard, that is, on Southern ambitions and pretensions. (They have more than made up for it since!) Old Andrew Elliot explained that the annoyance of publishers' travellers was becoming so great that "some of us" are talking of refusing to see them at all. However, he was paternal, and George, his son, was agreeable and slightly less pessimistic. Dan Macnivin deplored my purpose. Massie, of Douglas and Foulis, knitted his brow and was very economical of words. Old MacKenzie of Menzies snapped at me, but melted after a while. Harry Clifford, representing Edward Arnold, went in to Menzies one day to show his samples. He felt poorly, for he was hardly recovered from an attack of influenza. One of the clerks told him that by a coincidence old MacKenzie had just returned to work after a similar illness. Always start by putting your customer in a good temper.

"I'm sorry to hear you've been ill, Mr. MacKenzie. And what was the matter with you?"

"Just influenza." Very abrupt.

"And how did it take you, Mr. MacKenzie? How did it leave you, I mean? The after effects are very bad at times. How does it affect you?"

"In me legs, Mr. Clifford."

"That's curious, Mr. MacKenzie. It affects me in my head."

MacKenzie looked at him in a pitying way: "Aye, aye, Mr. Clifford, it aye affects ye in the weakest pairts."

But he gave Clifford a good order.

In spite of all this discouragement the full cold air of Scotland did not blow on me till I reached Aberdeen. There I called on John Rae Smith. He had his own ideas about publishers . . . I never went to Aberdeen again.

After Aberdeen, Glasgow, and there I paid by happy chance my first call on David Knox, then a comparatively young man and the proprietor of John Smith and Son. He must have noticed that I was bruised in spirit for he took me to his heart and remained my friend till he died, in spite of my wicked views, in spite of the fact that I was no teetotaler. He seemed to understand the difficulties I was contending against. Glasgow booklovers have reason to be grateful to David Knox. He kept a good shop till the day of his death and now his son, Bumpus-trained, is carrying on his work.

In Glasgow I called on the Maclehoses and made the acquaintance of James Maclehose who welcomed me as the son of a father whose pupil he had been at the City's University. The Maclehose shop and library were havens of quiet after the noise of the Glasgow streets.

It was against James Maclehose's wainscot that I saw leaning a picture that attracted me, a strange Monticelli-ish affair. I asked what it was. A Pringle. And who was Pringle? John Quinton Pringle was a working watch-maker and general repairer in the Saltmarket, Glasgow, a mechanic earning a humble wage. His hobby was painting. He exhibited with the other Glasgow men and was as interesting as the best of them, but he would not give up watch-making for painting, no, argued his fellow members of the Glasgow School never so cunningly, and in consequence, as late as 1902 in any case, his work was very difficult to find. He was a mechanic and he would remain a mechanic, and he would paint when it suited him. The Pringle on which I had stumbled James Maclehose had just bought at the Show, and he passed the bargain on to me at the price he had paid, five pounds. An extraordinary piece of painting. In 1924 a Memorial Exhibition of Pringle's work was held in Glasgow. The City had come to appreciate him more and more. Nevertheless, no one has ever been able to tell me what my Pringle represents. It is sheer colour laid on in the Monticelli manner. I have seen but little notice of Pringle's life or work in the Press—just one article by Hugh Monro in the *Scots Observer*—not Henley's *Scots Observer*—of June 25, 1927, from which I learned that although he had secured the South Kensington Gold Medal of the Glasgow School of Art for figure drawing and painting, he had had little academic training: "Pringle remained among his spectacles, binoculars, clocks and gasogenes practically to the end. He had the gifts of mechanical and artistic genius in equally great degree, and he was able to keep them apart so that the one did not suffer by the other. His physical powers were remarkable: his working day approached sixteen hours of the twenty-four; as a youth he worked ten hours daily at the bench, learning his trade as an optician in a back shop which had no windows, and was lit by gas in summer and winter alike; and thence he went, often unrefreshed by food or rest, to prosecute his art studies at the St. Mungo or the Haldane Academies.... He painted from early morning till breakfast-time, and in the evening after cessation of his toil at the bench, until bed-time.... With retirement, he hoped to devote his entire time and energy to painting, and he forsook the dusty surroundings of his shop for the more congenial air of Ardersier, in Inverness-shire...." In 1925 he died.

In some ways my first autumn was unlucky. One of the books I was carrying was E. V. Lucas's anthology, *A Book of Verses for Children*. I might have sold many thousands of it, for it was being well reviewed and it made a brave show with its gilded cover, its F. D. Bedford end-papers and title-page in colour. But a printer's strike had broken out in Edinburgh and I could not get deliveries. R. and R. Clark were printing it and Edward Clark, that burly embodiment of the Scottish commercial and sporting spirits, did all he could to get copies through for me, but he could not achieve impossibilities. He was not, however, going to subordinate his six feet and some inches to any compositors and machine hands, whether they were his or another firm's. He ran some good cargoes of printed matter, did Edward Clark, and many strikers had bloody knuckles as the result of attempting to stop him.

At the same time I made the acquaintance of Walter Biggar Blaikie (of Constables') of whom I wrote in my fourth chapter. He was a very different man from Edward Clark. They respected each other, the one a scholar, a dreamer, an artist; the other a man of action, a rider to hounds, a gentle-man-rider, a sportsman. Blaikie, who looked in 1897 as if he might be taken at any time, lived on, in indifferent health, until 1928. Scholar, historian, printer and man of affairs, he died at the age of eighty. His nurse, it is interesting to know, in view of his later connection with Robert Louis Stevenson, was that Alison Cunningham who, four and a half years later, was to nurse the author of *Treasure Island*. She lived to see the books that made one of her boys famous printed exquisitely by another in the Edinburgh Edition, the fore-runner of all the other "fine" editions of modern writers which, generally so inferior in appearance to the series which inspired them, have since taken up too much room on the shelves of second-hand booksellers. W. E. Henley dedicated to Blaikie that admirable anthology *Lyra Heroica* —"to Walter Blaikie, artist, printer"; and really *Lyra Heroica* is one of the most beautiful examples of commercial printing that Edinburgh has ever sent out. But perhaps Blaikie's chief claim to a place in literary history was the share he had, with his friend Fitzroy Bell, in founding the *Scots Observer*, that amusing, audacious and truculent weekly which is said to have cost its proprietors several thousand pounds a year. It was Blaikie who brought Henley to Edinburgh as the paper's editor.

When at the end of November my "journey" was finished, my sister came up to London and I took her, on the strength of my as yet non-existent profits, to Paris for a week. We had a good time. It was easier to have a good time in Paris then, and cheaper. We visited all the good restaurants I knew or of which I had heard—the Tour d'Argent, La-pérouse, Sylvain's, Foyot's, Marguery's. We could neither of us understand why it was that, with the exception of Mar-guery's, at no one of the restaurants I have named did we find more than two other clients, and in each case they were young clients, seemingly as young and inexperienced as we were ourselves. It may have been that in the first week in December people were already saving up for Christmas!

'And it was cold. Whatever the reason, we came to the conclusion that a young couple was a necessary piece of furniture in a Paris restaurant. You have only to look like a young couple to gain sympathy. I remember that, planning to go to Paris that time by the late afternoon boat, we found it was so rough at Dover that we could not cross and had to seek refuge at the Lord Warden. At about nine the waves lessened and a seaman came to announce the boat's departure. My sister and I, anxious not to miss a single hour in Paris, leaped to our feet—but it was not to be so easy.... Elderly ladies had observed us sympathetically and had come to the conclusion that we had been married that very afternoon. Some approached my sister to tell her that it would be indiscreet to travel in such a storm; others came to me and suggested that I was a fool....

It was Charles Whibley who recommended me to Lapérouse. It was a place he had much frequented with Whistler, his brother-in-law. I do not think it has greatly changed. Its Burgundies and Beaujolais were excellent. I recall a Moulin à Vent at four francs before the War. The bottle had no label; one was convinced at first sight of the lump of coarse red wax that sealed the cork that here was no commercial *monopole*. During the War Lapérouse became rather too transatlantic in its *clientèle*. My wife and I lunched there with Miss Meg Villars in one of those troubled years. The prices had been keyed up to the capacity of the richer Americans. No doubt that Moulin à Vent is finished.

VIII

WILL ROTHENSTEIN AND CHARLES CONDER–MRS. MEYNELL–G. K. C.'S FIRST BOOK

I HAD not in this first year of my work allowed my interest in painting to sleep. I had assiduously attended the more advanced exhibitions, had continued to sneer with the best of my contemporaries at the work of the Melbury Road school of artists, and I had, greatly daring, gone to the length of commissioning Will Rothenstein to do for me a series of drawings to be called *English Portraits*, which was to make a companion volume to, and be an advance on, the *Oxford Portraits* published by John Lane. But Rothenstein and Lane and I were, all three of us, in this matter, in advance of our time. The public was not yet ripe for such sincere, such uncompromising portraiture, or, perhaps I should say, for sincerity of that particular brand. I do not know how the Lane book went. Perhaps well, for it had a small and special appeal to the Oxford which was mirrored in its pages. *English Portraits* did not succeed–if by success one means sale. And yet it ought to have succeeded. Way printed the lithographs beautifully; the typography, influenced by Heinemann's manipulation of Whistler's letterpress, looked beautiful; the short character-sketches of the subjects, the work of various and distinguished hands, were, some of them, beautiful pieces of prose. I think that Rothenstein himself in his own Reminiscences tells the story of Sir Arthur Pinero's annoyance with the few paragraphs that "Max" had written about him. (I never knew how the playwright discovered the identity of his critic.) For some reason the publication was unfortunate; I quarrelled with Will about the portrait

67

of Grant Allen, for I did not like it; and altogether, apart from my pride in it as a publisher, I was not happy in the venture. And of course it locked up a great deal of money, locked it up permanently as it turned out. Some of the drawings were extraordinarily successful, those of George Gissing and William Archer in particular. I seem to remember that in the prospectus of the work both the artist and I, as the publisher, undertook that the drawings should never elsewhere be reproduced. Since then, many of them have been reproduced in all sorts of places, but it was not my fault. Let it be a warning to publishers not to make such rash promises, for one can never be sure that one's successors will respect them.

At that time Will, permanently established in London, was living in Glebe Place, at Number 53. We quarrelled; but not, thank heaven, for ever. In September, 1903, he wrote to me from 26 Church Row, Hampstead—trust him to find beautiful places in which to live: the top floor at Number 23 rue Fontaine, Paris, for instance, wanted some beating in 1892, although you might not think it to-day as you climb slowly the hill that takes you to the Place Blanche—that, having heard a year before from "Robert Ross of Carfax" that I was willing to part with the surplus stock of the *Portraits*, he would, if I liked, take it off my hands: "I think after six years there is no reason for us to look at one another like kylons at opposite ends of a chimney-piece—and we are both now fathers of families." I forget what did ultimately happen to the *Portraits*, and I know only one other man who has a complete set of large-paper proofs of them—Crosby Gaige of New York—but I do remember that Will had always a master's hand when he took up his pen to write even the briefest note. The volumes of his Life witness generally to his skill. I am glad that I have kept his letters.

I suppose it was through Rothenstein that Charles Conder heard of me. I had wanted to meet Conder ever since Will had described him to me and shown me the witty portrait that he had done of the elder man. Well, I had not been established in Henrietta Street many weeks when I was told that Conder had called. "Show him in," I said with delight; and in came the emaciated, overwrought, untidy and yet dandy-ish figure of the painter who was already fluttering so many hearts and dovecotes. He was nervous and so, in consequence, was I. He had a portfolio under his arm and I hoped he had come with some project with which, as a publisher, I might fall in. Not so, however. He had been led by some practical joker to think of me as an amateur of the fine arts, as a possible collector, as someone who was at least sure to be interested in his work and who might be induced to buy. And it was soon evident that he was determined that he would not leave my room until I had bought:

"But, my dear Mr. Conder, you've been deceived. I should love to have one of these beautiful paintings, but I haven't, and shan't have for years, any money for pictures. I've only just started as a publisher. Everything goes out; nothing comes in. I want every penny I have for my business—and more, a great deal more. . . ."

I might as well have been talking to a child, a wilful child —and perhaps this wayward genius was nothing more—for he wouldn't listen to me. I must have some of his paintings— small paintings on silk they were, some of the best that he had done—and it was absolutely necessary that he should go away with some of my money. At last, that he might see that it was useless to persist, I asked him how much he wanted for the fans and other small fragments of silk that I liked so much. I thought he would mention figures which I could straightway declare to be impossible and that I should be able to send him off unsatisfied but unoffended. But that was not, at least on that occasion, Charles Conder's way of doing business. No, not at all. He looked round my rather barn-like room in which nothing was for beauty save a cheap Turkish rug, a Bonnard screen—oh, such a jolly screen, Paris of that very day, all fiacres, nurses and playing children!— and a few Cheret posters; he looked round and, turning to me, asked whether as a business man I thought I should be able to do much satisfactory business in a great room without a window, without a picture, business, that is to say, with artists (for he would allow literary men to be artists), with men and women who were susceptible to atmosphere, to surroundings: "Why, it's impossible; it's an idea of the middle of the century. You see, Mr. Grant Richards, you need pictures on the walls; you must have them—and they must be my pictures. Besides, they won't cost you anything to speak of——"

I interrupted him: "But it would be a great deal for me to speak of——"

"No, no! You'll never speak of it; you'll be ashamed to say how little you've paid—you'll keep it dark for the sake of your own reputation——"

"Yes—perhaps. But you don't tell me how much you do want—for this one, for instance," and I picked out the "drawing on silk" which was afterwards chosen as the first of the reproductions in Frank Gibson's *Charles Conder: His Life and Work*, a painting which Cunninghame Graham, no doubt with his tongue in his cheek, declared, when he saw it, to be so improper that he wondered that anyone dared to hang it on his wall.

However, I was still some way from getting down to brass tacks with my eager artist. "It isn't a question of what I want for that painting, Mr. Grant Richards. Really, it isn't. . . . Look here! I'll be frank with you. There's a certain sum I must have. It isn't much. You say you can't afford to buy paintings. But you can afford what I want— even if you think of it as expended on furniture as necessary as these chairs and that desk. It's a question of what you want in exchange for seventeen pounds. . . ."

His sentence faded out. At first I didn't understand what he meant. He explained. I could take what I wanted and I was to give him seventeen pounds. The situation struck me then, and strikes me now, thirty-seven years later, as an awkward one. Here was Charles Conder, a painter, an artist, a considerable talent, a figure, needing for some reason or another this comparatively trifling sum; and here was I who, much as I admired the work he had shown me, couldn't afford to gratify my taste even to the extent of seventeen pounds. . . . From my point of view any one of these pictures was worth more than that! Conder looked at me and I looked at Conder. I wished to heaven that no one had thought of sending him to me. What good could come of it? But whatever the reason that moved him, whatever prank had got him into a scrape in which seventeen pounds was necessary, Charles Conder was not going to budge. "Look here, dear Mr. Grant Richards—you are going to give me seventeen pounds and I am going to make it worth your while, however careful you have to be. You give me a cheque and you can have that painting you like—no, stop: don't be in such a hurry—you shall have this *Prince Charming* that you like too, and this fan"—*The Peacock Fan*[1] it was—"and—"

I stopped him then. "You know you're making it very difficult for me—" I began.

"Not difficult at all—"

"I mean, these three pictures are worth a great deal more than seventeen pounds—"

"Try! They're not. I *have* tried. I know. I thought I'd get what I wanted for any one of them—but dealers aren't buyers, or English dealers aren't anyway! I tell you that if you take these three pictures—no, not 'if', for you *are* going to take them—I tell you that if to-morrow you go out and try to get seventeen pounds for them you won't succeed.

---

[1] Some sixteen years later the *Times* critic dealing with a memorial exhibition of Conder's work signalled out *The Peacock Fan* as one of his "finest inventions of delicate unrealities". The article began interestingly: "Guy de Maupassant said of Swinburne that he was the most extravagantly artistic being that he had ever met; and it might be said of Conder's pictures that they are the most extravagantly artistic that ever were painted. Like Swinburne, he belonged to an inartistic people, and his art was the result of a violent artistic reaction against his surroundings." Yes, I do seem to have been justified in diverting that seventeen pounds! Conder should have been contemporary with Ronald Firbank and have illustrated *Valmouth* and the rest.

You'd have to wait for the man who wants a Conder; *I* can't afford to wait!"

Yes, he was so frank and so sincere that I succumbed. I gave Charles Conder his cheque and he left my room apparently well pleased. And I was pleased too in a sense: I had three Conders; I should rank as a Conder collector. But I was not very well pleased. I could not afford seventeen pounds and most assuredly I felt that I had been forced against my will to take advantage of an artist's temporary lack of money. Anyhow, I was not proud.

Charles Conder's visit had a sequel—but its story is for a later chapter.

Alice Meynell was my next venture—could I hope to get a book from Mrs. Wilfred Meynell? Why not? She had always been gracious to me, kind indeed. I could try. But I had no very original idea to lay before her. Would she make me an anthology of what she herself believed the most beautiful things in English poetry? Would she make it without any capitulation to what other anthologists, other critics, had chosen or thought? I think she was rather pleased at the idea. It was to be called *The Flower of the Mind* and I promised that its dress should be worthy of its contents. Constable was to print it; Laurence Housman was to design the binding. I paid seventy-five guineas to Mrs. Meynell for her work. That book had its circle of admirers but it did not sell well, and I lost about ten pounds on it first and last; but I added to my reputation. The trouble was that there were, even in those days, quite enough anthologies on the market. I tried it in two forms—one of the conventional crown-octavo size and one in a small pocket form. Many of its critics were so shocked at the wilful omission of the *Elegy in a Country Churchyard* that they succeeded in making the whole thing suspect. Booksellers are shy of trying to sell a book which has what is from the point of view of the general a glaring defect. Robert Buchanan was one who did not like this "vegetarian anthology" and seized the opportunity of dedicating one of his *Latter-Day Letters*, "The Angel in the House as Précieuse", to the author of *Renouncement*. The Letter was a flagrant piece of work, committing almost all possible errors of taste.

But I must not run on in my pride about these books that I published in my first months. Many of them were good; some were very good; some were the first books of authors who have since made tens of thousands of pounds out of their work and sell now with each story they publish into hundreds of thousands; and some were the first efforts of writers whom their contemporaries believe to have secured immortality. Who am I that I should judge? I was not Laurence Binyon's first publisher but I was almost his first, with *Porphyrion*; I published the first Alfred Noyes—*The Loom of Years*—but that was not until 1902; and, yes, I was the first publisher of G. K. Chesterton. But that was almost an accident. It happened in the following manner:

R. Brimley Johnson, who died last year, was a man destined to live with books from the moment of his birth. A connection of the Macmillans, he went to Cambridge. He came down and seemed to plunge into the making of books. If you were ill-natured you would say he looked and was a hack, but he was more than a hack: he had enthusiasm and he was full of publishing ideas; indeed he set up as a publisher at 8 York Buildings, Adelphi, at much the same time as I started myself. But he hadn't much self-confidence and when it was open to him to publish a book of serious verse by a young friend, Gilbert Keith Chesterton, he brought the manuscript to me rather than run any kind of risk on his own account. The book was *The Wild Knight*. Brimley Johnson liked it and why he did not whip up his courage was always an enigma to me, for he did publish the humorous *Greybeards at Play* later on. When my book came out some of the critics declared that it was much influenced by John Davidson. Perhaps it was. G. K. C. has done a deal of influencing on his own account since those days! I never had occasion to meet Chesterton in connection with *The Wild Knight*, and no good fairy whispered to me that it would be very much worth my while to make some opportunity of doing so. Johnson carried things through for him. Indeed I never did speak to him or sit in the same room with him until some thirty-five years later—last year in fact—when large, jovial, bacchic and looking exactly like himself, he was a fellow-guest with me at a supper of Sir John Squire's Invalids, a club of wandering cricketers, at The Cheshire Cheese. Chesterton sat on Squire's right and drank burgundy, having the wisdom to prefer it to beer, and you looked at him and felt that he was a man. I wonder whether anyone else has noticed his likeness to Belfort Bax, as that dear and sybaritic old philosopher came to be in his last years. Well, I must not pretend that I foresaw in those late 'nineties what a writer and what an influence G. K. C. was to become. (Writing in the *New Statesman* of January 12, 1916, on the Need for a Coalition of the Intelligentsia, Bernard Shaw remarked in passing that "the War Office has not as much brains as the brim of Mr. Chesterton's hat".) The fact that his work had to be pressed on me by a rival publisher may have made me careless of the chance that had been vouchsafed.

My cousin, young Grant Allen, reminds me that when he left me he joined Brimley Johnson for a while as sole assistant. They would close the office at one and go out to lunch and often G. K. C. would choose that hour to call. When he did so he would leave no card in the letter-box but would draw his own portrait in coloured chalk on the glass door to show that he had been there.

It was at about this time that I made the acquaintance of a man who had in those days hardly an equal for knowledge, intelligence and cunning in the whole publishing trade. This generation knows him as Temple Scott. When I first met him he was working for George Bell and Sons and was called Isaac Henry Solomon Isaacs. He looked like Isaac Henry Solomon Isaacs too, and he also looked like a genius. Indeed

I am by no means sure that he isn't a genius. He managed
Bell's Colonial Library and used to come to see me about the
novels I published. He would buy for Bell—who, curiously
enough, published at that time no novels on their own account—a thousand or more copies of such stories as he
thought at all "likely" in "sheets"[1] at some low, but not
unprofitable, figure, would bind them up in a Bell uniform
binding—and then he would be sure of a sale—for the colonial
booksellers knew that they could trust the Bell imprint. Of
Grant Allen's *An African Millionaire* he took over four
thousand. It must have been a paying affair for Bell. The
finance was a simple matter, for each transaction was paid by
a six months' bill. It was a satisfactory method for a new
publisher who could have few accounts open with Colonial
booksellers; I fancy it has almost entirely died out nowadays,[2] although the Colonial bookseller, and the Colonial
book-buyer too, still buys, as he did then, his English fiction
—generally at least—at a considerably lower price than is
paid in England. As a result, of course, the author gets on
copies sold to the Colonies a very much lower royalty than
he gets on copies sold in Britain. Sometimes the same thing
happens with books which are not novels.

Normally Australia provides the best Colonial market.
The bookseller over there must have considerable difficulty
in providing his customers with anything like an up-to-date
stock. Of course he cannot afford to order books for a chance
sale when he is six weeks or so from his sources of supply.
Sample copies shown by the travellers of the London publishers do help, but then as often as not they do not reach
Australia until first copies of the book itself arrive. The
cable has to be kept at work, an expensive item even when
an elaborate code is used. There are agents in London
who buy according to schedule for their Australasian and
South African customers. These schedules used to make

[1] Unbound and unfolded copies, copies just as they came off the machines, in fact.
[2] Bell gave up their Colonial Library in 1918.

amusing reading. They provided a list of novelists who had any sort of popular appeal and indicated how many copies of each novelist's book might be sent out on appearance. In the old days Hall Caine and Marie Corelli had the largest figures after their names. The lists were subject to revision. A man would fall or rise on the list. It was curious to see how certain novelists of the highest reputation here had apparently no public at all across the Indian Ocean. . . .[1]

I had very bad luck with my Colonial trade in my second year. The sale of *No. 5 John Street* had been great even in the Colonies, semi-highbrow though it was, and one particular London agent had to take it in considerable quantities. He had also ordered my earlier books generously. I suppose Isaacs, never having heard of Richard Whiteing, had made no offer to secure the book for Bell's Colonial Library, so I dealt with the Colonial market myself. Suddenly that agent failed. Mine, of course, was a very small house with a small turnover, but the agent owed me not much short of four hundred pounds. It was a blow. My small capital would not have stood a repetition of such a blow. I attended a meeting of the creditors at the Cannon Street Hotel and heard the explanation that was made, and as it was my first experience of the kind, I felt very vindictive. One learns to take such things in a more sensible spirit. But that smash, happening when it did, was very awkward.

But to return to Isaacs. He would come in and talk to me by the hour about publishing and of how foolish publishers

---

[1] A correspondent settling in Kimberley wrote to me in November 1902: "Between four and five dozen copies of *The Unspeakable Scot* have been disposed of in this town to my knowledge by the two leading booksellers here. I got into conversation with one of them. . . . He sells twenty-five novels to one of any other kind of book. He orders direct from the publishers, and has standing orders for books by popular authors. Thus Hall Caine's publishers have to supply him with forty-eight copies of any new book of his; an Anthony Hope, twenty-four, and so forth. Still, he always orders a few copies of any new book which has caused a stir in England." He writes again four months later: "What people want here is the Marie Corelli style of thing. Price cuts very little figure in the sale of a book here."

were and of what they should do, and after a time my ingenuous bearing must have attracted him and he must have seen possibilities in me, for he wrote me in his tiny half-mediaeval hand a long letter in which he proposed to leave Bell and to come to me as manager and chief assistant. Together, he thought, we should conquer the world. He did not ask an unduly large salary and I took him at his own valuation. He taught me a great deal. If I had had a large enough capital I dare say we might have done wonders together. We were all young in that office. Young Grant Allen who was doing the country travelling, was very young indeed. The schemes that we evolved! We set to work at one time to secure from the public fifty or a hundred thousand pounds with which we proposed to revolutionise the trade in novels. It deserves a chapter to itself, that scheme. It shall have it one day.

IX

RICHARD LE GALLIENNE AND G.B.S.—*A SHROPSHIRE LAD*—
T. B. MOSHER

I TRY to remember how and when the name of Richard Le Gallienne first came into my consciousness. One knew him as "Log-Roller" of the *Star*; he succeeded Clement King Shorter as that paper's literary critic. Anyhow, it must have been very early. The name, once heard, was one to remain in the memory. Certainly when I was "doing the books" for W. T. Stead I read *The Student and the Body-Snatcher*, which Le Gallienne wrote in collaboration with Robinson K. Leather—whose name, by the way, comes first on the title-page. Who is Mr. Leather? What else has he done?—That was in 1890, and in 1891 I must have heard of some announcement of Frank Murray's (Murray was a Derby bookseller who might with a little encouragement have blossomed into an English Mosher) for I have a letter, dated August 28, 1891:

6 STAPLE INN,
HOLBORN, W.C.

DEAR SIR,

I have been out of town or I sh^d have answered your courteous letter before.

It chances that the new volume of which I spoke will be out immediately. I should not be surprised if a copy is in your hands at the present moment.

It is called *The Book Bills of Narcissus* and was written as a commission for Mr. Frank Murray, as a volume of a bookish series published by him.

I am now a little sorry that it goes forth to the world

in that form, as both that and the title really belie its contents, which I think you will see are far more human than dilettante, and really designed for a broad appeal. As Mr. Murray tells me his whole edition [only two hundred and fifty copies] is subscribed for, I shall now endeavour to win a wider audience by a larger and more accessible edition—that is, of course, if criticism encourages such attempt.

Forgive my troubling you with these matters, but you have shown yourself so sympathetic to my other work that I felt I should like you to know that my little book makes a more serious attempt than appearances might argue.

In a chapter on "The Children of Apollo" I "speak up" about modern Art-cant for which I think I shall have a sympathiser in the *R. of R.*

But enough

Believe me
faithfully yours
RICHARD LE GALLIENNE.

To Grant Richards, Esq.

Le Gallienne, as I say, was on the *Star*. Ernest Parke, then its editor, must have had an unrivalled nose for the critic who would serve his purpose, for Le Gallienne's particular mind, his sympathies and his interests, made him the very man to guide the aspirations of the earnest and half-educated youths—I was one of them—who read his paper, while "Corno di Bassetto" (George Bernard Shaw's name for himself) dealt with music in a way that made it fun to read his column even if one didn't know the difference between Handel and Tschaikovsky; and A. B. Walkley, who "did the drama" and who contributed Saturday articles, made the theatre more interesting to me than any other writer has ever done. The name of the art critic, "Artist Unknown", hid the identity of Joseph Pennell. In course of time we lost Le

79

Gallienne to America, but "Corno di Bassetto" became Bernard Shaw and Walkley, after being "A. B. W." in Henley's *National Observer* and in the *Speaker*, went to *The Times*. Parke believed in pushing his young men along. To get them talked about must have been his principle, and he had, from the point of view of publicity, a brilliant idea when he gave *The Book Bills* to G. B. S. to review. Shaw fell on it heavily —on September 12. After declaring that "if an unusually fine literary instinct could make a solid book, Mr. Le Gallienne would be at no loss for an enduring reputation", he goes on to hope that his erstwhile colleague would "gain knowledge otherwise than through his books, and with it temper, bias, one-sidedness, bigotry, and everything that is fatal to the negativeness of perfect taste. No doubt that is only an opinion of mine; but I do not think the readers of the *Star* will under-value any opinion which appears over the once-familiar signature of Corno di Bassetto."

When a year later Le Gallienne's *English Poems* appeared Ernest Parke and G. B. S. repeated the same experiment, Shaw being allowed a column and a half in which to deal faithfully with the young poet—and, according to his lights, he made full use of space and opportunity, guying his victim in a friendly but rather disconcerting manner and quoting stanza after stanza in such a way and with such comment that it is a wonder that the book did not at once secure the sale of the more surprising of the early Swinburnes—and all this no doubt with the idea both of doing Le Gallienne good and at the same time making him the talk of the town and a success. I must quote from the review:

"I wonder why I of all *Star* reviewers, should have been asked to deal with this book—I, di Bassetto, most prosaic of critics. For I do not enthuse readily over the smaller fancy wares of art: the builder, not the jeweller, is the man for my money; and your miniatures and fan paintings, your ballads and *morceaux de salon*, make but a finnicking appeal to the Bassettian spirit, nursed upon cathedrals, frescoes and giant Wagnerian music-epics. Besides, it is against my vow to let any man off cheaply in the arts. I am no smirking verger to let all comers who look good for a tip into the choir and among the tombs of the mighty dead, there to pose and scratch their names until Time, Death and Judgment come down out of Mr. Watts's picture, and inexorably eject them. Rather let me stand at the gate I guard, fell, grim, and venomous, not to say downright unpopular, holding it against all who are not strong enough to make a doormat of me. And yet Mr. Le Gallienne is such an uncommonly likely young man, and so easily able to do me a good turn one day—for is he not a professed log-roller—that I am half tempted to do what so many of the other vergers do and make a pretty exhibition of tact and good nature by passing him quietly in after a little coquetry with his claims. But in England this cannot safely be done without a careful investigation of the applicant's moral character; and I regret to say that the most cursory examination of Mr. Le Gallienne's hymn-book is enough to convince any verger that a more abandoned youth has seldom presented himself at the choir gates of an English cathedral. Just listen to this, for instance, from page 91, the first and third verse (the second is too awful for quotation)."

There follow two stanzas of *Neæra's Hair*, which, by the way, also shocked William Archer's sense of the proprieties.[1] G. B. S. proceeds:

"Now I ask, is this proper? Is it moral? . . . I wonder what people would say of me if I wrote such things. . . . Mr. Le Gallienne ought to know that a writer should never read anything but the book of life. . . . It really does take a most tremendous equipment to survive oneself as a poet. In fact, the demand is so unreasonable that I do not myself consider immortality worth having at the price. For you

[1] See *Poets of the Younger Generation*, by William Archer, 1902.

must not only make good verses, but you must write poetry which the very cleverest poets of succeeding generations shall not be able to renew and replace. . . ."

Le Gallienne's admirers were not, of course, going to let this Shavian criticism go by default. "A Disgusted Reader" wrote to the *Star* to liken G. B. S.'s opinions to "the disagreeable attentions of a Newfoundland dog newly come from gambolling in the mud, so offensive is his ungainly beslaverment of Mr. Le Gallienne. . . . He does not pretend, he says, to be a judge of jewellery and perhaps it would have been better if Mr. Le Gallienne's pearls had been cast before some more discriminating critics for appraisement". In the meantime the book, of which only eight hundred copies had been printed for England and America, did sell fairly well. The collector should try to find a copy in which is loosely laid a four-page leaflet, *Three Poems Printed for Private Circulation Only*, and bearing a quotation from Herrick:

I write of youth, of love, and have access
By these to sing of cleanly wantonness.

I am reminded that Herrick himself was treated by Mr. A. W. Pollard, his editor, and Laurence and Bullen, his publishers, in the same manner, when in 1891 his Works appeared in the Muses' Library, for his "coarser epigrams and poems" appeared in a separately printed appendix, which had neither title on its wrapper, nor title-page, nor printers' nor publishers' name.

In that same autumn of 1892 G. B. S. was indeed busy in his correction of the young poet, for, a month or more earlier, in the *Daily Chronicle*, he had fallen foul of Le Gallienne over the use of "and which". The curious will find on September 2 a letter " 'And which' etcetera". A day or two before, it seems, the poet had contributed to the famous literary page of the *Chronicle* a review—anonymous, it is true—of George Saintsbury's *Miscellaneous Essays*, in which he must have protested against colloquialisms which, in certain circumstances, have always had Shavian support. G. B. S. took up his pen in a letter to the editor:

"If you do not immediately suppress the person who takes it upon himself to lay down the law almost every day in your columns on the subject of literary compositions, I will give up the *Chronicle*. The man is a pedant, an ignoramus, an idiot, a self-advertising duffer. . . . Your fatuous specialist, driven out of his 'and which' stronghold, is now beginning to rebuke 'second-rate' newspapers for using such phrases as 'to suddenly go' and 'to boldly say'. I ask you, Sir, to put this man out. Give the porter orders to use such violence as may be necessary if he attempts to return, without, however, interfering with his perfect freedom of choice between 'to suddenly go', 'to go suddenly' and 'suddenly to go'. See that he does not come back: that is the main thing. And allow me, as one who has some little right to speak on the subject, to assure your readers that they may, without the slightest misgiving, turn their adverbed infinitives in any of the three ways given above. All they need consider is which of the three best conveys by its rhythm the feeling they wish to express. . . . Be advised by me, Mr. Editor; send him adrift and try an intelligent Newfoundland dog in his place."

It is of course not unlikely that G. B. S. had no idea whom he was attacking, although in his role of guardian of the gate it would not have made any difference. Not that H. W. Massingham would have been wise in taking the Shavian advice. Le Gallienne was, even from the commercial point of view, a very valuable member of the *Chronicle* staff in those "renascing" days. He had enthusiasm and he was able to impart enthusiasm, and, in any bad sense of the word, he was no log-roller. He was, as a critic, first and foremost, a stimulus to the enjoyment of letters, and it is certain that if his scholarship was neither wide nor deep (and indeed he would have been the last to suggest that it was) his love of books was something that lay far deeper than scholarship. I turn over the pages of two little privately printed pamphlets of his, *Limited Editions* and *Thomas Bird Mosher*, and I recall vividly the young Le Gallienne of the little house in which he lived with his first wife and then of Mulberry Cottage, Boston Road, New Brentford, where he lay night after night struggling with asthma and yet using every sleepless minute in reading and writing.

Where now can youth feed his ardour for literature as he could in H. W. Massingham's famous *Chronicle* page? The secret of such an achievement seems to be lost—or perhaps the necessity of appealing in every line of the popular newspaper to the taste of two million possible buyers has made it commercially impossible. That famous page hung together; in one cunning way and another it supplied day after day the continuous interest of a good serial story.

I had my difficulties with Le Gallienne of course; and I made my mistakes. I have told elsewhere how I lost him a manuscript and an income. That was not a mistake; it was a crime. My idea of inducing him to try his hand at a new rendering of Omar was a mistake.

The letter of Le Gallienne's that I quoted just now was written from Staple Inn, which has housed a procession of literary men. When I first began to earn a living in London I had a friend in Staple Inn—Tom Heslewood, the painter, the designer of stage costumes, the actor—and my ambition was to occupy his rooms and ultimately to live in the Inn. My mother frowned on the idea. Heslewood had a complete skeleton as a companion, and we evolved the notion of hanging it out of his first-floor window where, with its legs and arms manipulated by strings, it would end by stopping the Holborn traffic while we, with the outer oaken door sported, would be secure from interruption at least until the guardians of the Inn, the Police and the Fire Brigade, could bring ladders and fire escapes. Alas, it remained a notion.

Another man of letters with whom I have reason to associate Staple Inn is E. H. Lacon Watson, who had chambers in an inner court and existed in the ideal manner of a man

who could afford to be careless of the outer world, to live
with his books and his fine wines, and to loaf and invite his
soul. I published one book of Lacon Watson's—*Benedictine*
—which deserved far more notice than it secured.

I associate Le Gallienne rather with Verulam Buildings,
across the road in Gray's Inn, than with Staple Inn. For
there lived his sister, Sissie Welch, with her husband James
Welch, the actor, and there or thereabouts was a little colony
of Bodley Head authors to know whom was to be in the
literary movement of the day. For people talked incessantly
of the *Yellow Book* and of Lane's authors—and Heinemann's.
Just then books were fashionable!

Le Gallienne, as "Log-Roller", was always making discoveries in the *Star*. Perhaps he was too ready to praise. So
were most critics of his age and school. In the *Academy*,
under J. S. Cotton, and in the *Athenæum* under Vernon Ren-
dall, however, praise was not so easily come by. Lionel
Johnson was, for instance, not the "smirking verger" of
G. B. S.'s review, nor did Theodore Watts or poor Edmund
Gosse put themselves out to find new talent—although it is
fair to say that Gosse was one of the first passengers on the
Kipling omnibus, and he "tumbled to" the importance of Ibsen almost as soon as anyone else, although he could not have
been called helpful in the matter of the Norwegian dramatist.
Still, in spite of Sir Arthur Pinero's phrase—"always, blame,
blame, blame; praise, never"—there was a good deal of lauda-
tion floating about. Too much for some people. And then of
course Sir Sidney Colvin always had a protégé of some kind.
Once you have had a man like Stevenson attached to your
apron strings, I suppose you have always to be looking about
for a successor. Stevenson's successors in the Colvin nursery
were not always the successes Sir Sidney hoped for. With
Le Gallienne praise was a matter of temperament. He was
always exhibiting his own pleasure in some writer of the past
to whom the appearance of a new edition gave him an excuse
to burn incense; or else discovering some entirely new man.
Norman Gale, published off the map, so to speak—that is to

say, at Rugby by George E. Over—did not escape his quick
and appreciative eye; and he was up to his ears in the Stephen
Phillips boom. There were others—novelists, essayists, short-
story writers. Not all of them came off, but Le Gallienne has
an unusually creditable record. Knowing infinitely more
about literature than I could ever learn to know, he influenced me profoundly in my early likes and dislikes. Such
taste as I showed in the early days of my publishing owes
much to his *Star* articles; the paths on which I set my feet
were often indicated by his enthusiasms. He almost turned
me into a book-collector; indeed, I became a sedulous reader
of second-hand booksellers' catalogues, secured copies of the
early and obscure Norman Gale volumes, and even found a
first edition of Sir Thomas Browne which, years afterwards,
being more than usually short of money, I sold to Bumpus
for something like a profit. I rather gave up searching for
rare books, however, when one day, coming home to Rossetti Gardens Mansions, where I shared a flat with my cousin
Frederick Whelen—coming home late, as he had had a meeting of some socialist committee in the room in which my
books were housed and I, having reached what seemed to be
the end of my socialist interests, having no wish to arrive
in the middle of it—I found that he had used the cover of
Norman Gale's *Primulas and Pansies* to inform me very in-
sistently that I should find the whisky in the dining-room.
The book was spoiled. Whelen had a host of books of his
own, for he had been one of the founders of the Browning
Society, an early Fabian, and was, and is, a seriously minded
person in every way—as audiences all over the world can
testify; but his books were for use; they were not the accu-
mulation of a would-be collector.

Le Gallienne it was whose writing first told me of *A Shropshire Lad*. I find I devoted to it what nowadays seem to me
very odd lines in the *Review of Reviews* of August 1896: "A
new writer, A. E. Housman, a very real poet, and a very
English one at that. . . . Simplicity is the note of Mr. Housman's style—simplicity and a dignified restraint. Open at

86

page 38 and read the poem that begins 'Is my team ploughing?' and then tell me if you do not consider Mr. Housman
a distinct acquisition to the little body of young men who
are worthily doing their best to keep alive the tradition of
English song." Ingenuous words; to-day I blush to read
them! Kegan Paul published the book—at half a crown:
there were five hundred copies. In those days Kegan Paul
published dozens of books of verse every year—and generally
the author paid the bill. In the case of *A Shropshire Lad* the
manuscript had been offered to Kegan Paul on that basis,
just as it had been offered to Macmillan. Macmillan would
have none of it! They had a reason: they did not find an easy
sale for poetry! Charles Whibley said that John Morley was
responsible for Macmillan's verdict! It was Arthur Waugh
who "read" the manuscript for Kegan Paul and it is a source
of wonder to me, a wonder to which I often return in the night
watches, that he, of a younger generation than John Morley,
did not insist on Kegan Paul securing all possible rights in the
first book of this new poet. Surely Waugh did his best? Con-
tributing some reminiscences to *John o' London* of November 8, 1930, he says briefly for the benefit of bibliographers
that "the original manuscript bore the legend 'By Terence
Hearsay', which explains the fact that the final poem begins
'Terence, this is stupid stuff'—a reference not easily intelligi-
ble when the pseudonym has vanished from the title-page".

I also find it strange that Arthur Waugh, with *A Shropshire Lad* in his mind, in his very next sentence indeed, describes the fact of being the publisher of Austin Dobson as
"the greatest privilege" he experienced at Kegan Paul's.
Tastes differ. But surely the very pretty verses of the author
of *Proverbs in Porcelain* are not so good as all that! Of course
they are not, although no doubt Dobson was, as Waugh says,
a "Prince of Courtesy". I met Dobson once. Bidden to lunch
at the National Liberal Club, as a very young man, by Edmund Gosse, I found that Dobson was my fellow-guest. I
had to fetch my host at the Board of Trade, and I have an
idea that, on that day at least, both he and Dobson were

working in the same room. I carried away no memory of hard work in the service of the country. There was a very leisurely atmosphere, and the lunch was very leisurely too. I thought of Charles Lamb and his experience of the Civil Service. No doubt things are different to-day. Dobson was courtesy itself, and patient with youth. I thought of him as solid, double-chinned, gentle. Why did Gosse ask me to lunch? I have no idea. Heinemann, who liked me, might have told him that I should be encouraged. I saw very little of Gosse thereafter, but in the first or second year of the century he wrote a letter accompanying the manuscript of a poetic drama, *Gaston de Foix*, which he suggested I should read myself and publish. He had praise for it and for its author, and made prophecies as to its author's future. That author was Maurice Baring, but I doubt whether Gosse foresaw the direction his protégé's talent would take. Of course I took his advice—I always took the advice of mandarins like Gosse in those days. Within a year of publication I sold a hundred and sixty copies, but that sad fact does not detract from the lustre that comes naturally to one of the earliest English publishers of Maurice Baring's work.

The article of Arthur Waugh's from which I have just quoted reminds me that when E. V. Lucas was preparing for me *A Book of Verses for Children* and I had hurried up and sold the American rights to Henry Holt, through Waugh, Holt, an enterprising and educated publisher but one who was always reluctant to leave author and manuscript alone, thinking his role was both that of editor and publisher, kept "butting in", being anxious to have his say in the book's contents. Mr. Lucas "did not much appreciate American interference", but Arthur Waugh was, and is, much of a diplomatist, and that English anthologist and American publisher did not quarrel is shown by the fact that Holt also published Lucas's second anthology, *The Open Road*.

Writing of Frank Murray just now I wrote the name of Mosher. Thomas B. Mosher was an American publisher who, fitly enough, carried on business at Portland, Maine, a state whose coast, indented, according to my atlas, with creeks and rich in islands and rivers, is, apart from its climate, the very place for pirates. He produced charming little books and a periodical *The Bibelot*. Yes, Andrew Lang was not incorrect in calling him a "pirate" in that he made full use of the fact that at the time he greatly flourished the English writer had little or no copyright protection in the United States. But it is difficult to see why the word "pirate" should be used in any opprobrious sense, since all that he did was to avail himself of his legal rights. Besides, much of what Mosher printed was "chosen from scarce editions and from sources not generally known", while at all times he used material that was, according to the law of his country, within the public domain. However, pirate or honest man, Mosher was more or less a scholar and had as high a standard of book production and, apparently, as fine a sense of literary values, as any bookmaker or publisher working in the United States in his day. He did much, in that long dreary period which Miss Dorothy Dudley so well describes in *Dreiser and the Land of the Free*[1], to keep the literary torch alight in the forty-five States of the Union. In one of Lang's protests—to the *Critic* of New York—he falls particularly upon the reprint of *Ballads and Lyrics of Old France*. What would the purchaser of the pirated reprint get that he could not get with propriety in the ordinary editions of his books—"One or two badly-done early translations from Villon, which I did not think worth reprinting; one or two from Passerat, Hugo, Musset, and the ballads, a deplorable sonnet, a twaddling lyric, and some misprints. . . . A few trifles which even the author thinks worthless." On that occasion Mr. Lang's modesty was extreme: "an unpopular twitterer" is the way in which he describes himself. In the following year—in Frank Harris's *Saturday Review* on December 5, 1897—this "twitterer" falls under George Moore's displeasure, but Moore uses no such opprobious epithet. Here is his letter:

[1] In America this book was called *Forgotten Frontiers*.

AUTHOR HUNTING

MR. ANDREW LANG AS CRITIC

SIR,

In this month's *Longman's* Mr. Andrew Lang comments somewhat strangely on my article entitled *Since the Elizabethans*, published in *Cosmopolis* for October.

It happened to me to spend a few days last summer in an English village. As I drove from the railway station to the lodging which had been hired for me, I noticed a pleasant river, which seemed to promise excellent fishing. I mentioned the river to my landlady.

"Oh yes, sir," she said, "there is very good fishing here —many people come here for fishing."

"What kind of people come here?" I asked distractedly.

"Literary gentlemen come here very often, sir: we had Mr. Andrew Lang staying here."

"Oh, really ... does he fish? Is he a good fisherman?"

"Yes, sir; he fishes beautifully."

"Really! Does he catch much?"

"No, sir; he never catches anything, but he fishes beautifully."

Yours truly,

GEORGE MOORE.

Frank Murray of Derby, I suppose, had not such financial strength as Mosher, and, moreover, he had the cares of three bookshops. But he did make his mark although he was at the business of book production for only a short time. He helped to keep William Sharp on the map, for instance—he published *Vistas* at the Moray Press in 1904—and was surely the first man to put Fiona Macleod between covers—yes, Murray did that, no doubt on Sharp's advice. It is a coincidence that Le Gallienne, writing about Mosher after his death, was able to state that the inception of Fiona Macleod's fame was largely due to the American pirate's devoted appreciation. Mosher and Murray were linked in that enthusiasm.

X

A SHROPSHIRE LAD

IN the early days of my literary enthusiasm I developed the grangerising habit to the praiseworthy extent of cutting out and keeping in their proper places important reviews of the new books in which I was specially interested. I do not find that I have any reviews of *A Shropshire Lad*, and I therefore assume that it was not received with salvos of critical artillery, that it slipped more or less unheralded from the press and that few of the people whose business it was to recognise and welcome the appearance of a new poet had hastened to notice and proclaim its qualities; it was reviewed neither in the *Athenæum* nor in the *Spectator*. In fact it did not have the immediate success that Will Rothenstein attributed to it in his *Men and Memories*, nor, as a result of its appearance, were "people who had sneered at minor poetry . . . silenced". Curious this apathy, since two (younger) Housmans had already established themselves in London's Book Fair, and it should have occurred to every competent literary editor that talent might go on repeating itself more than once in the same family. Laurence, A. E. Housman's brother, was a man whom most of us knew. Draughtsman, poet, critic, he had a finger in many pies; I myself had gone first to him when I had wanted decorations for the covers of my early books or designs for title-pages and initial letters. Later I was to publish three of his books of verse, *Spikenard*, *The Little Land* and *Rue*. Clemence Housman, his sister, had an unusual distinction as an engraver on wood, and wrote —her *Were-Wolf*, a successful attempt at a re-casting of the old legend, appeared first in *Atalanta*. I doubt nevertheless

91

whether there were many besides Le Gallienne to associate
these other Housmans with that one whose name figured
on the title-page of *A Shropshire Lad;* Le Gallienne must
have been one of the few quickly to cry aloud the merit of
the book. It was difficult to get by Le Gallienne in those
days. He smelt a good book from afar. The dress of *A Shropshire Lad* was in its favour: its modest, unprecious binding,
its brevity, its sincere, unpretentious page, must have combined to make it fairly certain that however many volumes
of verse were jostling for his attention, he would spare a
minute for its closer examination. William Archer, too, was
an early admirer. In 1902, in *Poets of the Younger Generation,* which must surely have been a gathering together of a
series of articles written and presumably published during
several preceding years, he ends an article on Housman with
assurance and hope: "There is no reason why Mr. Housman
should not put off his rustic mask and widen the range of his
subject-matter. I trust he will do so in other and larger
volumes. But even should he be content to remain merely 'a
Shropshire Lad', his place among English poets is secure."
Archer lived to see another if not a larger volume, and,
moreover, one in which the rustic mask was put off, but I
do not know his reaction to *Last Poems.*

Of the first edition of *A Shropshire Lad* five hundred
copies were printed and the type was distributed. I. am
helped to my belief that it enjoyed no immediate success by
the fact that it took some two years to dispose of the edition.
The date of the first edition was February, 1896; it was not
reprinted until September, 1898. The original price was half
a crown, and a copy was sold, at auction in New York before
the slump, for four hundred dollars. All book values have
been steadily dropping since then; to use the language of
the Stock Exchange, weak holders have been shaken out, but
a really good copy of that first edition would be difficult to
find to-day under fifty pounds.

Now when I commenced publisher *A Shropshire Lad* was
perhaps of all books the one I most wanted for my list.

Kegan Paul having published it, not at his own but at its author's expense—the fact was generally known in literary and publishing circles—there was little to prevent any other publisher approaching Mr. Housman in the hope of securing it for his own list. Lane, I believe, had that idea; he had already many Housman affiliations. I, as I say, had it too. So one day I sat down and wrote a letter to A. E. Housman at University College in Gower Street—by then the world that cared had discovered that he held the Professorship of Latin—and begged in as diplomatic a way as possible that I might be allowed to be his publisher, and no doubt indicated politely that whatever arrangements had been made when the book was first issued I should wish to be financially responsible for the production of future editions. And I received a most polite reply, written in a hand whose equal for legibility and uneccentric beauty you will hardly find if you search through the collections of the autograph manuscripts of men of letters either here or in America. But it was the letter's tenor that excited me. Housman did not reject my proposal; nor did he accept it. He replied briefly and simply to the effect that many copies of the first edition still remained on its publisher's shelves, and that it would be time enough to discuss a second edition when they were sold. He gave me reason to hope that I might hear from him again.

Well, I am so constituted that, while I did not take it for granted even for an hour that I was sure to have my way, yet I did most distinctly feel that if I sat tight and avoided making a nuisance of myself by further enquiries the chances were in my favour, and, in a way, I dismissed for a while the matter from my mind and devoted myself to other affairs. Of course, now I come to think of it, I should have been clever and myself have hastened the exhaustion of that first edition. I ought at once to have bought copies here and there singly at this bookseller's and at that, so that the question of a second edition would come up before my name had had time to fade from memory. I dare say, though, that I played the wiser game. You see, I had experience of the scholar's mind; I had too many classical scholars and dons in my own family not to recognise that their mental processes are generally not of the kind that obtains in Whitehall Court and Paternoster Row.

It must have been more than a year later that, sitting in Henrietta Street, I was surprised and elated at having brought to me a card bearing the name of A. E. Housman.

"Show him in." Of course I was elated: he could only have come about one thing.

And I was right. Yes, I might have *A Shropshire Lad;* the first edition was at last exhausted.

"And the terms? What royalty shall I pay? What business arrangements are we to have?"

"Royalties? I want no royalties. You may produce the book—that's all."

"But the profit? The book will become better and better known. It won't take over two years to sell the second edition.[1] There is bound to be profit."

"Well, if there is, then apply it to a reduction in the price of the book. I am not a poet by trade; I am a Professor of Latin. I do not wish to make profit out of my poetry. It is not my business. The Americans send me cheques. I return them."

"But there is no separate edition of the book, is there, no 'pirated' edition?"

"No, not as far as I know, but there's a magazine—*McClure's*—which every now and then fills up one of its pages with a poem from my book. I suppose I couldn't prevent it even if I wanted to. There's a man on the staff who seems to like it. It's he who is responsible for such appearances as I make there."

"And they send you cheques and you send them back?"

"Yes, and I shall no doubt continue to do so; by and by they'll no doubt learn to save themselves the trouble."

[1] It did not. But it "did not go off with a bang". Published in September, 1898, the sales in that month were 115; in October, 98; in November, 107; in December, 77.

I wondered. I had never before met an author like this. He didn't want money, refused it even . . . !

"But, this is a little awkward," I took heart to say. "We may not get on together; you may not approve of my stewardship. If I am to pay you nothing for your share of the profit, however large it may be, then you must have some compensating advantage of one sort or another. You must be free to take the book away. I hope you'll never want to, but, if you do, then you must be at liberty to do so without trouble or delay. We shall have to have some sort of written agreement or exchange of letters. We must put that condition in—that if for any reason or at any time you want to take back your rights in the book, then they are yours for the asking. . . ."

And so the matter was arranged, quickly, informally, pleasantly. . . . And A. E. Housman went his way.

What manner of man did I find A. E. Housman on that first visit? It is not an easy question to answer. Adjectives come to the end of my tongue only to be rejected. Remote. Dry. Unenthusiastic. Unkindling. No, they are none of them of any use. Precise. Yes, precise perhaps, in the way that a scholar may be precise, precise in speech, bearing, clothes. But not precise in any uncomfortable way. Certainly his spirit showed no signs of effervescence and he did not use ten words where five would do; and perhaps his aspect was, until I had seen his smile, a little sombre. I am not sure. That he should be sombre would be in keeping with his work. Apart from other things too the teaching of young men is likely to make one sombre. My father was a teacher of youth and he was very sombre,[1] save when a smile lightened the bleak aspect of his face. There was, and is, nothing eccentric about Housman in appearance, habit or clothing;

[1] In other circumstances my father would have been far from sombre, I fancy, although his philosophical outlook could have been no other than it was. He read the modern French novelists for his pleasure. Indeed, I believe his favourite light reading were the novels of that old rip, "Willy".

95

he is, one may suppose, respectability itself; he carries no surface secrets. Yes, people who have known him well have described him as silent, especially in his London years, but he was not unduly silent with his few associates. It is true that there are stories illustrative of his tendency to avoid the society of useless chatterers, but I believe them to be apocryphal, although I do remember Professor Platt, his colleague in Gower Street, telling me that his Pinner landlady, sorry though she was to lose him, had declared that she couldn't help being glad that her lodger was going to Cambridge and to live in a college as it would take him out of himself, shake him up, force him to chatter like the rest of the world. . . . In 1931 an experienced observer and literary hand, writing in the *Spectator* under the pseudonym "Amicus", described Housman as "having a partly military, partly academic appearance". The second adjective never occured to me; perhaps it is just.

The second edition of *A Shropshire Lad*, my edition, appeared in 1898—I am afraid that these memories of mine are hardly following a proper chronological order, but it cannot be helped—and from that time until the present day, I believe, the book has year by year increased its rate of sale. There have been in this country and in America editions of many sorts, shapes and kinds. Apart from a Mosher "pirated" edition—a delicate and pretty edition, perhaps too pretty—there were in America in the early years an edition I sent over in sheets to Mitchell Kennerley, a publisher of so much vision and originality that I was always being surprised that he was never willing to sink some of his wealth in producing an edition of his own contrivance; and an edition, also sent over by me, with coloured illustrations by William Hyde, an artist who had done for me the end-papers to *The Open Road* and to Wilfred Whitten's anthology *London in Song*, and had "illustrated" the poems of George Meredith. It is possible that America appreciated *A Shropshire Lad* even more than England did. *McClure's Magazine* had an enormous circulation and it must have made admirers for the book of many of its readers.[1] I have heard of missions from the Middle West to lay addresses and wreaths at the poet's feet. Nobody in England thought of such tributes—but then, in spite of the existence of The Browning Society, they are not the English way.

Among American publishers there was a general interest in *A Shopshire Lad*, and some feeling of having missed the boat. Such of them as I knew best would year after year ask me whether I would not do what I could to secure for them its successor. Its successor! I had no reason to believe that there ever would be a successor, and, after Kennerley had seemed to slacken in his interest or had largely gone out of business, I answered each one in turn, from Ferris Greenslet downwards, with my assurance to that effect—"but", I added, "I'll do one thing: I'll promise to do all that I can to secure you the successor *if* you'll go back to America and bring out an edition of *A Shropshire Lad* set up by your own printers and in every way manufactured on your side. You can't call it The Copyright Edition since there isn't any copyright, but you can announce it as the one edition author-ised by the English publisher. The present situation isn't satisfactory any way. . . ."

Their faces would brighten then and they would say that they would return to New York or Boston and would as a matter of form look into the matter, but I could take it they would do as I suggested. And the steamers would carry them back and their enthusiasms would wane and their colleagues would tell them that there wasn't much in poetry any way—

---

[1] Beverley Nichols tells a story of the surprises that America has for the traveller: "Then there was another man, heavy-jowled and extremely plain, whom I met in Providence. He had manufactured, during his life, a depressingly large number of braces—those articles which in America are whimsically termed 'suspenders'. We sat in the same hotel, while I informed him, in general terms, of the braces situation in Europe. He was not very interested until he learned, from a chance remark, that I wrote books. And then a light came into his eyes. He can into the hall, got his bag, and produced from a nest of braces a first edition of *A Shrop-shire Lad*, which he knew by heart. I have seldom heard poetry recited so beautifully."

97

except Noyes—and they would write to me that they did want me to understand that they were just as keen in their admiration as they had ever been, and so on and so on, but that the fact remained that Mosher had an edition and that Kennerley had had one and they couldn't be sure that the market wasn't sufficiently "catered to" and that anyhow they'd like to wait, but that I must not forget that when the new book came along they were sure they'd be able to suggest a satisfactory agreement. . . . Yes, they all said that until I made the acquaintance of Lincoln MacVeagh, now the American Minister at Athens but at that time—1913, I think—the manager of the new book side of Henry Holt's business, a man who was all enthusiasm for literature and experiment. He saw at once the advantage of my proposal, and Holt's became as a result the recognised publishers not only of *A Shropshire Lad* but also, in course of time, of *Last Poems*. I am prepared to bet a depreciated dollar that in spite of the timidity of all their eminent rivals, their edition of *A Shropshire Lad* made money for them from the first season. At the time this bargain was struck, I, in order to show willing as it were, bought an editon in sheets of one of their books—Robert Frost's *New Hampshire*. The more intelligent critics wrote, and still write, about Frost, but over here people did not, and do not, buy his books. I doubt whether they buy any American poet at all freely nowadays —no, not even Longfellow.

So much for *A Shropshire Lad* in America. In England I quickly met Housman's wish for a really cheap edition, for in 1900 I made one that would fit the waistcoat-pocket, bound in cloth and costing sixpence. That, with a willing public, was not a difficult thing to do in the years before the War—especially with the work of a man who would accept no royalty! And, besides the Hyde illustrated book, of which I was never very proud, there was at the other end of the scale an edition designed by Philip Lee Warner and brought out as one of the Riccardi Press Booklets by the Medici Society—an edition of one thousand and twelve copies, the odd twelve, "printed on vellum, bound limp Kelmscott vellum", costing a pretty penny, twelve guineas each to be exact! Housman disapproved of such numbered productions —of his own work at least—and I do not remember how I secured his permission.

There was also an edition in Braille.

Not always of course did I find Housman so easy. For instance, I had had the temerity, or lack of tact, to include his book in a series of small volumes which for lack of a better name I called *The Smaller Classics*. The poet, in order, I think, to avoid giving me trouble, permitted the offence for a while, but when, later, a crisis came in my affairs, he not unnaturally seized the opportunity to protest and insisted on the edition being suppressed. Here is the letter he wrote:

1 YARBOROUGH VILLAS
WOODRIDINGS, PINNER
17 *Aug.* 1906

DEAR SIRS,

Mr. Grant Richards included my book *A Shropshire Lad* in his series of *The Smaller Classics* without consulting me, and to my annoyance. I contented myself with remonstrating, and did not demand its withdrawal; but now that I have the chance, I take it, and I refuse to allow the book to be any longer included in the series. I hope that you will not be very much aggrieved; but I think it unbecoming that the work of a living writer should appear under such a title.

I am yours faithfully

A. E. HOUSMAN

Having, as I felt, failed with William Hyde as an illustrator, I rather put the idea of a pictured *Shropshire Lad* from my mind. I knew that its author would have to like the work of the artist very much before he would approve such a thing. Some day, perhaps, the right man would turn up. I need not look for him. But Joseph Thorp, the strange and marvellous fellow who is dramatic critic for *Punch*, artist-printer, expert in advertising value, inspiration to his friends and heaven knows what else, came to me with the suggestion that Lovat Fraser, whose work he controlled, should be "turned on" to the little Housman book and allowed to make it, from the point of view of the decorative artist, a thing of beauty. I consulted the author who would say neither yea nor nay; he was, however, not unwilling that Fraser should try. In due course Thorp sent me the result, a "dummy" partly complete. Certainly it had charm, although it was a charm that one gets a little tired of after a while if one sees much of it, and anyhow one hardly wanted one's *Shropshire Lad* decked out like a valentine. But the countryman in A. E. Housman saw at once that the rural decorations were inaccurate in detail, that, let me say for example, the chestnut did not flower—no, I cannot find an example: I am not rural enough. Anyhow the "dummy" went back to Thorp and soon thereafter Lovat Fraser died. There was talk of someone else using the pictures, but I cannot remember that anything came of it.

I will leave *A Shropshire Lad* for a while.

XI

FIGURES OF PROFIT AND LOSS

I HAVE just been looking over the first of the ledgers in which, from January, 1897, onwards, I kept what was in effect a balance-sheet of every book I published. Depressing reading, some of it. Book after book locked up more money than I could afford. Of course there are cheerful pages, but there were not enough of them to make me feel that publishing was the royal road to content and success I had hoped for. Thus, even out of a novel like Grant Allen's *An African Millionaire*, I made in the first year of publication an actual gross profit of only one hundred and sixty pounds. When you remember that the phrase "gross profit" means that from it has to be deducted the book's share of all the office expenses—rent, salaries and so on and so forth—you may begin to see how necessary a considerable initial capital is to the young publisher. Not every one can hope to have Martin Secker's luck and to start right off with a *Passionate Elopement*. Robertson Nicoll used to say that no publishing business could hope to turn the corner till four years had passed. Still, I did have my successes, and the fact that Grant Allen's books came to me as a matter of course was a great source of strength, although some of them, the Historical Guides for instance, took a long time before they showed even a balance-sheet profit. At the moment, however, the fact that the Guides went off slowly was more than set off by the good that their publication did to the reputation of the new firm. A publisher, new or old, has to keep that consideration in his mind. If he has any reasonable ambition in him he must bring out some books for the good of his reputation even though he is more than dubious of their chances of commercial success. Woe betide him, however, if he allows himself too many luxuries of the kind![1] Of course, too, a fair proportion of books—even books published from purely sordid motives—disappoint one's expectations. I, for instance, was sure that I should make money by publishing (in July, 1897) the new Maeterlinck, *Aglavaine and Selysette*, a book that, naturally, I was proud to have on my list. Translated, on royalty terms, by Alfred Sutro, with an introduction by J. W. Mackail, and a title-page design by W. H. Margetson, it ended in my losing several pounds. Again, the Winchester Edition of Jane Austen made no one a real profit unless it was the booksellers and, in particular, the secondhand dealers, who did quite well with it after it had vanished from the regular trade. That, when you come to think of it, is curious. Why should a remainder-merchant be able to make a success of a book or a series with which the original publisher has failed? Perhaps because their campaign is better planned and is more persistent.

In religious publishing I seldom if ever dabbled, but I did have the folly to experiment, at the suggestion of F. S. A. Lowndes, in a Bishopage, if I may coin the word. *Bishops of the Day* resulted in a loss of fifty guineas, but I had the consolation of knowing that my friend made thirty-five pounds out of it.

E. V. Lucas's anthology *A Book of Verses for Children* makes brighter reading. As I have said, I paid the editor fifty pounds for the copyright, and in its first autumn, printer's strike notwithstanding, it made me a gross profit of a hundred and seventy pounds, which, however, was never greatly added to. For some inscrutable reason it never became a classic as did the same editor's *The Open Road*, which, published a couple of years later, was a steady seller and, being issued on one of the many variants of the half-profit system, not only brought E. V. Lucas a very much larger profit than had the children's book but also a great deal more than it

[1] See p. vii.

brought me, even on a "gross" reckoning. Then *Cakes and Ale*, the book which had suggested itself to me as a result of my assiduous Saturday reading of the *Pink 'Un*, put me about a hundred pounds to the good; I made fifty pounds on one of the countless novels of G. B. Burgin; and I entered into some curious arrangement with Alfred Harmsworth by which I was to publish for the Harmsworth Brothers *Convict 99*, the extraordinary, and extraordinarily successful, serial by Marie Connor Leighton and Robert Leighton, and to take for my trouble fifteen per cent of the profits. As a serial, *Convict 99* had had no small share in helping the early Harmsworth publications to success. It was used again and again, in one paper after another. It helped to swell my "turnover", but it never attracted anything like as large a public in book-form, and my share of the profits was small. On George Egerton's *The Wheel of God* I made sixty pounds, on Grant Allen's *The Evolution of the Idea of God* in the autumn of 1897 about a hundred and seventy, on W.T. Stead's *Real Ghost Stories* about fifty, a little on Sir Hugh Clifford's *In Court and Kampong*, a trifle on Vernon Lee's *Limbo*, about one hundred and twenty on Grant Allen's novel *Linnet*, about ninety on Joseph McCabe's *Life in a Modern Monastery* (You can be sure of a book with so sensation-revealing a title! My error was that I did not follow it up with a similar work on a modern nunnery!), a little on *Mrs. Turner's Cautionary Stories* in the series of *Dumpy Books for Children*, twelve on *A Shropshire Lad* in the autumn of its publication, a little on Haldane Macfall's *The Wooings of Jezebel Pettyfer*, ninety out of M. P. Shiel's *The Yellow Danger*, twenty out of an edition of the *Rubaiyat*, a trifle on W. J. Stillman's essays *The Old Rome and the New*, about twenty pounds on Le Gallienne's translation of the *Rubaiyat*, and a trifle on Laurence Housman's *Spikenard*.

If you had before you that first ledger of mine and added together the actual gross profits on all the business of the first couple of years—after deducting copyright values and stock values, mind you, because in a balance-sheet they figure as valuable, yet they are not immediately realisable —you would not find that the result was a considerable sum.

Now let us look at the losses in the first two years, or the apparent losses—for some of these books justified themselves and my belief in them in years subsequent to 1897 and 1898. I lost money on, or locked money up in, Maeterlinck's *Aglavaine and Selysette*, on Jane Austen's novels, on Leonard Merrick's *The Actor-Manager* and *One Man's View*, on almost all the children's books I published and especially on those excellent picture books in which the pictures were by Mrs. Farmiloe and the verses by E. V. Lucas (I even lost money on that delightful little nursery classic, E. V. Lucas's *The Flamp*), the Grant Allen Guides, *Bishops of the Day*, E. H. Lacon Watson's *Benedictine*, Will Rothenstein's *English Portraits*, Mrs. Meynell's *The Flower of the Mind*, on Eugene Lee-Hamilton's translation of the *Inferno* of Dante,[1] George Fleming's *Little Stories About Women*, Wilfred Whitten's *London in Song*, Carveth Read's *Logic*, Lady Gilbert's (Rosa Mulholland's) *Nanno*, no less than two hundred and fifty pounds on *Politics in 1896*, and Benn's *Philosophy of Greece*, R. Murray Gilchrist's Derbyshire stories *A Peakland Faggot* and *The Rue Bargain*, much on the anonymous *H.R.H. The Prince of Wales*, something on Laurence Binyon's *Porphyrion*, F. Anstey's *Paleface and Redskin*, Laurence Alma-Tadema's *Realms of Unknown Kings*, a fair-sized sum on *Tom Unlimited*, a children's story in the Lewis Carroll manner by Grant Allen but published pseudonymously. I must say in candour that I lost small sums on many other books, but they are not books the names of which anyone will now remember. Of course I lost money on an

---

[1] Indeed this was just the sort of book to seduce a young publisher from the commercial path. Its author looked so very romantic lying on his bed in the Florentine sunshine and pretending year after year, year after year, to be too ill to move—until one day he took it into his head that, after all, it might be worth while to get up and walk about! *Sonnets of the Wingless Hours*, the fruit of his self-imposed "horizontalness", is worth taking from the shelf and reading. Lee-Hamilton married, years later, Miss Annie E. Holdsworth, a Heinemann novelist of the more conventional kind and a protégée of W. T. Stead.

attempt to emulate the French and to produce fiction in paper covers, even though I did have my wrappers designed by Maurice Greiffenhagen! How many publishers before me and since 1898 have experimented in the same way and have had to kick themselves for fools! And of course I ought to have been told to avoid purely opportunist and trifling publishing such as little books on the Poetry of Robert Browning. And then, to be fair to myself, I ought not to have given such good terms as I sometimes willingly gave, and sometimes was browbeaten into giving, both to authors and to artists. I gave Gordon Browne, for instance, a hundred and fifty pounds for the illustrations to Anstey's *Paleface and Redskin*, which works out at a shilling a copy on the first three thousand sold, and there was in addition a royalty for the author of fifteen per cent on the first two thousand copies and then of twenty per cent. It was a six-shilling book.[1] Then I paid Bernard Shaw a twenty-per-cent royalty on the five-shilling volumes of *Plays Pleasant and Unpleasant*, and the same in the case of *The Perfect Wagnerite*, a three-and-sixpenny book. George Fleming asked and was given fifteen per cent on the first seven hundred and fifty sold and then twenty per cent. (She only sold about seven hundred and fifty!) I do not complain. I did these things with insufficient experience, but with my eyes open.

It was not to be wondered at that by the time I had been a publisher for two years I had made intimate acquaintance with anxiety.

[1] At Sotheby's in May, 1934, the manuscript of Anstey's *Vice Versa* was put up for sale. Most dealers seemed to be present because my uncle's Keats letter was in the catalogue, and I doubt whether anyone expected the Anstey item to fetch more than a score or so of pounds. The bidding began quietly enough. The pace quickened. There was excitement. After a tussle between two dealers the little packet of sheets was knocked down for five hundred and twenty pounds. Presumably it went to America. English booklovers have never collected Anstey. His brother Dr. Leonard Guthrie wrote a book, *Hospital Sketches*.

XII

WILLIAM ORPEN AT TWENTY—THE OMAR KHAYYAM CLUB
—CLEMENT SHORTER

IN my eighth chapter I said that my visit from Charles
Conder had a sequel, although I did not recognise it as a
sequel until I was told the secret many years later. Conder
had been satisfied with the results of his raid on Henrietta
Street. His intimate friends knew of it and one day one of
them, William Orpen (whom I did not know then, but of
whom later on I was to see a good deal in Hugh Lane's
company), needing money, came to the conclusion that it
would do no harm if, with variations, he repeated Conder's
experiment. It was he himself who, many years later, told
me the story. Perhaps he exaggerated the fact, but it doesn't
matter. Here is the story as he told it. He and Conder were
both on the rocks. What was to be done? ... Grant Richards
again? They might try. But I shouldn't want any more fans!
... What would be a good method of approach? Orpen bethought himself of some coloured drawings he had made in
illustration of the *Rubaiyat*. Yes, he could find them. Bun-
dling the pictures together, the two conspirators set out from
Chelsea to the Strand and Conder took his friend to the door
of my office and left him with a prayer for his success.

Orpen appears in my room. His name was familiar to me.
Had not D. S. MacColl years before told me that Orpen and
Augustus John were the two men who would thereafter ring
the bell? I assumed my most intelligent expression and sought
to appear as welcoming as I felt. Orpen throws open his
portfolio, tells me he has long had in mind the illustration and
decoration of the *Rubaiyat* and suggests gently and gradu-

ally that he would like a commission to complete the work, that his terms would be reasonable, but that they must include an immediate payment on account. The story shall proceed in his own words:

"You took the pictures, which really weren't at all bad, and looked at them with an owl-like intelligence. Your eyes showed appreciation and then you shook your head. You were play-acting just as much as I was—I knew that. Of course they were a little difficult; to reproduce them adequately would mean a lot of separate printings and would be costly. They lacked definition, outline; in short they were not illustrations. After a while you handed them back: 'They're no good to me. Altogether too indefinite. Dreams, not pictures. I like them; oh yes, *I* like them very much; but the colour-scheme must be simpler. Omarians must be able to see what you are driving at. In short, my dear boy, you'd better run off and try again. The ability is there, but not the technical knowledge. I'd like to see your new attempts——.' And I who had no more idea of reviving my student-notion of illustrating Omar, unless it was made very much worth my while, than of flying—well, I went off knowing that anyway that cock wouldn't fight. At the corner of the Street my accomplice met me, hope in his eyes. 'No use!' He, Conder, shrugged his shoulders. 'Ah,' he criticised, 'you don't know how to play your fish! A pity I couldn't have done it for you. Well, let's go and have a drink anyhow'; and we went down Bedford Street to the Bodega and did our best to drown our anxieties."

The strange thing is that until Orpen reminded me I had forgotten all about the incident. But it came back to me. All the same, I do not believe that I called him "My boy"—even though he was six years my junior.

Later, as I say, I saw a deal of Orpen—in those days when he shared a house at 5 Bolton Gardens South with Hugh Lane. I often regret that our acquaintance did not ripen into friendship. Lane, who was running his compatriot for all he was worth, told me again and again that I was a fool not to have him paint my portrait or at least to buy something he had painted. I was. As Lane said, it would have been a comparatively easy thing to arrange at that stage of his career. I might even have bought the famous *Hommage à Manet* which stood for so many months in the studio in which he painted and in which Lane gave his tea-parties. But no; I always answered that I could not afford it. Lane would guffaw: "Not afford it! Why, if you would only spend on pictures the money you pour down your throat month after month, year after year, in the shape of food and drink, you could have as many paintings as I have!" There was some truth in the gibe. Lane ate in A. B. C. shops, grudging every penny that he had to spend on his inside and making the effect of any good meal that came his way, or that he gave—for he was very hospitable—last over into the next day. The *Hommage à Manet*, perhaps Orpen's masterpiece, is now at Manchester. Its portraits of Wilson Steer, Walter Sickert, D. S. MacColl, Tonks, George Moore and Lane himself, grouped before and discussing Manet's *Mademoiselle Eva Gonzales*, make as perfect a conversation-piece as its century has produced, the scene being, not Lindsey House, where Lane went afterwards to live, but the Bolton Gardens studio. Clearly the painting was inspired by the memory of Fantin Latour's *Hommage à Delacroix*. The *Gonzales* itself is at the Tate Gallery, where, let us hope—dare I who was one of Lane's executors say so?—it and its companions will remain until the end of time, however furiously the Irish may struggle for its transfer to Dublin.

I have been much amused by an Orpen caricature—Arnold Bennett drinking his third or fourth or fifth glass of Hospices de Beaune 1906; *A Memory of Deauville* the painter calls it. I do not believe that anyone except Orpen ever "saw" Arnold Bennett looking like that, so perhaps it is all the more my duty to reproduce it here. Lord Castlerosse, who was there when it was drawn, seems to have had his doubts: "I must explain", he says, "that Arnold was really very abstemious, and that this is only Orp's little joke." You are to understand, of course, that Arnold Bennett was one of Orpen's greatest admirers. "Singular freshness of vision, evoking a truly remarkable vivacity of invention. . . ." Yes, clearly the vivacity of invention is shown in the caricature! "A supreme craftsman."[1] If you should ask me how I know that it is a Burgundy that is responsible for the novelist's aspect I would answer that, the scene being France, the large glass makes the character of the wine obvious.

After the passage of many years I came to discuss with Orpen—by letter this time—the possibility of his doing some work for me. I was in June, 1928, lodging for a while at Southwick, and by a coincidence found George Moore waiting for his train on the Victoria platform—a coincidence, for Southwick was the scene of *Esther Waters*. On this occasion he was on the way to Worthing. We travelled together and all the way he talked, talked without lowering his voice, talked without cessation and with complete frankness in that fascinating, emphatic manner that he had, about several subjects that interested him. No one of the other four passengers, middle-aged and wealthy-looking, paid the slightest attention to what he was saying. Yes, there was no reason at all why I shouldn't publish something of his. Why not *Perronik the Fool?* It was, I remember, a question of producing something beautifully—limited edition, fine printing, signed copies, and so on. I think it was I who suggested pictures by Orpen. Moore warmed to the idea. Yes, I could write to Orpen. I did. And in a day or two I had an answer from the Majestic in Paris:

6.12.28

MY DEAR GRANT RICHARDS

Moore and Tonks have been at me for a long time about the business and Moore has sent me books—but the one he wants illustrated is the holiday one—and I think myself

---

[1] "War: Paintings and Drawings Executed on the Western Front by Major Sir William Orpen, K.B.E., A.R.A. With an Introductory Note by Arnold Bennett," 1918.

it lends itself more than the others for that purpose—(that is as far as I have studied them, I never read them before from the standpoint of illustration).

I think I know what Moore wants me to do, but I am not at all sure I can do it—these bright fleeting sketches done in "ten minutes" take a long time! And I have got to be paid—but I would be willing to work for a quarter price to be allowed to illustrate a book by the Master.

Yours ever

WILLIAM ORPEN

Somehow the idea came to nothing. George Moore was old, and was at the time convinced he would soon end his days; at that moment he was interested only in finishing the one book on which he was engaged. Then he would write nothing more. I couldn't get him to move. It was a pity. *A Story Teller's Holiday* illustrated by Orpen would have been a great possession.

And before I leave Orpen I must repeat one story about him which Barnard Lintott told me. The painter came into the Club one night when George Lambert was playing. "Hullo, Billy," said Lambert, looking up from the billiard table; "is there anything good at the International?" "Yes," replied Orpen; "six." "Have you anything there, Billy?" "Yes, six!!!" That must have been another of "Orp's little jokes".

Omar Khayyam! For what a lot of sins that hoary "old poison-pot" has been responsible! And for how much make-believe! The Omar Khayyam Club for instance—although I write of the Club, to which I once belonged, with becoming reverence. I have under my eyes a collection of its menu cards—for it is a dining club—and I look at them now with curiosity and astonishment. The first card I have commemorates a summer dinner at Ye Olde Bell Inn (*sic!*) at Hurley in 1894. The names that interest me are George Whale, Edward Clodd, Grant Allen, George Bird, T. J. Wise and one or two of C. K. Shorter's artists. Grant Allen contributes verses to the card. By the Spring of 1896 the twenty diners present in 1894 have increased to sixty-two, Shorter, one of the four founders, has a firm hold on the Club, and Edmund Gosse, Coulson Kernahan, the Rev. W. Robertson Nicoll, the Rev. S. R. Crockett and several other eminent subscribers to the Omarian gospel and way of life have joined the party. Only that ripe old hedonist, Sidney Colvin, is missing and he, one notes, turns up a few months later. One would like to think that on that occasion Sir Sidney Colvin wore vine-leaves in his hair and that the Restaurant Frascati jeopardised its license! But no. . . . The party was respectability itself. Indeed the only hint of rebellion is in a letter declining an invitation to be present written by Swinburne to Clement Shorter:

"As to the immortal tent-maker himself, I believe I may claim to be one of his earliest English believers. It is upwards of thirty-six years since I was introduced to him by D. G. Rossetti, who had just been introduced himself—I believe by Mr. Whitley Stokes. At that time the first and best edition of Fitzgerald's wonderful version was being sold off at a penny a copy[1] having proved hopelessly unsaleable at the published price of 1s. We invested (I should think) in hardly less than sixpennyworth apiece—and on returning to the stall next day for more, found that we had sent up the market to the sinfully extravagant sum of twopence, an imposition which evoked from Rossetti a fervent and impressive remonstrance. Not so very long afterwards, if I mistake not, the price of a copy was 30s. It is the only edition worth having—as Fitzgerald, like the ass of genius he was, cut out of later editions the crowning stanza, which is the core or kernel of the whole. As to the greatness of the poem, I can say no more than I have tried to say in print. I know none to be compared with it for

---

[1] "At Hodgson's a fine copy of a rare nineteenth-century first edition of Fitszgerald's translation of Omar Khayyam, fetched £890." Iolo Williams on "The Sale Room in 1933" in *The Observer*, December 17, 1933.

power, pathos, and beauty, in the same line of thought and work, except possibly 'Ecclesiastes'; and magnificent as that is, I can hardly think the author comparable to Omar either as philosopher or as poet."

In the autumn of the same year a smaller party gathered together at Great Marlow at The Crown. To me it is distinguished because once more Grant Allen is its laureate, although I, who know now more about wine than he did, would now prevent him from suggesting that liveliness is a desirable quality in a Pommard. The poem, though, is a notable one: it contains the lines,

> If systems that be are the order of God,
> —Revolt is a part of the order.

I most remember the Summer 1897 dinner at Marlow, a dinner notable for the verses Sir Frederick Pollock contributed to the card, and also notable to me for the fact that thereafter a horrid rumour was bruited abroad to the effect that a member of the Club had not only so far forgotten the conventions of the time as to drink just a little too deeply of "the ancient Ruby" but had even allowed his guests to do likewise. And I—*I*—was the peccant member. *I* was accused of having filled too often for myself and them

> The Cup that clears
> To-day of past Regrets and future Fears—

I couldn't believe the rumour when I first heard it. Getting drunk was not in my way. I was twenty-three and I had never been drunk in my life. My father, it is true, when an undergraduate, had locked himself up in his rooms with a bottle or two of claret in order to see what it felt like to be drunk, but I had never had so much scientific curiosity! It was my aunt, Mrs. Grant Allen, who told me the story of my behaviour. Appealed to, her husband, who was one of the most abstemious men I ever knew, supported it! He was sorry to say so, but Edmund Gosse had drawn attention to the uncertainty of my steps and those of my guests. Clement

King Shorter too. The matter might even be brought before the Committee of the Club! Mind, this accusation did not go further than that: the "uncertainty of our steps"! Really! And my fellow-members and my guests' fellow-guests were Omarians, believers in the doctrine of

> The Grape that can with Logic absolute
> The Two-and-Seventy jarring sects confute.

Perhaps I should add that I had on that occasion two guests. Either of them could have put away a bottle of "the Ruby Vintage" without embarrassment and without becoming the "sot" that Grant Allen abjured in his poem. One, Archibald Ripley, was a "pet" of the Savile. He was thinking of becoming a publisher, of joining me as a partner. He had an affection of the leg which made him limp slightly. I think the story began from that: on his way home, he stumbled as he stepped into the railway carriage! The other, Ethrayne Bicknell, was my sister's husband. I never saw him the worse for drink. Not that I am concerned to defend either myself or my guests. If we wanted to get drunk why, in the name of the Tent-Maker, should we not do so? Is not the very idea of Mr. Edmund Gosse frowning, as President, on a slight and cheerful inebriety very absurd? But of course the members of the Omar Khayyam were all of them—as far as the world knew—painfully respectable. There was not an *homme moyen sensuel* among the lot, unless it was A. B. Walkley. Why, they would have shrivelled up at the idea of sporting with Amaryllis in the shade, or of sitting with the woman of their choice and a jug of wine under any bough, figurative or otherwise! I can even remember that at one of their Great Marlow banquets these middle-aged men arrived at The Crown with their amiable wives. It was true that these ladies were not allowed to sit at the meal itself, but there they were, almost in sight, in an upper room. . . . A little later on they were released, and were permitted to stroll about the garden with their true spouses. . . .

No, no, no, the Omarians were not Omarian in their practice, whatever they were in their precept and philosophy. All the same—yes, all the same, many of their dinners were very enjoyable. One even forgot Omar in the speeches of L. F. Austin and Augustine Birrell, and in the conversation, at once agreeable and learned, of one's neighbours . . . and one caught almost the last train or omnibus back to one's respectable home,

And one by one crept silently to rest.

The extreme conventionality of the early Omar Khayyam Club members has not lessened the admiration for the poem.

Last December, at a luncheon given to J. A. Craig, the Editor of *Great Thoughts*, to which in my teens and early twenties I used regularly to contribute, I found myself to my great satisfaction seated next to David Williamson, once assistant to Clement King Shorter on the *Sphere* and now the Editor of the *Daily Mail Year Book*. Not having seen each other for thirty-five years or more, we fell to talking of the past, and of that past figure, the aforesaid Shorter, and, going home and looking among my papers, I found Shorter's account of the Omar Khayyam Club, contributed to—of all papers—*Great Thoughts* itself. Here is a passage from it: "In its origin the Club was unpretentious enough. Three friends, two of them lawyers, the third a journalist, wanted an excuse for dining together now and again, and a common interest in FitzGerald's translation seemed to offer that excuse. The Club came into being when Mr. George Whale, of Woolwich, Mr. Frederic Hudson and the present writer, with some three or four others—one of whom was Mr. Arthur Hacker—invited between us about a dozen of our friends well-known for their interest in the astronomer-poet to dine at Pagani's." Another passage: "Mr. George Meredith once gave me a picturesque description of sitting at the door of his then home in Surrey, when he observed Mr. Swinburne running wildly towards him, waving a pamphlet. 'I did not suspect Mr. Swinburne of being a Revivalist or a Total

Abstinence Agitator,' said Mr. Meredith, 'and I was mystified by his excitement, until he recited to me some of Fitz-Gerald's booklet, when I speedily caught the contagion.' "
And again: "Perhaps the most significant gathering" [of the Club] "was that held at Burford Bridge Hotel, a few yards from Mr. George Meredith's residence. Mr. Edward Clodd was the president who engineered this entertainment, and he was rewarded by seeing Mr. Meredith on his right and Mr. Thomas Hardy on his left at the dinner, both the great novelists making excellent speeches."

Clement King Shorter was a good journalist but a difficult fellow to get on with. He did not like me. I, who like nearly everyone, knew this, and was awkward in consequence. When *Black and White* started I described its pictures as being more attractive, but its letterpress as being far less attractive, than those in Shorter's *Illustrated London News*. He never forgave me that. He let pass no opportunity of paying me out. Such chances as the editorship of the *Sphere* gave him of sticking knives into me in connection either with my torts or my misfortunes, he eagerly seized. Indeed, I was driven to pay a visit to the *Sphere* office, to complain to Mr. George King and even to threaten legal action. I was promised that it should not happen again. It did not; and after a time Shorter and I met as if nothing had happened. He was at heart not at all a bad chap—and he did love books. Also I should have liked him for the understanding he had of many sides of Grant Allen's character. They had Celtic blood in common—or so Shorter claimed! What he had to say of my uncle (in the *Bookman* of December 1899) was in many ways the best piece of writing called forth by his untimely death. It read true.

I like to believe a story someone told me of a lady who, early in the century, gave a garden party to meet an Aztec prince and princess. When it was too late to postpone the party these royalties fell ill. But they were hardly missed. Many of the guests as they bade their hostess good-bye thanked her for the pleasant afternoon and added that they had found the Aztecs not only interesting as strangers from a little known land, but unusually well-educated and well-informed. It was not until this had happened again and again that the hostess, looking round in bewilderment, espied the Shorters and realised how the mistake had arisen.

Shorter was neither an Aztec nor a Celt but a Jew if general opinion went for anything. But he disliked being thought a Jew. Alfred Harmsworth when he wanted to make him angry would refer to him as a Jew. And there must have been black blood. I myself believe him to have been a white negro.

XIII

PLAYS PLEASANT AND UNPLEASANT

FIRST catch your hare. . . . Well, I had caught my
Bernard Shaw and to me to-day, looking back, one of
the great wonders is that the fields were not full of hunters
bent on securing the same prey. Perhaps if they gave any
thought to the matter it was to feel that after all the country-
side was full of spirited young leverets or, in other words,
that the newspapers and weeklies had among their contemporaries bright young men by the score, and that talent was so
common that a publisher need not employ any great amount
of energy in looking for it. In those days London was not
overcrowded with publishers; as a trade, publishing was slow
and fairly dignified. The publisher, with few exceptions, sat
and waited at the receipt of custom rather than went out and
searched the hillsides and coverts. Moreover, such publishers
as had heard of Bernard Shaw no doubt remembered that
Walter Scott had had his try with G. B. S. as a novelist—
Cashel Byron's Profession—and that Henry had experimented
with him as a dramatist who should be read—*Widower's
Houses*—and as a critic—*The Quintessence of Ibsenism*. No
one of these books had exactly set the Thames on fire, and it
was then, as it is now, a defect in the publisher only to run
after successes. (I remind you of the case of Richard Whiteing.) But I—well I, at the time that Shaw burst into journalism, was at a receptive age, my sympathies were all left-wing
and I read the *Star*, which I am sure that very few of my
rivals did at all regularly. And every week, A. B. Walkley,
the critic on whom I pinned my faith, strengthened my
Shavian prejudices. We have seen[1] that as far back as the

[1] See *Memories of a Misspent Youth*, by Grant Richards, 1932.

117

summer of 1890 Shaw had read a paper on Ibsen to a little party of whom "A. B. W." was one. Walkley's criticisms helped Shaw in more ways than one: they had minds so dissimilar. Shaw was restive under the play of the Walk-leyan dart. I do not think that, although he paid much attention to his criticism, Shaw ever gave Walkley his due. In the *Academy* of January 16, 1897, in a review of Ibsen's Borkmann play, he writes of Walkley rather lukewarmly as "one of our best dramatic critics".[1]

Shaw and Walkley were always good friends; but Walkley would never admit that Shaw was a real playwright, nor Shaw that Walkley was a real critic. After Walkley's death, when I raised the question of the influence of Walkley's

[1] Not long before, A. B. W. had written in the *Star* (November 2, 1895) —I wish I had not omitted the context of the paragraph: ". . . That, I am sure, is why Mr. G. R. Sims, an incorrigible romanticist and a warm-hearted man, says he 'loves' barnstormers! And I confess I would rather love them with Mr. Sims than dissect them, as if they were dried speci-mens in a museum, with Mr. Bernard Shaw. 'Why the deuce', asks Mr. Shaw, 'do you persist in talking about theatrical people as if they were children, and let their dishonest tricks and shifts and incorrigible lying and swindling pass with an indulgent laugh? Why does Mr. Sims say he *loves* them, although, as a dramatic author, he objects to their im-provising their parts and paying no authors' fees? Just because you imagine you sympathise with them when you only fail to realise that they are human beings like yourself, and not mere playthings for your sym-pathies.' This is Mr. Shaw all over! He imagines that all human beings are like himself—which simply means that he has no imagination. He has no bowels of compassion; the word 'love' is not in his vocabulary, nor warm blood in his veins. He would ratiocinate us out of all our instincts, and deny everything that cannot be reduced to a syllogism— or a sophism. I am heartily ashamed of him. For two pins I would treat him as a mere plaything for my antipathies. But I will refrain, and only offer him a piece of advice—which is, to try and realise that there are human beings who are not like himself, that sentiment is not a fiction merely because he has never experienced it, and that there is such a thing as a heart, though he may not (except for mere blood-circulating pur-poses) possess one. My advice is not disinterested; if taken, it will increase my own pleasure some day. For the humanising of Mr. Shaw will mean that he will ultimately succeed in getting real humanity into his plays. His characters will be able to feel for feeling's sake and not for the sake of arguing about their feelings. Indeed, he might do worse than join the barnstormers—as 'theatre-poet', say, and critic-historiographer—and learn a thing or two from the university man."

criticism on his work, Shaw's reply was: "The truth about A.B.W. is that *he was not a critic at all.* He was a preacher. His sermonettes were entertaining; but he never could feel that English actors and playwrights were gentlemen, or the theatre an institution to be taken seriously. I knew this and never paid the slightest attention to his criticism, though I immortalised him as Trotter in *Fanny's First Play.*" Whether Shaw is right or wrong in this pronouncement I cannot say, but I do know that I felt very strongly that after Walkley joined the Garrick Club and began to use it regularly the value of his criticism lessened, much of the virtue went out of it.

I have printed on page 12 the letter with which Shaw responded to my first advances. It seemed to suggest a fair wind and a flowing sail. But I soon discovered that there were to be many obstacles to overcome before my first Shaw volume would be in the booksellers' shops. There was the question of waiting until after theatrical production before printing. This was a natural consideration for the author, who had to tread warily because of the possibility of losing by English publication his American dramatic copyright, but it was a consideration over which I, the publisher, would have preferred to take chances. I dare say I argued to myself that Shaw had not yet had from the commercial point of view any theatrical success worth boasting about, and that if he waited until he had made his American copyright safe he might be sacrificing the substance for the shadow; and I must also have had it in mind that he would be standing between me and my projected coup. For, like the author, I had enormous belief in his advertising value and his ultimate drawing power. The difference between us was that he knew it would pay him to wait, while I thought that neither he nor I could wait and was all for "cashing" him (as Kennedy Jones used to say). Of course I was wrong. After a while the difficulty was overcome. There were few difficulties that G. B. S., verging on middle-age, could not manage— and he has not grown less clever with the passage of nearly four decades. I cannot remember how the matter of securing simultaneous publication in America was settled. It was all very well for Shaw to say that there was more at the time to be made out of his name in America than here, but I did not find it so then, as I will tell directly. The production of the little play at the Lyceum came to nothing, as we know, but in the raising of this small point one sees the artist who is also the born man of affairs.

Shaw and I went on corresponding, and in the spring of 1897 I must have been asking for manuscript and have also suggested the reprinting of *Cashel Byron's Profession*, which had by then, I fancy, rather disappeared from sight, for he wrote to me:

29 FITZROY SQUARE W.

27th March 1897

It is my private belief that half the book-selling trade in London consists in the sale of unauthorised *Cashel Byrons*. However, I presume Scott has some copies of his stock left. I shall ask him how many presently.

I suppose the thing may as well be republished. I read the copy you sent me.[1] The comedy in it amused me; but the fundamental folly of the thing sickened me.

I'll bring round *The Philanderer* on Monday. I wish we could get six plays in one volume. I propose to call the issue *Plays Pleasant and Unpleasant*. Vol. I, *Unpleasant*, 3/6, Vol. II, *Pleasant*, 5/-. Both together, half a crown. If we could get all six into one volume, I should have the unpleasant ones printed on light brown paper (Egyptian mummy colour) in an ugly style of printing, and the pleasant ones on white paper (machine-hand made) in the best Kelmscott style. Nobody has ever done a piebald volume before; and the thing would make a sensation.

G. BERNARD SHAW

Cashel Byron was republished, but not until 1901. It sold about six hundred copies in its first year. Not that this

---

[1] What happened to that copy? I swear he never sent it back to me!

republication exhausted the public's interest in the book or G. B. S.'s interest in boxing. In December, 1919, he went to the Great Fight—the match between Georges Carpentier and Joseph Beckett—and wrote about it in the *Nation* of December 19 a long article, *The Great Fight*, an article which Mitchell Kennerley privately reprinted in New York under that title and as "by the author of *Cashel Byron's Profession*" in June, 1921. I wonder how many copies exist of that sixteen-page pamphlet. Again, on September 3, 1921, G. B. S. went to the Leicester Square Cinema and saw the film reproduction of the Carpentier-Dempsey fight for the heavy-weight championship of the world—"I had", he says, "a much better view of it than nine-tenths of the people who saw it in the flesh from Mr. Ted (*sic!*) Rickard's benches in New Jersey"—and described what he saw in two columns of small type in the *Observer* of September 11 and in the *New York American* of about the same day:

"I must warn those who have seen Monsieur Carpentier only at New Jersey or in this film that they have no idea of what he is like and what he can do when he is at the top of his form and master of himself and of the situation. The film only shows what he can do when he is sandbagged. This is no excuse for his defeat. It was Mr. Dempsey's business to sandbag him, and it was his own business to prevent Mr. Dempsey from sandbagging him. Instead of doing so, he offered Dempsey (who will allow me to drop the ceremonious Mister) every facility for the operation and got it very literally in the neck. That he nevertheless put up a tremendous fight is true: Dempsey escaped defeat again and again only by a millimetre; but in boxing a miss is as good as a mile...."

G. B. S.'s further criticisms are professional:

"... the referee being in his proper place out of the ring,[1] and bent on having a display of boxing as distinguished

[1] In the Dempsey-Carpentier fight the referee remained in the ring.

from pollywogging. This is the old English style; and none of its ancient practitioners ever heard or dreamt of hitting or being hit on the back of the neck. In modern American practice, however, the occiput seems to be the favourite mark. It is *de rigueur*, when you have led off, or countered a lead-off, to crouch, clinch, and begin pounding your man on the atlas process, or banging him over the kidneys, trying meanwhile to hold his arms locked under yours until the referee, who is in the ring all the time, takes part in the combat and violently tears the clinchers asunder. (Incidentally I may say that if ever I act as referee in an American glove fight I shall demand at least an equal share of the gate money and cinema rights with the rival champions, as I shall have to work just as hard and get no glory by it.) At this game Dempsey is consummately skilful, cold, systematic, indefatigable, and ruinously damaging. Carpentier, his superior at out-fighting, cannot touch him at it. . . . If Carpentier had not had a demon of endurance and determination in him he could not have got through the first round. As it was, he went to his corner a desperate man, without having given a single demonstration of the classical pugilism that has made him the idol of artists as well as of bruisers."

One wonders whether, things being as they are in the boxing of to-day, G. B. S. has kept his interest in the sport. He ends his article:

"For my part it would greatly revive my interest in boxing if the order 'seconds out of the ring' were to include the referee, and if crouching and occipital pile-driving went the way of up-and-down fighting, and all the other practices that once made the ringside no place for a gentleman, not to mention a lady. Ladies are becoming as common at glove fights and the films thereof as at polo matches. At the Leicester Square cinema several ladies saw the fight when I did; and they were ordinary ladies, not Leicester Square ladies. Possibly this criticism may help them to understand what they are seeing, and encourage them to protest against American in-fighting as dull, ugly and indefensible as a propagandist spectacle. It produces decisions, because it produces disablement; and decisions are necessary to betting. But betting has always been the bane of honest boxing; and now that the star pugilists draw the same fees whether they win, lose, or draw, they would be well advised to make their films as spectacular as possible by cultivating exhibition boxing, and leaving the minor practitioners to make more money by selling fights than by winning them."

Well, having been to fights about half a dozen times in my life, I am all for the referee being kept out of the ring! But obviously I cannot set up as one whose opinion is worth a tinker's curse. I have been taken to a fight by the Hooligan of Clarence Rook's *Hooligan Nights*—a fight in which he himself was beaten—that took place in a railway arch somewhere down Lambeth way; and to more ambitious affairs by C. B. Cochran and by Sir Harry Preston, but I never could abide the clinching or the referee's dancing about in the ring. However, I dare say there is something to be said for it. I also saw the afternoon "fight" between Carpentier and the Belgian champion at Monte Carlo, which no one seemed to take seriously, for I met one of the protagonists walking away cigarette in mouth just after lunch, from the Galerie Charles III, as I made my own way just before the opening to the Capitol, the building in which it was held; while the Café de Paris had the ill-taste to parade the hall with banners announcing that that same evening the French champion would be present at the gala dinner. They might at least have waited till after the fight! It was always on the cards that the Belgian would land one where it would hurt most! There was a lot of falling down in that fight. One of the combatants seemed very nervous of a chance blow getting home and spoiling his beauty, and adopted the falling-down habit in order to make it impossible!

It is a pity that G. B. S. was not at the last fight at which
I was present. He would indeed have seen enough crouching, clinching and occipital pile-driving to strengthen him in
his convictions. Len Harvey *v.* Tarrante was not at all the
sort of fight that G. B. S. likes. But he was on the way home
from New Zealand[1] and saw neither that display nor the
exhibition boxing of Carpentier, who revisited that night the
English ring for a few minutes and looked as if he would
have no great difficulty in "coming back" even to-day and in
his forty-first year. By the way, G. B. S. mentions in *The
Great Fight* the presence of "men with an artistic interest in
the display like Robert Loraine, Granville Barker, Maurice
Baring and Arnold Bennett". Well, at my recent fights I
have found myself at the side of an apparently very knowl-
edgeable critic of boxing, and on enquiring who he was I
discovered the violinist, Albert Sammons! Who would associate violins with boxing gloves? I once induced A. E. Housman to accompany me to an important race-meeting at
Auteuil, but he showed no signs of caring either for the
spectacle or the racing.

Shaw had in those days an idea that his books should be
cheap. But when it came to the point, the price charged
for the two volumes of the plays was ten shillings, and the
volumes were sold separately. I should, considering all
things, have expected the "Unpleasant" volume to have sold
the better of the two. It did not.

With *Plays Pleasant and Unpleasant* the period of gesta-
tion was a long one. We spent time discussing the agreement.
Not that G. B. S. was not at work. I am sure he was. And
he would raise fresh points. I wanted the books to be in their

---

[1] At what stage was it that G. B. S. started to like travelling the ocean,
to become indeed a cruise addict? He did not so begin. His first voyage
in the Mediterranean—Athens, Villefranche, Syracuse, Algiers: that
kind of thing—in 1899 began by seeming "a success in itself but"—indeed
more "buts" than one developed: "G. B. S. is impatient of the confine-
ment of the ship's life. We shall both be glad to get back", I am told
from the steamer (off Algiers) on October 23, 1899.

way beautifully printed; he had the same wish, but would have them printed by a Union house. I suppose I doubted whether a Union house could do justice to my ideal. I had few notions of what made a Union house. I do not think I had a Union house on my list. The problem shifted to the question of fair wages, and R. and R. Clark were approved. On May 21, 1897, I received this letter from which I might almost deduce that it was I who suggested the famous Shavian introductions:

LOTUS, TOWER HILL, DORKING

21st May, 1897

Thanks for *Philanderer*.

Clark is all right—a first-rate house. I enclose a letter which you can hold as your certificate of your compliance with my Fair Wages Clause.

Yes; separate introductions to the volumes by all means, and separate portraits if you like. Evans[1] has an assortment which includes both tragic and comic masks.

The best people to give the portrait to are Walker and Boutall, 16 Clifford's Inn, E. C. Emery Walker, the senior partner, will look after me like a brother. He is the guide, philosopher and friend of many publishers in the matter of illustrated books; and you ought to make his acquaintance anyhow. He is also a first rate authority on printing, and personally an almost reprehensibly amiable man.

If you have a copy of one of Walter Scott's volumes of Ibsen's plays you will see how the style of thing I want works at three plays to the volume. In Scott's edition the

---

[1] Frederick H. Evans, a bearded bookseller, who, when I was young, dictated to the City of London what it should read. His shop was that of Jones and Evans in Queen Street, and it still exists, and flourishes, under W. T. Whittaker. Evans retired years ago. He was a fine bookseller and took admirable photographs. He showed the liveliest interest in the Shaw venture, and if every bookseller had sold in proportion as many copies as he did of *Plays Pleasant and Unpleasant* it would have been a fin de siècle "best seller". His habit was to whip up orders beforehand for books in which he was really interested.

block of letterpress is not properly set on the page; but otherwise it is not so bad.

In drafting the agreement I should have made the five years start from the date of publication.[1]

November will do as well. Probably we shall have to add something about the American business when we find out what can be done. In it I take it that you will not meddle in the publication there yourself, but virtually act as my agent and take a percentage on what you can get for me. Or have you any other plan?

The Man of Destiny is quite available if there is room for it.

The Quintessence[2] has been skimmed a good deal. Hadn't you better wait and see whether I sell well enough?

I am writing by this post to Henry and Co.

Yrs ever

G. BERNARD SHAW

The American business to which G. B. S. refers did not prove easy. The New York publishers were found on investigation to know less of his name and fame and the value of his work both artistically and commercially than his November letter had led me to believe. My own acquaintance with American houses was at that time slight. Charles Scribner had called on me; so had Craige Lippincott who was to become later on one of my warmest friends; and Maynard Dominick, of Frederick A. Stokes Company, came too and encouraged me with his advice and with his appreciation of what I was trying to do. I wish he came over here nowadays. Every Englishman who knows him has a warm affection for him. I cannot remember all the houses to whom I talked about *Plays Pleasant and Unpleasant* when it at last reached the proof stage, but I do well recollect that I offered it eventually to the Lippincott house and that Craige,

[1] We had settled that the agreement should be for five years. Lane in those days had clauses to that effect in his agreements. I do not think they are so general now.

[2] *The Quintessence of Ibsenism.* I must have suggested republishing it.

the head of the firm, a very American from the crown of his head to the soles of his feet, a Philadelphian, radiating a sense of comfort and geniality, pink-faced, eupeptic, must have been told of it and that he sat down and wrote me a personal letter with his own hand urging me from the wealth of his experience, from a sense of expediency, and, yes, from the prompting of his sense of decency, to have nothing to do with the issue of the "Unpleasant" plays, however much I might believe in the literary value of the "Pleasant". He added that he was surprised that I should have thought the book a suitable one to offer to a firm of their standing. Poor dear Craige! He could no more prevent the tide coming up than could Canute or the first Mrs. Frank Nelson Doubleday. I remember how, later on, I had much the same experience when I was trying to find a home in the United States for Thomas Burke's *Limehouse Nights*. More than one house returned it to me with a protest against my having thought it possible that it could be published in their country. That was in 1916; *Plays Pleasant and Unpleasant* ante-dated it by eighteen years. By the way, John Murray took the same view of *Man and Superman* as Craige Lippincott had taken of the earlier plays, and thereby drove Shaw into publishing on commission.

To return to Shaw. There was a new firm in Chicago—Stone and Kimball—who were more forward-looking and who had a keener insight into reality and a surer hand on what was happening in the art of letters than almost any of their older rivals. Kimball I never met. Herbert Stone was a man whom to know was to like, a fellow of infinite charm. He loved books; he loved life. In later years Elliot Holt reminded me of him. A young man, he threw himself into publishing with zest, and he had no small share in founding the tradition which has made the comely American book to-day as fine as anything that is produced in this country or on the Continent. Herbert Stone was over here in that 1897; he read Bernard Shaw, and he succumbed. Shaw wrote to me on August 7 from The Argoed, Penallt, Monmouth, that "before leaving town" he had "applied" his "mind to business for a day. Among other matters I considered our American project; and I came to the conclusion that Stone and Kimball's offer is good enough as such business goes. If you like to close with them without looking any further do so. S. and K. are as keen as any Americans on my work: we shall do no better with Putnam,[1] as far as I can judge." So Herbert Stone's firm was to introduce Shaw to the United States. The arrangement lasted for a few years; but the upshot bore out Shaw's cheerful habit of predicting bankruptcy for any publisher rash enough to put him on his list. The Stone firm crashed; and their Shavian successors persisted in pursuing Shaw's claims in a Jarndyce lawsuit in which the assets were entirely swallowed up by the costs.

In the meantime I was plugging away at the Edinburgh printers and working at proofs. I little knew what those proofs were to let me in for. Those were the days when William Morris was revolutionising modern printing by his Kelmscott Press. Shaw, up to his eyes in Socialist propaganda with Morris, was intensely interested in his artistic enterprises, and was enchanted by his books and his rules for making printed pages pictorial in themselves. Better printers than R. and R. Clark of Edinburgh under the late Edward Clark and Peter Begg were not to be found; and I had, I thought, proved my own good taste in the design of books already published. But the Morris revolution, with Shaw as its fiercest fanatic, burst on us like a typhoon. We were willing to learn; and the new margins, the elimination of "mutton quads" and all the rest of it, justified themselves in the result; but our docility was sorely tested, as will presently appear. Even the rate at which Clark worked was not good enough for Shaw. He writes again, no doubt led

---

[1] I see the name of Putnam here with surprise. I should have to be convinced that the Putnam house of those days was keen about the Plays. George Haven Putnam had many excellent qualities but he belonged to an old scholarly tradition and his mind worked more freely in Oxford college gardens and Cambridge common rooms than in the advanced theatre and in the reading of subversive literature.

on by the fact that I had been spending a quiet fortnight at St. Moritz, which had in those days no such excited winter season as it has now:

THE ARGOED, PENALLT, MONMOUTH

26th August 1897

This letter of yours comes well, Grant Richards, from a man who has been bounding idly up the Jungfrau and down the Matterhorn to an exhausted wretch who, after a crushing season, has slaved these four weeks for four hours a day at your confounded enterprise. I have sent three plays to the printer, transmogrified beyond recognition, made more thrilling than any novel; and he has only sent me proofs of one, of which it has cost me endless letters and revises to get the page right, to teach him how to space letters for emphasis, and how to realise that I mean my punctuation to be followed.

I had no idea of the magnitude of the job. Anything like a holiday is out of the question for me. Must I endure in addition the insults of a publisher for whom I am pre-paring, with unheard-of toil, a gigantic Triumph? Read *Mrs. Warren;* and then blush for your impatience if you can.

Stone and Kimball's offer, as described to me in your letter of the 9th Apl. (doubtless negligently and lazily composed before going up the river) mentioned neither the price nor the royalty after 10,000 copies. The latter I assume to be 20%: the former not less than 75 cents at least. A princely affluence will accrue to S. & K. on these terms; but I desire to make the fortune of one American publisher in order that I may spend the rest of my life in plundering all the others!

Shall I draw them an agreement? If they prefer to do it themselves, warn them that I wont assign copyright, but simply give them exclusive leave to publish in the U.S. for 5 years.

yrs, overworked to madness

G. BERNARD SHAW

129

I laid in that August the foundations of my ill-merited dislike of Switzerland. I found it a dull place; I was ill-equipped with clothes of the kind that Switzerland demanded of its visitors or, more likely, that its visitors demanded of one another; an affair of my heart was not progressing as it should do; I was surrounded by rich and intelligent and Henry James-ish Americans (at the table d'hôte my neighbour was a charming old American lady, Miss Grant, a sister of the General. She asked me to see her again. I wish I had been able to do so) who talked too much. American was the dominant language of the hotel, and I caught the accent so badly that the winter was well advanced before I recovered my own English. Most of my time I spent wondering whether my second six months' business would be better than my first, why, for instance, Sir Hugh Clifford's *In Court and Kampong* was not selling as well as it should and whether I couldn't do something to expedite the appearance of the Shavian plays. Returned to London, I was kept up to the mark by G. B. S.:

THE ARGOED, PENALLT, MONMOUTH
28th August 1897

By the way, a good many of the corrections so far (I have only sent back one sheet, and that chiefly to get the page right and to settle about spacing the letters for emphasised words instead of italicising them) are corrections of Clark's departures from my copy, in spite of my straitest injunctions, in the matter of punctuation. However, I am now knocking righteousness into his head; and I shall feel deeply humiliated if my corrections are not under rather than over the Carlyle-Balzac average.

I'll presently send you a sheet with the corrections of Clark's misdemeanors in red ink and of my own in black. You may charge me for all corrections over and above 95% of the total cost of production.

G. B. S.

P.S. Have you seen the translation of Diderot's *Neveu*

de Rameau just published by Macmillan? The paper on which it is printed is the sort of thing we want for the plays, except that it might be well to have it toned instead of white.

I am doing a sparkling study of Napoleon by way of preface to *The Man of Destiny*.

Then G. B. S. seems to have left Penallt for Moorcroft. Still we are arguing about the price at which the books shall be published:

MOORCROFT, MONMOUTH

25/9/97

Grant Richards, my boy, do not deceive yourself. Ibsen's plays sell at three & sixpence the volume of three plays. The first issue of a new play at 6/- by Heinemann fetches the rent of Ibsen's unique European position, which I have not yet reached. The point of a six shilling volume is the length of time it takes to read. The man who buys a six shilling book expects that he will not have to buy another for several Sundays; and he looks strictly to the quantity of matter supplied. Now a play is a very short business owing to the dialogueiness of it; and that is why every attempt to charge more than eighteenpence for a single play fails in England. The six shilling public will just go the seven shillings for our two volumes: make it ten, and you will not sell a thousand copies all told. At the three & six you will not lose; and you *may* land a really large circulation. An edition de luxe—two volumes in a case for a guinea—is the only real business alternative; and that would not pay *you*, as your interest does not lie in getting a reputation for that sort of thing, especially in connection with *Mrs. Warren's Profession*. Our original plan is the right one, and the only one in which there is any money. Sit tight therefore and trust my judgment. I mean this book to break out far beyond "my public": that is why I'm squandering hard work on it.

G. BERNARD SHAW

131

I still believe I was right. The cost of each individual volume, after printing a first edition of twelve hundred and forty copies, was about two and sevenpence. All the experience I have since had leads me to suppose that if we had reduced the cost of production by doubling the number printed in the first edition and had made the books three and sixpence each instead of five shillings, we should not have sold a much higher number within six months of publication. We did sell seven hundred and fifty-six copies in about that time, which may be said to have supported G. B. S.'s prophecy, but which I think proves rather that it took a long time for his kind of reputation to reach the book-buying public.

And a few days G. B. S. writes again:

29 FITZROY SQUARE W.

8th October 1897

DEAR G. R.

You have an india rubber mind: as fast as I stretch it to the TWO volumes, it contracts to one. If it were a question of 3/6 and 5, or even 6 shillings, I should not hesitate to go the larger figure; but it is a question between SEVEN shillings and TEN. Ten is a prohibitive price: you wont sell your 2,000 copies at it—perhaps not even 1,000; whereas at seven you will either sell upwards of 10,000 or the whole project will be a failure. I tell you the next price to seven shillings is a guinea for the two volumes in a case, which would get you a pornographic reputation.

My old circulation of 1,000 was attained when I was comparatively unknown by an essay on "Ibsenism", with an unpopular title. And that was not a ten shilling circulation, but a half crown one.

I object strenuously to gilt tops.

If on thinking this over, you still feel suicidal, I am not sure that my best plan will not be to back my opinion by manufacturing the book myself, taking over Clark's contract from you and getting you to publish on commission. At any rate, it is a thing to be considered. There is an enormous section of bookbuyers who regard 10/– as a price absolutely outside their means, and 7/– within it. Evans's [1] notion that they will give ten as soon as seven only applies to people who will give fifteen as soon as ten. 7/– is only silver: 10/– is gold. I believe in going for a large circulation, even if the paper is cheapened. Anyhow, Globe 8vo is too small for a big price, unless it is *de luxe*.

Do think it over a bit. The enterprise is really not worth undertaking at all if you limit your aim to 2,000 circulation: at least not from my point of view. Allowing me the moderate tariff of £25 for the prefaces, I should get £25 apiece for the plays. It takes six months to write a play. Therefore the dramatic author would get less than £1 a week—say five shillings less than a dock labourer—4½d an hour for writing masterpieces. It's sweating. Sell 10,000 at 7/– and I shall get 1/3¾ an hour. Do you grudge me that modest reward?

Yrs arithmetically

G. BERNARD SHAW

Here I must pause and explain. It was no part of my plan when I began this book in general and this chapter in particular to print so many of Bernard Shaw's letters, but having them before me, I feel sure that the best way to carry on the narrative is to quote his exact words rather than to condense and to paraphrase. I hope he won't mind. It does seem to me that I ought, having the opportunity, to show the Shavian machine at work, to disclose one side of the Shavian mind. Besides, much of what he says will help the education of every printer in this island and in America. For instance this letter:

29 FITZROY SQUARE W.

23rd *October* 1897

DEAR G. R.

I return a couple more sheets—all I've got—for press. If you look at pp. 17, 25, 6 & 7 you will see that I have

---

[1] Evans, being a bookseller, ought to have known.

made a faint protest against the whiteness of some of the lines. You might suggest to them that they need not justify to avoid dividing a word at the end—that it is better to divide a word than to have a loose line making a streak of whitey grey through the black. Caxton would have printed your name Gr-ant Richa-rds at the end of a line sooner than spoilt his page with rivers of white.

The great thing is to get the color even. Besides, since we are substituting spaced letters for italic in underlined words, it is important that the spacing should be regular and rather narrow, so as to make the spacing distinctive....

G. B. S.

With regret I omit some technical letters which follow the last, only quoting a sentence from one of December 9: "By the way, are you going on with *The Political Year Book?* I trust not; but if you are going to come down on me for an article, give me warning." I have already told how grievous a frost *The Political Year Book* was. G. B. S. had a nose.

Plays Pleasant and Unpleasant did manage to come out early in 1898. I was as proud as Punch. The look and feel of it gave me intense pleasure. But it did not make me rich. As I have shown, its rate of sale was entirely incommensurate with the amount of notice it attracted and with the reputation it helped to make for its author. I know little of its sale in America. On Stone's failure Shaw chose Brentano as his publishers because that firm had "pirated" more of his books than any other house. The compliment was irresistible. In the end Brentano also failed; and Shaw, though bombarded with invitations, transferred himself quietly from the most advanced of the newest publishers to the ancient and ultra-respectable house of Dodd, Mead and Company.

XIV

MORE G.B.S.

SOME time in the early spring of 1898 I became engaged to a young Italian lady; in May of the same year we were married. I shall have, I think, no need to mention that marriage again, so I will confine myself to saying that my wife bore me children and that the union was dissolved. It was in the summer of 1898 that Bernard Shaw himself married. He tells me about it beforehand, but I am "to keep it dark":

29 FITZROY SQUARE W.
23rd May 1898

DEAR G. R.

This upset of mine[1] has knocked the Wagner pamphlet out of time. I have written a lot of it; but the operation stopped me dead: I was forced to lie there and feed myself back to life. As it is, I cannot do much until I can be moved to the country. I have chucked the *Saturday* and am spoiling to get on with the pamphlet; but I have given up all hope of being in time for the cycles at Covent Garden. I have written 12,000 words; so I have no doubt the total will be at least 20,000, if not more. . . .

What on earth do you want to get married for, at your age? As a matter of fact I am going to get married myself as soon as I can get round to the workhouse (where the registrar officiates); but then I am 42. Keep this dark until I have done it. I only tell you to keep you in countenance.

G. B. S.

[1] A reference to the accident to his foot.

135

I did keep the secret. What G. B. S. refers to as the Wagner pamphlet was in fact *The Perfect Wagnerite: a Commentary on the Ring of the Niblungs* that he had hoped to finish in time to be of use to Covent Garden audiences. By the middle of June the secret was common property. On June 19, 1898, he writes me a post card, which bears the Paddington postmark 12.5 a.m. and which has printed on its top left-hand corner a precise and characteristic indication of his address and plans:

"Until the end of October Mr. and Mrs. Bernard Shaw's address will be Pitfold, Haslemere, Surrey. Telegraph office: Shottermill. Railway station: Haslemere (Waterloo line), 1½ miles. Permanent London addresses as usual: Mrs. Shaw at 10 Adelphi Terrace, W.C.; and Mr. Shaw at 29 Fitzroy Square, W. (Telegrams: 'Socialist, London')."

10 Adelphi Terrace had been the London address of Miss Charlotte F. Townshend before her marriage. I need not make too much of the fact that to the best of my belief G.B.S. never did return to Fitzroy Square to live. Small blame to him! Mrs. Shaw, I suppose, made him too comfortable. Besides, the period during which he had to be nursed was unexpectedly lengthened as will be seen from the words he wrote on the card:

My wife has been having *such* a delightful honeymoon! First my foot had to be nursed and the day before yesterday, just as it was getting pretty well, I fell downstairs [1] and broke my left arm close to the wrist. I am afraid this will make a hopeless mess of the Wagner book. I had got to work fiercely again when it occurred, and had actually carried the exposition to within one act of the end of the Ring; but in my present smashed condition I daren't attempt to work against time. I am very sorry, as I had hoped to complete the MS. next week.

G. B. S.

[1] He tried to come downstairs on his crutches, and shot himself out into space, crashing on the tiles in the hall.

Within three weeks G. B. S. writes again (on July 8): "The Wagner book is progressing; in fact half of it is already revised and the other half ready in the rough; but I think I will get a fair copy typewritten and go over it all again so as to reduce the corrections in proof as far as is possible." Six weeks later, on August 20, he writes:

DEAR G. R.

I send you herewith, by parcels post, the complete MS. of the Wagner book. I compute it roughly at 35,000 words. This, in the type of the preface to the plays, would make 100 pages. I think, however, that it should be got up as a book of devotion for pocket use, and not bulked out as a treatise. I want to secure the American copyright: do you think Stone will venture upon it?

I have not made up my mind about the title. The Perfect Wagnerite seems to me the best. It might be *announced* as "The P.W.; or the New Protestantism." Quintessence won't do: it would be a weak repetition, and would suggest an explanation of all Wagner's works, whereas I have dealt with the Ring only. A sensible title would be "Wagner's Ring: What it Means"; but nobody would read a book with a sensible title; and quite right too.

We had better have a specimen page or two. If we decide on a biggish book like the plays, the type should be small pica Caslon set solid, like the prefaces to the plays, in which, however, three lines might be knocked off with advantage to the lower margin. If we carry out the idea of a pretty little book of devotion, the type should be as in the plays.

Get it into type as soon as possible, as I have no complete copy; and if the MS. gets lost or burnt there is an end of it forever.

Shall I have to do a prospectus for you?

My foot seems to be filling up in a business-like way at last; I hope to be able to walk in a few weeks.

Yrs ever

G. BERNARD SHAW

Apparently neither my idea of a book suitable for pocket use nor R. and R. Clark's idea of a suitable page agreed with G. B. S.'s for my reply to this letter of his called forth another characteristic effusion on 25 August, 1898:

Who on earth is your tailor? He must have a mania for making large pockets. Walk down Bond St. with your coat bulged out by a volume of the Plays and you are a lost man. What I mean by a pocket volume is a little Imitation of Christ affair about as large, at most, as the envelope of this letter.

Had we not better get the first set of proofs in galley slips? I want to insert a passage which may be long enough to upset the paging. Clark is the only printer I ever heard of who made any difficulty about galley proofs. They ought to be cheaper instead of dearer than paged ones.

You sent on the Glasgow letter to me all right. The writer is not used to my habit of leaving letters unanswered for eighteen months or so.

I will draft the prospectus presently.

When you are next in these parts . . . be sure to look in on us.

Yrs ever

G. BERNARD SHAW

And my reply found G. B. S. in the same good humour:

28th Aug. 1898

What mean you? I have received no specimen page: your previous letter contained no enclosure. Let this hideous omission be instantaneously repaired.

It is quite plain that this book, if turned out in the plain style of the plays, would not look worth three and six. My "book of devotion" conception involved gilt edges, leather binding, clasps, and a bookmarker of perforated card with a text worked on it in wool. An edition de luxe in mother-of-pearl, in Russia leather case £2.2.0. I think that the right notion.

G. B. S.

G. B. S. never persisted in unreason. That is one of his qualities. He seemed then to be coming round to my point of view:

31st Aug. 1898

DEAR G. R.

God has forsaken Clark: those lines are not a bit too long; but *nothing* could make a page look well with such margins. Further, you cannot judge the look of a book by contemplating half of it: the open book presents two pages, which, taken together by the eye, form the complete picture to be aimed at.

I am inclined to favour your notion of the larger page and larger type. But we must have a sample. Ask Clark to send us a couple of pages, set with the margins as I have indicated. Implore him to believe that the lower margin simply cannot be too broad for the world's thumbnail, and that the top must be narrow, and that the top *is the first line of the page and not the title*. We can compare the two samples and decide. Don't tell him to cut off the m: that's not what's the matter. . . .

Did you ever see the Clarendon Press *Pilgrim's Progress*, bound in Russia leather, 2⅛″ by 1⅞″, 418 pp.? It is not as big as a watch. That would be the style of thing for Covent Garden.

Yrs ever

G. BERNARD SHAW

One more letter I must quote for the sake of the advice it gives to me and to young publishers in general:

4th Sept. 1898

DEAR G. R.

Of the two, there can be no hesitation in choosing the smaller type, No. 2. It looks very well now with the margins right, though so far from the page being at all "squat," the line would bear another m if we want to economise in the number of pages, which of course we don't.

No. 1 is out of the question as it stands: the type is too large for the page. But if you hanker after the big fount, get them to try again, adding three lines to the length of the page, and two ms to the width. You will find it will then look much better. *Don't* be in too great a hurry to try these experiments. You will learn from them the only part of a publisher's business that is real. Nobody wants to read the book, or cares a straw whether it is published next month or next century. Besides, you will soon know exactly what to order—only you *must* experiment. Why publish my books if you don't mean to learn from them? You don't expect to make profits on 'em, do you?

If you can't wait, No. 2 will do me well enough though I expect you'd like No. 1, if corrected as suggested.

ever

G. BERNARD SHAW

It is Mrs. Shaw who writes to me next, on September 7— to tell me that they have taken Pitfold on till the end of October but that the doctor "has ordered us to the seaside for change of air. We go to Freshwater Bay Hotel, Isle of Wight, on Saturday for about ten days and we hope that will just put the finishing touches to my patient's recovery". Two days later G. B. S. addresses himself to a further stage in my education:

9th Sept. 1898

DEAR G. R.

We have now got the two specimens right, one being as good as the other, in its own way: the question remains, which will we choose. Or rather, which will *you* choose; for far be it from me to force your inclinations when you have taken so much trouble.

Oddly enough, the larger type is the harder to read, partly because the line is too long to be taken in at an eyefull, partly because its size and clearness are positively dazzling. That is the only point to be considered between the two over and above their good looks. Now please yourself: I leave the decision to you. One will please me as well as the other.

(If you choose the big type [as I anticipate from your letter you are likely to] then you must impress upon Clark that every defect in the printing will be ten times more glaring with the larger than with the smaller. There must be no holes and rivers of white patching the page. As a first step to attain this, the huge gaps left at the beginning of each sentence on the sample page must be vehemently forbidden. The spaces between the words must be kept as narrow and even as possible: it is better to divide words at the end of the line with hyphens than to spoil the line by excessive spacing merely to "justify" without dividing, as some printers make a point of doing. There should be no greater space between the point at the end of a sentence and the capital, than between the last letter of one word and the first of the next within the sentence. In short, the color of the block of printing should be as even as possible. The printing of the sample couldn't possibly be worse in this respect.)[1]

For the big type, a rougher paper and cloth than we used for the plays will be advisable. I suggest rough holland sides and a blue back, with your favorite rough edges.

If you choose the smaller type, the format had better be the same as the plays, with perhaps a different colored cloth, to distinguish the volume of criticism from the volume of fiction.

Tomorrow (Saturday) we go to the Isle of Wight for some days.

[1] Those who are both interested in typography and G. B. S. should read his letter to the *London Mercury* of September, 1925.

I am getting on with my play at last. When it is finished, there will be two in hand for the next volume.

Yrs ever

G. BERNARD SHAW

Of course, in spite of his compliment—for it was he who had taken the trouble, not I—I did my best to carry out his suggestions to the letter. All the same, I have never liked the appearance of *The Perfect Wagnerite*. It seemed to me an error in policy to give it an outside so dissimilar to that of *Plays Pleasant and Unpleasant*. Not that we didn't go on scrapping about the book's binding—and its interior too —for a few more weeks. Thus, having changed his Haslemere address, he writes still from the same neighbourhood on 5th December:

> BLEN-CATHRA, HINDHEAD,
>
> HASLEMERE

DEAR G. R.

. . . The binding exhibits a hellish misconception of my suggestion. The holland should come right up to the back, leaving no margin of blue; and the blue should not be glistening ribbed sticky silk, but a kindred material to the holland, and really blue in color, which this adulterated horror is not. . . . I suggest a large paper edition at ten shillings, with a portrait of Wagner.

If there is time still, I think it would be well to alter the cases and use thicker (or tougher and better) paper for the rest of the edition. That blue stuff is a most blasted fabric. Besides, don't you see how that accursed margin makes the book look small and narrow and worth only a shilling? With the full 4¾″ width of holland it would look worth five. Why, oh why, didn't you send me a case before deciding? . . .

When are you coming down? Will next Saturday to Monday suit you? If not, say when,

Yrs ever

G. BERNARD SHAW

But before that G. B. S. had had another accident. We must go back to 3rd October, sixty-three days earlier than the date of the last letter:

PITFOLD,
HASLEMERE

DEAR G. R.

I am sorry to delay the proofs so long; but my ill luck is not yet exhausted. I sprained my ankle the other day, and found it worse than ten operations or two broken arms. The third sheet is only half finished; and I have had such a bad night that I shall not attempt to do anything at it today, proof correcting requiring one's clear and capable moments. I enclose the first and second sheets.

The only item in the a/c which is utterly immoral is the charge for proof correcting. I enclose *my* a/c under that head, in the best Publisher's Association style and spirit.

Yrs ever
G. BERNARD SHAW

It is characteristic of G. B. S. that in one of his moments that he had described as neither clear nor capable he had worked out his joke—his account under the head of proof correcting. In rendering to the author my account for *Plays Pleasant and Unpleasant* I had charged him with an item of ten pounds six shillings for "author's alterations and extra proofs", an item which, in the circumstances, was correct and according to custom. (Some authors—Thomas Carlyle, I believe, was one of them—re-write their books on their proofs. I myself had a bill from the printer for over sixty pounds for the corrections to my *Memories of a Misspent Youth*. Publishers therefore have to protect themselves against writers so excessive and, in this respect, so incompetent. G. B. S. was not of that kind: he had already in connection with *Plays Pleasant and Unpleasant* referred to "the Carlyle-Balzac average" for corrections.) But he would have none of it. Here is his account:

143

30th Sept. 1898

G. BERNARD SHAW

PITFOLD

HASLEMERE,

SURREY,

in a/c with Grant Richards

	£	s.	d.
Minimum customary allowance to Author for proof correction			
Pleasant Plays	10	0	0
Unpleasant Plays	10	0	0

Services rendered as Typographical Expert by Author to publisher

	£	s.	d.
Choice of type . . .	5	5	0
Design of page, margins, etc. .	2	2	0
Choice of paper . . .	2	2	0
Design of title page . .	10	10	0
Inspection of proofs . .	52	10	0
Choice of binding . . .	2	2	0
Consultations with publisher .	105	0	0
Letters of Instruction . .	63	0	0
Personal instruction (no charge)	—		

	£	s.	d.
	242	11	0
Extra proof corrections in style of typesetting in the interest of the Publisher's reputation	21	0	0
	283	11	0
Less amount charged in Publisher's a/c for "Author's alterations and extra proofs"	10	6	0
	273	5	0
Interest at 6% for 6 months . .	8	3	9
	£281	8	9

Two days later, on October 5, without reference to my unhappy account or to his correction of it, he takes the opportunity of setting down the correct practice in this matter of alteration to proofs:

PITFOLD,

HASLEMERE

DEAR G. R.

I enclose the third sheet. It would be well to mention to Clark that I have made the corrections with the greatest care so as to take out of a line no more and no less than I put in, or, where that is impossible, to readjust the correction within a line or two. Some compositors, when they see a correction, will knock a whole paragraph to pieces and spoil the symmetry of the first setting quite needlessly, though the author may have racked his brains for ten minutes to save overrunning. . . .

G. B. S.

After the beginning of October, if slowly, G. B. S.'s health progresses, for on December 2 he writes to me from Blen-Cathra: "When are you going to look us up in our new quarters? My operation is postponed indefinitely, as my health is improving so much according to the operator (and he is right enough, unless I flatter myself) that if I am patient and keep quiet I shall either escape an operation altogether or else reduce its magnitude very considerably."

With convalescence—if convalescence continued—and with the publication of *The Perfect Wagnerite* came a period of Shavian calm, helped perhaps by the fact that in February, 1899, I paid my first visit to the French country, going to Marseilles, the Riviera and the Rhone Valley and spending three weeks away from London. William Sharp and Thomas A. Janvier collaborated in drawing up my itinerary. I must write of it one day. Returning to London on March 12 I had soon a refreshing tonic in the shape of a characteristic letter, the result, I suppose, of having sent in an account showing the sale of the book. (I should explain that while he

145

had wanted it priced at half-a-crown I had issued it at three and six):

12 *March* 1899

BLEN-CATHRA, HINDHEAD

HASLEMERE

SURREY

DEAR G. R.

You are the most incompetent publisher I ever heard of. In my obscurest days I have always had 20% on half crown books paid without a murmur; and here are you putting a shilling on the price and declaring that you cannot spare me twopence out of it. I blush for you. You should dismiss your clerk at once for making out such statements. Better bring out another edition at once for use at the opera next season: besides, I want to correct my blunders. You must sell some more copies, and turn the loss into a profit. Harmsworth would have sent me a cheque for £250 instead of demanding a reduction of my hardearned royalty. Why don't you advertise? Spend a few thousands on the book and the plays, and then you will begin to see something.

Come over next Saturday week and I will talk to you most paternally.

Yrs ever

G. BERNARD SHAW

The Shaws stopped on at Blen-Cathra, but I have no record of their welfare and activities until July, when, on July 2, Mrs. Shaw writes that "G. B. S. is *much* better; nearly quite well, and I don't mind leaving him now. He is very troublesome about going away *anywhere*, but I think he will go to Cadgwith for a bit. I want to have a talk with you about that". And then on July 4, my cousin, young Grant Allen, having suffered a minor operation and having been kept in bed for a long time, writes to me that "the Bernard Shaws often come up to see me". (He adds "and so does Conan Doyle. He brought me up a gramophone which he's

146

lent me for a few days". Gramophones must have been rare at that time.)

The Shaws did go to Cadgwith[1] or rather, as it turned out, to Ruan Minor, where G. B. S. got "*very* well"—"but we found it too far from the sea and smelly Oh so smelly!! However we stayed there nearly a month, so you may argue from that that we hadn't much to complain of". I should think not indeed! They lodged with Mrs. Dening in the last dwelling-house but one before you turn down the hill to Cadgwith. I appeal to Sir Laurence Binyon, to Finley Peter Dunne ("Mr. Dooley"), to E. V. Lucas, to declare that Ruan Minor when Mrs. Dening ruled was worth suffering a few smells in. Yes, G. B. S. in Ruan Minor was "nearly quite well" and in spite of broken arm and sprained ankle swam me out to sea and brought me into terror of my life from drowning, so skilful he was and intrepid.

At the time the Shaws were at Cadgwith—or, rather, at its sister village—the E. V. Lucases were of the party and the F. C. Constables. Constable was a retired Indian judge who wrote several books, the best being *Aunt Judith's Island*, for which Lucas and I had great admiration when we read it in manuscript—a humorous novel which, while it would hardly bear reprinting, would repay a reading by the curious. I had to leave Cadgwith before my friends, and after my departure Lucas wrote to me:

Monday.

My dear Richards,

We hope your journey was not very tiring and that you are well. Here the skies are still blue and the waters fair. We bathed twice to-day and swimming is but an inch or two beyond my grasp. Mrs. Shaw came off her bicycle on the way to Poltesco and hurt her foot a little, but otherwise received no injury and is now whole again. Without you—its squire—Cadgwith droops. We all went in Jane's boat on Saturday evening. Everything went well until

[1] See *Memories of a Misspent Youth.*

Shaw and Constable plunged into an argument on the modern stage with particular reference to a recent play at the Haymarket. It was then observed that our oarsman was becoming more and more uneasy and at the same time erratic in his movements. After an embarrassing five minutes it was discovered that he resented the phrase "The Manœuvres of Jane",[1] which everyone had been using very freely. Only a promise of a copy of *Aunt Judith* and *The Quintessence of Ibsenism* could placate him.

The Constables drove off this morning and we go on Wednesday. I don't know what, but there is something about this coast and these people which get into the blood. We are—and shall be eternally—obliged to you for giving us the Ruan secret. If it is any pleasure to you to hear it, let me tell you you have been much missed.

Our kind regards.

E. V. L.

It should be explained that the Jane to whose boat reference is made was a fisherman who bore that name, the Janes being a family much honoured on that stretch of coast. They had been my playmates, my mentors, my tutors in the ways of the sea, since my childhood. In a very recent note Lucas reminds me of something that his more retentive memory has yielded up of those far-off days: "How often I recall our joint reading of Dooley on the Dreyfus case as we jogged along in a wagonette". Mr. Dooley—Finley Peter Dunne—had been taken by me to Cadgwith in the previous year.

Soon after leaving Cornwall, the Shaws went on a cruise. Mrs. Shaw, writing to me on October 5, 1899, from the *Lusitania*,[2] "off Syracuse", says that "a young fellow of the name of Lethbridge came on board at Villefranche who seems to know you and the Grant Allens very well. He said he had been present at the first performance of *The*

[1] Henry Arthur Jones's play.
[2] The big ship's predecessor, not the ship that was sunk in the war.

Devil's Disciple. So odd to find someone out here who had been at it! How it can have been a success, I *don't know*, as there can have been practically no rehearsing; the actors only got their parts the day before we left London!"

And then, once more on the move, Shaw writes to me from Wales:

30 MARINE TERRACE, ABERYSTWYTH,
24th December 1899

DEAR GRANT RICHARDS,

Stuart Glennie, of whom I spoke to you at Cadgwith, tells me he is sending you his essay on the New Drama. He is a disciple of Buckle, and a Philosophy of History man, strong on the Conflict of Races, and regarding all history subsequent to 8000 B.C. as a matter of a few recent episodes. As you ought to have a learned man in your menagerie of authors, he may suit you. I suggest that as he is a good pamphleteer, he might apply his Conflict of Races theory to the South African war to the extent of doing you a saleable firework on the subject. The real difficulty with him is his age. Not that he is at all past working; but he has been so suppressed all his life because of the heterodoxy of his science that he does not realise how freely he can speak out now on questions of marriage, religion, etc. He wants to found a "Kosminian Brother-hood" of men who look at the world from the high scientific and philosophical point of view. If you tell him that you are game to publish anything that is at once respectably learned and breath-bereavingly scandalous, urging him to go ahead to the utmost length of his tether, he might give you something that would be as much of a success in its way as Kidd's *Social Evolution* in *its* way. But you will have to publish the New Drama to begin with, to give him confidence. He tells me he has shortened the essay, which is just what he oughtn't to have done. If you can get him to make it more aggressive, do.

French, the theatrical bookseller (really Hogg), has

been talking to Edward Rose about my plays—wants to have them published separately for the use of amateurs. Heinemann had, and no doubt has, an eighteenpenny edition of Pinero in paper covers for this purpose. I have not thought the matter out; but it seems possible that a demand of the kind may arise, and that it might possibly be met by not selling the separate copies to the general public but by selling them to amateur societies paying fees for a performance; in other words, selling them through French. Hogg declares that he pays Pinero £100 a month in author's fees; but this I take to be an explosion of the theatrical imagination. Fees for amateurs, however, total up to an appreciable part of a popular dramatic author's income; and it might come to French (Hogg) playing bookseller to your publisher for an acting edition.

I shall be back in town in the first week in January. I came down here to lecture; and as there was neither fog nor snow I thought I would stay over Xmas.

How I should like to do a pamphlet on the war! Only it will be over before I could find the time.

G. BERNARD SHAW

For one reason or another—my own indiscretion and my own greediness, according to Shaw—I did not get on with the old but interesting man who was Stuart Glennie; at that time at least nothing much came of the idea of selling the Shavian plays separately; and the war—well, it dragged on for another twenty-nine months—but then, as we have seen, the Boer War was one of the very few things about which G. B. S. proved wrong—that is to say, he had greatly underestimated the trouble that the Boers would give. (I have already shown how in 1896 he had written that "any of the Great Powers could—if the others would allow it—swallow up the Transvaal as a whale swallows a herring".) You will realise why it is that I, being human, like to get this jibe in before I come to quote (on page 152) what G. B. S. had to say to me about my brief traffic with Stuart Glennie! And indeed, I find another small blot on his record! Two months later—on February 20, 1900—G. B. S. does not do something that he had previously thought should be done. I had asked him about the revision of, I think, *The Perfect Wagnerite*, in view of the fact that another edition was required. He is back at Adelphi Terrace and yet he answers "No: I *haven't time* to undertake a revise. It had better be reprinted as it stands." Needless to say the italics are mine.

Re-reading in proof the last paragraph, I felt it would be an advantage to get from G. B. S. a statement of what his attitude had been on the Boer War, and on May 23, 1934, he tells me exactly what I wanted to know:

DEAR G. R.

. . . Within a few years before the war, Cronwright Schreiner called on me; and I, taking the view of Kruger's theocracy that, as I learned, later, was taken by Ibsen, urged upon him strongly the importance of overthrowing Oom Paul and replacing him by Joubert and the more modern party. Schreiner said they knew all that quite well, but must wait until the old man died, which must soon happen in the course of nature. I did not agree. I said it might be too late then; and it *was*.

When the war broke out I was expected as a matter of course to go pro-Boer with Ramsay Macdonald, Chesterton, Lloyd George, and the group which left the Fabian Society because the utmost concessions I could make to it in drafting and amending *Fabianism and the Empire* did not satisfy it. But though I was under no illusion as to the commercial basis of the war, I for my own part answered Ibsen's question "Are we really on the side of Mr. Kruger and his Bible?" in the negative. The line I led the Fabian Society into taking (with plenty of assistance: I was only the draftsman and spokesman) was justified by events, just as my 1914 war manifesto, which I did singlehanded, has been justified.

Fabianism and the Empire must therefore rank as a success.... The quarrel was finally settled on our lines. Some of the incidents of the war were, of course, horrible; but for a wonder the victory was not abused as the 1918 one was, and the victory of the North in America in the sixties.

Always yrs

G. BERNARD SHAW

Here, to go back, is the Shaw letter that deals with Stuart Glennie. It may as well come out now as later! Of course it is not so much the Glennie part of the letter that gave me a pain. (By the way, note in the first paragraph the use of the word "candid": I am glad I was candid; it is better to be candid in such cases):

IO ADELPHI TERRACE, W.C.

8th May 1900

MY DEAR G. R.

Glennie told with great gusto, in his highest register, the tale of your candid statement of the financial result of your proposal. But what I want to convince you of is that you shouldn't have made it. If he were rich, it would be an absurd bargain for him, since he could publish on commission; if he were poor, it would be an absurd one for you, since he could not buy the remainder. Of course you have wasted good time in the matter. Also his. Also mine. You should never make a bad bargain with a man except under very special circumstances; and you should never *under any circumstances* let a man make a bad bargain with you. In this instance you would probably have done both but for my interference.

And now, what about *Three Plays for Puritans?* It is going to involve a lot of composition, and at least three plates, at the old price. You have not done so amazingly well with *Plays P. and Unpl.* (an edition of 1200 in two years) as to feel certain that this book is going to be a treasure. I offer to pay for it (instead of Clarke), and hold you harmless. The public and the press won't know. The honor and glory of the thing will be the same. You do not deign to reply on the point, possibly because your feelings are hurt. I don't care about your feelings, except in so far as they seem likely to ruin you, which would be extremely inconvenient to me. I want to know definitely and at once, because if it is to be commission, I must set about the printing at once; and if it is to be as before, I must draw up an agreement, which, this time, must be properly considered and executed in spite of your shrieks. If you won't be businesslike with other people, you *shall* with me: I'll make you, if only for the sake of your education. *Do* wake up.

G. B. S.

I do not remember, and I cannot after all these years discover, what proposal I did make to Stuart Glennie, but I suppose that, having G. B. S.'s opinion of his work to give me confidence, I offered to publish his essay on the New Drama at his own expense or, possibly, against his guarantee that I should sell enough copies to cover not only the cost of production but also the cost of handling, that I should be sure to make something out of the transaction. Essays on the New Drama were not any more marketable in 1900 than they are to-day. Read, they might be; discussed, they often were; sold, they seldom were. What G. B. S. says about his friend's essay opens up the whole question of "commission books", books published at the expense of the author. We have seen that *A Shropshire Lad* began by being published at the expense of the author; Grant Allen published at least two of his books, the books that in his early years as an author he thought most of, at his own expense; all the books of Samuel Butler were published at Samuel Butler's own expense—until, that is, I had the good fortune to make his acquaintance. Perhaps it would be a good thing if no books were published unless a publisher were willing to pay out of his own pocket the cost of production. Perhaps. Perhaps not. Perhaps it would be a good thing if every infant which at birth looked as if it could come to no good were put out of the way. Grant Allen has dealt with that question in *A Child of the Phalanstery*.[1] But in that case what would have happened to Pope and to Byron?

Did Fitzgerald pay for the first edition of his *Rubaiyat?* I forget.

I imagine that Shaw must have astonished every kind of tradesman and professional man with his knowledge of the practices of the trades and professions with which he was successively brought into contact. We have seen how much he knew about printing. He showed signs of knowing as much about publishing and bookselling. Thus when, on May 31, 1900, we were discussing an agreement, and fixing dates for the rendering, and payment of, accounts for *Three Plays for Puritans*, he writes from Adelphi Terrace:

MY DEAR G. R.

Very well: let us make the accounts up to the 30th June and 31st Dec. and furnish them with a cheque on the 25th March and 29th Sep. That will enable you to get in your accounts—a process consisting for the most part of taking ready money across the counter from the bookseller's boy for three John Streets, nine Dooleys and a Puritan.

I shall do just as much proof correction on this volume as on the last one—probably more. My corrections were in no way extravagant; and the few trial pages we had when I was doing your work of inventing a presentable format after the blighting failure of your own perfunctory attempt, cost you a few shillings and me many days in which I might have earned guineas. The extra proofs for the copyrighting performances I was perfectly willing to pay for with 150% profit for you. The price I did pay would have provided me with complete volumes on Japanese paper. Anyhow, this time I shall need no such copies; and I shall spare no expense (to you) in achieving the

---

[1] *Strange Stories*, by Grant Allen.

utmost accuracy and elegance of composition from Clark & Co. If you demur to the tiniest comma, I shall instantly offer to take over the whole cost of manufacture and revert to a commission basis. If at the last moment I think I can rewrite all the plays with advantage I shall do so on the proofs without a throb of remorse. So there!

Yrs resolutely

G. BERNARD SHAW

P.S. I go down to Blackdown Cottage, near Haslemere, by the 11.25 a.m. tomorrow and hope to stay there for the next three weeks.

The gibe at the end of the first paragraph of this last letter is based on the fact that at that time a publisher would sell thirteen books at the price of twelve and that the thirteen books need not all be the same book as long as they were all published at the same price. "Dooley" is of course the more or less immortal essays of Finley Peter Dunne.

When next he writes Shaw tells me that when he goes to Fitzroy Square he will look for and lend me Havelock Ellis's *Studies in the Psychology of Sex* ("It is quite unfit for you to read"); and on June 27 he shows a knowledge of warfare:

10 ADELPHI TERRACE, W.C.

27th June 1900

DEAR G. R.

The sooner you raise the Pleasant and Unpleasant to six shillings, the sooner I shall get one and fourpence instead of a shilling; so fire away.

Will you instruct Clark to supply me with as many special extra proofs of the Devil's Disciple as I ask for, and to charge me for them—that is, send the *a/c* to me, only charging you with the ordinary proofs for correction. Forbes Robertson wants to begin rehearsing for his provincial tour; and I shall have to supply him with copies for stage use. . . .

155

Who wrote the New Battle of Dorking?[1] Not Arnold Forster, surely? Only a professional soldier could be so grossly ignorant of warfare.

ever

G. B. S.

It is amusing to see G. B. S. here conniving at the increase in the price of *Plays Pleasant and Unpleasant* after his vehement advocacy of a lower price than was first adopted. *The New Battle of Dorking*, I should add, was a book that I had commissioned in the hope that it might have the same kind of success that its predecessor had had three or four decades earlier. It was written, I may now say, by Colonel Maude. It did not succeed. There had been other books of the same kind.

Then on July 10, still from Adelphi Terrace:

Puritans be blowed! Rehearsals of the Devil's Disciple have stopped everything except a fabulous output of extra proofs. However, the play itself is passed for press. The preface has not yet reached that stage; but with it as it stands and the play, you can make a dummy copy for the travellers. By the way, the paper should be like that of the American edition, light and tough, and not the cheap blankets on which we printed before. A thick woolly paper will make the vol too bulky.

Do you mind giving the illustrations to Walker and Cockerell to do? Walker will find out all about the Burgoyne portrait etc. for me; and his new partner Cockerell[2] (vice Boutall retired) is almost equally full of information. . . .

G. B. S.

At that time my engraving was being done by the Swan Engraving Company, then under the direction of the versatile Harry C. Marillier, who has done so many things so very well, from exposing the Harness Electric Belt swindle

---

[1] *The New Battle of Dorking* was anonymous.
[2] Sir Sydney Cockerell, now famous as curator of the Fitzwilliam Museum, Cambridge.

in Harry Cust's *Pall Mall Gazette* to managing the William Morris business, from writing good verse to pontificating as an art-critic. Shaw's reason for wanting me to employ Sir Emery Walker rather than the Swan emerges in his letter of the 20th July:

> ... H. H. C. [the late H. H. Champion, the socialist] is undoubtedly (or at all events *was*) a remarkably clever, resourceful, plausible, smart man, excellent company and authentically wellbred style. You might do worse if you want anybody in that capacity [as agent in Australia].
>
> What about Walker and Cockerell? I saw Walker the other day. He undertakes to do the work no better than the Swan, and to charge quite as much; but the real point is that he told me straight off about the authentic busts of Caesar, the one in the Museum being doubtful, and the accepted ones being in Egypt and Berlin. He will also hunt down Burgoyne for me, which will be a bit of a business.
>
> I am now writing a series of remarkable historical essays to follow the plays under the pretext of Notes. The setting up of that book will absorb your entire capital.
>
> G. B. S.

Three days later G. B. S. develops an idea that became a favourite one with him: that I was neglecting my business. It was based on nothing more reliable than the fact that now and again it would chance that when he came in to see me at Henrietta Street he found me out or even away. He was a great man for dropping in unheralded. But as for neglecting my business, I might just as well have accused him of neglecting his business as an author and as a publicist had I dropped in on him at the very hour that he was looking for me:

> DEAR G. R.
>
> I have been round to Henrietta Street, but found you neglecting that unfortunate institution as usual.
>
> H. H. C.'s wife was a Miss Goldstein, daughter of an official—a Jew. She is a capable and auspicious consort, and has conducted the only of C.'s enterprises that sur-

vived the last financial crash. This is a library at which you can read every book published for a penny per book. You go in, make a deposit to cover the risk of loss, get the book, read it (if possible), bring it back, and receive your deposit less a penny. When every other enterprise in Australia perished, this weathered the storm.

C. is a man fertile in schemes and hardy in speculation: consequently, if you propose to stake much capital on him, it is an open question whether you would not get more fun out of it at Monte Carlo. But with this reservation, you could hardly do better than jump at him. He is really a very clever chap.

Yrs

G. B. S.

P.S. By the way, what is your number in Great Marlboro St? I nearly called the other day, but did not know which house.

I wish he had known my number in Great Marlborough Street. It was in those days a pleasant place in which to live. I had gone to Number 51 from Rossetti Garden Mansions as the nearest approach that I could manage to the kind of house the Archibald Ripleys inhabited in Golden Square, and on the general principle that if I had to live in London rather than the country I had better do so as nearly as possible at its centre rather than in its abhorrent suburbs. My house was in effect next door both to a church and to a fire station, and as in those days motor-cars were almost unknown, the big merchants of the City had not invaded the street's quietude, and as at the Poland Street end it had no straight run through, it was very calm and gracious as a place in which to live. I had the whole house except the ground floor and paid a hundred and seventy pounds a year for it, including rates. Rents in that quarter have grown up since then! Great Marlborough Street was higher than Chelsea, and from the moment I went to it my health improved. Three of my children were born there.

A FABIAN SOCIETY MANIFESTO

Three Plays for Puritans continues to occupy much of Bernard Shaw's time. He writes on August 5:

DEAR G. R.

I have sent the proofs direct to Clark for the following reasons.

1. The book is of such extraordinary quality as to absolve the author from all common obligations as to keeping faith etc.

2. It is important that you should be able to plead, when indicted for blasphemous libel, that you had no opportunity of reading the proofs.

3. There was, in the case of the Devil's Disciple, no time to send round by Henrietta St, and I duly advised you of the same.

4. No other proofs save those of the D's D have passed.

5. I have kept those which did pass for you.

6. Had I sent them to Henrietta St, there is no reason to doubt that they would have been lost there.

More reasons, equally convincing, if required.

Have you instructed Walker and Cockerell yet?

ever

G. BERNARD SHAW

With the end of August the Shavian theatre has receded for the moment:

10 ADELPHI TERRACE, W.C.

31st August 1900

DEAR G. R.

I have just drafted an Election Manifesto for the Fabian Society. It is still far from complete; yet it runs to 11,600 words—out of the question for a magazine article or a penny tract. It is full of ideas about the Empire, China, etc. Whether the society will swallow it or not I cannot say; certainly not without a struggle. But if they will not have it, I can still publish it on my own account as my personal election manifesto, I being a party of one. Are you disposed to speculate in this? You would have to supply 700 proofs at cost price to begin with, since every blessed member must have a copy before it can be passed. And you ought to be prepared to put it in hand at high pressure speed next Friday (the 7th), on which day the Executive will decide what to do. I am suggesting this on my own responsibility, and cannot answer for what they may order. Even the Executive cannot answer for the Society; but at worst the stuff belongs to me and can be published as my own. In that case I should suggest your making it as cheap as you presently can, and calculating how many copies, without royalty, would give you a fair profit on the enterprise. I should licence you to sell that many; and if any more were wanted you could pay me an exorbitant royalty. If you publish it for the Society, they may want a royalty all through, or they may consent to the plan I propose for myself. Anyhow, let me know what you think of this.

There is no time to be lost. The election may not be until February or March; but it may and very likely will be in October. In any case the public will proceed on the assumption that it will come promptly.

I return to Blackdown Cottage, near Haslemere, Surrey, tomorrow evening. Up to town again on Wednesday, probably. Meanwhile I am at 29 Fitzroy Square, W. I presume you are at Ruan and that this will be forwarded.

Yrs ever

G. BERNARD SHAW

Things moved quickly:

BLACKDOWN COTTAGE

HASLEMERE

2nd September 1900

DEAR G. R.

Penny be blowed! sixpence, a shilling, half a crown, twelve shillings, large paper edition two guineas, anything it will bear.

Sixpence, probably, is the price most to be considered; but I did not contemplate anything below that. And since sixpence is beyond the reach of the penny public, and a shilling is not beyond the reach of the sixpenny public, and the main thing is to get the thing reviewed and quoted and discussed promptly, you had better make it a shilling if you cannot command the sixpenny organization. By the way, ought we to ask Pearson or Harmsworth instead of you? Or can you do a deal with them over it? The thing is to get at the newsagents, if it is to be sixpence and a big circulation. . . .

Yours ever

G. BERNARD SHAW

But not so very quickly. I suppose that the Fabians in counsel were true to their name:

IN THE TRAIN—GOING TO

BLACKDOWN COTTAGE, NEAR HASLEMERE

13th Sept. 1900

DEAR G. R.

There is no time to waste on preliminary proof corrections of that Manifesto. The Chiswick people must take the most violent measures to get 800 proofs delivered at the Fabian Office at the earliest possible moment—say Monday midday at latest.

The form of these proofs is most important; they ought to be galley proofs, so that they may not be available afterwards instead of a copy of the book. This can be managed by printing them in long forms and cutting them galley-wise. Margins should be wide enough for corrections.

Further—and this is also vital—there must be no page heading or galley slip heading to betray what the document is or where it comes from. Each slip should be headed "Copyright matter. Strictly private and confidential. All rights reserved". This, I think, will prevent any editor into whose hands a copy may fall, from making free with it.

161

The proofs should not be leaded. It will save paper and bulk to print them solid and insert the leads (if any) afterwards.

Yrs, very tired

G. BERNARD SHAW

Shaw, back at Adelphi Terrace, writes on September 21:

DEAR G. R.

Will you get the enclosed corrections made. . . .

I also enclose a preface, which will, I hope, help to get over some of the objections which are pouring in, to my utter and distracting confusion and overwork. Of this preface a couple of hundred proofs will be wanted for distribution at the meeting. Send 'em to Pease; but let me have a few—say half a dozen. I go down to Blackdown tomorrow evening, but shall come up on Tuesday; so post anything to Adelphi Terrace.

Tell the Chiswick people to be very careful to return my corrected proof with the revise, as I shall have to move all the corrections as amendments, and I have no other record of them.

I can't tell you how sick and brainblasted I am with the accursed thing.

G. B. S.

Two days later he writes from Blackdown Cottage: "I hate the thing more than I can say, the weather being out of the way glorious, and my brain needing rest." I am not surprised. The prospect of moving "all the corrections as amendments" must have been as fatiguing as anything he had ever done. Three days more pass:

10 ADELPHI TERRACE

26th Sept. 1900

3 A.M.

GRANT RICHARDS,

Observe the hour: the early village cock hath thrice done salutation to the morn.—Shakespear.

The Manifesto has passed: all is well save its shattered author.

I enclose proofs which, though not absolutely final, are nearly so enough to justify you in paging and preparing for press. If you divide into chapters as I have directed, it will not only make the book thicker and please the printer in search of fat, but it will prevent serious running over in case Webb and I at our final survey of it tomorrow should have to make alterations extensive enough to upset the lines much.

I shall drop this into your letterbox and then to bed.

Yrs ever

G. BERNARD SHAW

With the beginning of the month, on October 2, 1900, finished copies of the *Manifesto* are actually in its author's hands. Was any author more active? The writing finished, he sets to work on securing reviews, not, as in Hall Caine's case, reviews for his own aggrandisement, but reviews for the good of his cause. And in the midst of it all he pauses to suggest something to help on the success of Havelock Ellis's *The Nineteenth Century* which I had recently published to the satisfaction of my pride but the detriment of my pocket. Myriad minded man! (Shaw, I mean, although the phrase might be applied also to the other fellow as well.)

BLACKDOWN COTTAGE, HASLEMERE

DEAR G. R.

The Chiswick Press sent me six advance copies of the Manifesto on Saturday. I used them to secure good notices, concentrating myself chiefly on the Morning Post, which has promised a column notice and a leaderette. This cost me two copies. I planted the rest on the Star, Leader, and Westminster Gazette: the other papers must take their chance in the ordinary course.

If by any chance your 5000 copies go off like hot cakes, I suggest that you might do worse than go to Pearson or Harmsworth at the first sign of the least slackening in the demand, and find out whether they would make an offer of a lump sum for an unlimited penny edition. If they did, and we accepted, you could collar ten per cent and do a good action into the bargain.

By the way, if you print any more you might stick in Havelock Ellis's book among your advertisements, as his Nineteenth Century sounds rather like a book the Fabians would buy.

Yours ever
G. BERNARD SHAW

And there for a time we will leave G. B. S. and his correspondence. I did not realise how many of his letters I should wish to quote, or how much I owed in those years to his criticism, his patience, and to his ability to keep me up to the mark or, for the matter of that, how much he entered into my life.

XV

FIFTH AVENUE ENTERPRISE–FRANK NORRIS AND
THEODORE DREISER

AT the beginning of May in 1901 I paid my first visit to
America, going out in the old *Umbria* and finding the
journey neither comfortable nor enjoyable. I did not know
the ropes, and not to know the ropes on a transatlantic voyage is a cause of unhappiness. I had books to sell in America
and I wanted to buy books. That is to say, I had books, either
in being or in prospect, of which I wished to sell the American rights or to sell an edition in sheets; and I was keen to
make the acquaintance of more American publishers and of
as many American authors as was possible. By that time Frank
Doubleday was a friend of mine, and so were the head of the
Dodd, Mead firm and John Macrae of Duttons. I spent much
of my time with, and in the office of, the Stokes people, and
was successful in selling them an edition of W. E. Henley's
Edinburgh Folio Shakespeare. I am afraid they did not do
very well with it. Nor did I for the matter of that. The
Stokes crowd were very cordial. Recently they had published a book by David Graham Phillips, who later on wrote
Susan Lenox, and, suggesting that I might like to see over an
American newspaper office, asked the young novelist, who
was then on the staff of the *World*, to take me round. I remember him as rather English than American, as wearing
an English straw hat with a club ribbon and as being very
polite. No one then thought that one day he would be described, at least by Frank Harris, as almost the great novelist
America was waiting for. I myself was to publish two of his
books, *Golden Fleece* in 1903 and *The Master Rogue* in 1904.

Neither made any impression or was profitable in England; I suppose they escaped Frank Harris's notice at the time.

New York was to me a strange place. I had been told to go to the Holland House, but I did not find that it was so remarkably modern or so specially comfortable. Certainly it had no sumptuous air, and the dial contrivance by which you could in theory tell the people downstairs what you wanted, from a Bronx to a copy of the *Sun,* and have it brought to you in half a brace of shakes, never worked properly for me.

I had not been in the Holland House twenty-four hours when the post brought me an impressive but reticent envelope which I opened with some curiosity. It did not look as if it came from a publishing house. Nor did it. The handwriting of the address made me expect an invitation to dinner. From whom? Few hostesses knew I was in New York. Here is what it did contain:

"THE MARTINGALE"
(incorporated)
SANATORIUM
2 EAST 30TH STREET
(one door from Fifth Avenue)
NEW YORK CITY

A FEW FACTS
"any port in a storm"

is a well known saying, yet some ports prove most disastrous to the staunchest craft.

The following appeal is simply a "beacon light" carefully planned, as a means of protection for those very seafaring crafts, "the ships that pass in the night". All men have a weakness of one kind or another, most "thoroughbreds" (and those who train with them) show their weakness by a "too" too penetrating glance into the flowing bowl, or an incessant desire to flirt with "Col. Corkscrew", whose name and effect is legion.

The result is the same in every clime. They fall "hors de combat", but if they happen to fall in the "RIGHT"

PLACE there is no harm done, and no one concerned need be any the wiser, just as the "ships that pass, etc., etc.".

And it is right here we wish to suggest a port for those seeking a SAFE harbor when "storm beaten":

"THE MARTINGALE"
and what it offers

A strictly high-class private house (one door from fifth avenue), absolutely up to date in all its appointments, where every guest can anchor (as does the ship) and be assured of the personal supervision of the "captain", otherwise superintendent, Margherita Martin, a lady who speaks Spanish and French, and whose capability can be attested to by many of the most influential people of the day.

It often happens that GREAT CARE must be exercised in the treatment of a patient, in which case the Superintendent will assign a special nurse to each guest (like unto the ship's pilot), whose duty it is to look after the comfort and welfare of the patient.

When it is a case of sobering up as soon as possible (to continue on life's voyage) the most modern scientific devices are used—hot air baths, vapor baths, electrical treatment, massage, etc., etc.

It is a well known fact that many men, who, on account of weak hearts, bad kidneys and other troubles, have been warned by their physicians against drinking, yet do disobey.

In such cases the House Physician will assume the personal direction.

OUR SPECIALITY, HOT AIR AND VAPOR BATHS—WHAT THEY WILL DO: "WILL CURE"

Obesity, Rheumatism, free the system of tobacco, liquors, opium and morphine. They give new life to every organ. In a word, will make "Richard himself again".

Respectfully,

"THE MARTINGALE"

2 East 30th Street

Telephone 1092 Madison Sq.

I was soon to find that American hospitality—I refer, of course, to hospitality of a less specialised kind: hospitality in the ordinary sense of the word, in fact!—is of a kind all its own, and I learned to blush when I thought how inadequately it is returned when our American hosts come to England. The way in which they make you free of their Clubs, for instance; and again, the way in which they open their homes to you! I have no space to attempt to explain away our English reticence in these matters, but I hope my American friends do realise that it is not lack of politeness, no, nor lack of appreciation, that makes so many of us here seem so much less forthcoming.

An office in which I soon found myself at home was that of the Doubleday people. I had met Mr. and Mrs. Doubleday often in England and had known them well. The Doubledays were people whom to meet was to like and to see often was to love. In those days they would arrive in London with their two attractive but obstreperous boys, Felix and Nelson, at Brown's Hotel in Dover Street, would be American without ostentation and, if I may say so, English without losing their American character. I, who at that time lived at Number 51 Great Marlborough Street, saw much of them, as I did of their English representative, Henry Chalmers Roberts, who was for a time a portly uncle to my children and a friend on whose clever judgment I could rely and whose qualities as a "mixer" must have made him invaluable in helping to build up the Doubleday connection in England. The Doubleday family lived in those days at Bay Ridge, and it was exciting to me, an Englishman used to going home in an omnibus, to be taken by Frank Doubleday across the Bay through a real sea. The Doubleday home was a teetotal one, but on landing, the old man—he was by no means old, of course—took me into some water-side club and gave me a long and potent drink. I thought at the time that he did not realise its strength. I am sure I didn't or I shouldn't have drunk it all! The next morning, before the day was aired, he was up and away down to Philadelphia to bring off some deal with the *Saturday Evening Post* people. I never saw a man with more business energy.

The Doubleday, Page office was then at 34 Union Square. It was not long after the original Doubleday, McClure Company had split up, Doubleday going one way and McClure another. Arriving one morning in Union Square, I was at once haled round to the Doubleday town residence in East 16th Street to one of those round-table luncheons where privileged visitors met not only members of the family but heads of the various departments of the firm: Walter Page, later, during the War, to be Ambassador to Great Britain, who had just started *The World's Work*, the first of the Doubleday magazines; Sam Everitt; H. W. Lanier, the son of the poet, Sidney Lanier; and others. Round the luncheon-table projects were threshed out and criticisms offered in the freest and frankest spirit. I could not at the time see quite the same thing succeeding in England. But we have improved since then.

One of my chief purposes in going to America was to secure, if I could, the English rights in the future books of Frank Norris, one of the earlier of the Doubleday discoveries, whose *Moran of the Lady Letty* I had purchased in London from Roberts and had brought out under the name of *Shanghaied*. It was not easy; Norris had to be convinced that I was the man to handle his books. However, I did convince him, and when everything had been arranged he lunched with me at the Waldorf-Astoria and talked about his ambitious and perhaps rather French-flavoured literary plans, "the many magnificent conceptions that lay about loose in his brain", as the *New Yorker*, who cannot be old enough to remember, calls them, and, more immediately, *The Octopus* and the other volumes of his wheat trilogy:

"But, Grant Richards, I want to tell you something. You think I'm the man to go after—and you've got me. Well and good. I hope we shall both be satisfied. Listen! I can tell you of an author worth two of me. If you can get him—and you ought to be able to—you can go back to England satisfied with your trip."

The ardour of the hunter blazed up in my veins. "Who is he? I'll go after him this very afternoon. But perhaps he's already fixed up."

"No, I'm sure he isn't. He's a Doubleday author—but that doesn't mean that it's all plain sailing. No, indeed. His name's Dreiser—Theodore Dreiser. From Chicago. I read his novel in manuscript. Magnificent stuff. I'd give everything I have to be able to observe and write like that. *Sister Carrie* it's called."

"Why didn't any of them mention it to me? I asked so particularly if they hadn't someone else they believed in."

Norris smiled. "Yes, that's where the difficulty comes in. You see, my report on the book—I read manuscripts for them, you know—was so enthusiastic that I had him come through from Missouri and they signed an agreement right away. Most of the bunch read it and were as keen as I was. It was set up in type, printed off, ready to bind——"

"Well, I'll go round and get a copy——"

"Don't be in such a hurry—you won't easily get a copy there, anyway. You see, the Old Man's wife got hold of a set of proofs one day and read it and then—well, she kicked like hell. She wouldn't have her husband's name on the title-page of a book like that! Every puritan, old-fashioned, instinct she had was outraged. It was a shame. She's a very nice woman, but, my word, she doesn't believe in the modern spirit in fiction; I don't suppose she'll stand for my work long. She made 'Effendi' [F.N.D. = Frank Nelson Doubleday: the name 'Effendi' had been invented by Rudyard Kipling; in the original it meant one who had earned the right to command] read it and of course he caved in. The book must be given back to Dreiser; the contract must be cancelled; the firm would cut its losses. Anything to prevent the Doubleday name appearing on its title-page!"

"And what's happened?"

THEODORE DREISER EMERGES

"Nothing settled yet. They think it is, but it isn't. Dreiser's heart-broken, of course; all hit up over his disappointment.[1] But I've told him to sit tight—that is, to hold them to their

[1] He had already had disappointment with this first novel. In an interview printed in the New York *Evening Post* on a Wednesday a week or two after *Jennie Gerhardt* appeared he is reported as saying that after reading H. B. Fuller's *With the Procession*, Will Payne's *Story of Eva*, Brand Whitlock's *Thirteenth District* and Norris's *McTeague* (Something wrong in the chronology, isn't there?) he felt that, although "the critics with one accord damned these books and their authors as immoral because they dared to speak out frankly about real relations of men and women, nevertheless this was the kind of work I myself had to do. So I wrote *Sister Carrie* and left the first part of it with a publisher for reading. When I came for his decision, I found that not only would he have nothing to do with my book, but that he would have almost as little to do with me. I was a dog it seems, who was trying to tear down that beautiful American reserve. The critics felt the same way about me. That was as late as ten years ago." In *A Traveller at Forty* he contents himself with saying, "Eleven years ago I wrote my first novel, which was issued by a New York publisher and suppressed by him. Heaven knows why. For, the same year they suppressed my book because of its alleged immoral tendencies, they published Zola's *Fecundity* and *An Englishwoman's Love Letters*." Dreiser must have taken the immoral tendencies of *Fecundity* for granted, for, interviewed by Almer C. Sanborn in the New York *Morning Telegraph* on November 12, 1911, after saying how much Balzac, Hardy, Tolstoi ("from them I learned what in my judgment really great books are"), Daudet, Flaubert, Turgenieff, de Maupassant and George Moore had influenced him, he says, "I have never read a line of Zola, unfortunately." He also goes out of his way to rank "our own American *Quicksand*, by Hervey White, as one of the great books of the world". That same far interview is illustrated by an interesting drawing of the Dreiser of 1911 by Arthur N. Edrop. Nine days later, interviewed by the New York *Sun*, while remarking that W. D. Howells "won't see American life as it is lived; he doesn't want to see it", he goes on: "so that great stretch of country which is universally called to mind by the term 'American', in which a real and a throbbing life exists, has been allowed no literary expression. If one wanted to put finger on the name of the man who first recognised this, strove to work true to his ideals, and pioneered the way to a real American expression of American life, I should say put it on the name of Henry B. Fuller". Then he repeats the names he had already given: "These are all names of pioneers who were blazing the trail in the ten years or so immediately following my reading of——". Mr. Dreiser then realises he has said more than in his first guarded moments he had intended to say, but having said it, he sticks to it. "What's the use, any way, of trying to do anything unless you try to do it the way that strikes you as being right". By the way, the *Evening Post* interviewer was incorrect: Dreiser left the whole of *Sister Carrie* with the disapproving publisher.

171

agreement to publish. I'll get a copy of the book somehow and send it you. Mark my words, the name of Frank Norris isn't going to stand in American literature anything like as high as Dreiser's. I really don't know what the Doubleday people will do. I think if Dreiser refuses to budge they'll get over the lady's scruples—I hope so, anyway. It's a wonderful book . . ."; and Norris continued to urge it on me. Then I read the copy he sent me, and I did think highly of it but, somehow, I couldn't see it in England and made no offer for it, and, worst of all, did not see Dreiser for some years.

What happened to *Sister Carrie* is well known. You can read all about it, from the Dreiserian point of view, in Miss Dudley's *Dreiser and the Land of the Free*. Mrs. Doubleday did not change her opinion; she would not surrender anything to expedience, and, although Dreiser stood to his guns and Doubleday went through the motions of publishing, it was really so eighth-hearted a publication that very few critics knew of its appearance. It was, so to speak, kept under the counter. Such things have happened to English books over here, but not quite in the same way or for the same reason. The truth is that Mrs. Doubleday was a very strong character. If she said a thing had to be, it had to be, and I have no doubt she was more often right than wrong. Her share in building up the Doubleday business could not be over-estimated. She must have been more than a support, she must have been an inspiration, to her husband. And then the books she wrote under the name of Neltje Blanchan: they were invaluable to the list. Perhaps she lived to see Dreiser's work more justly, but I doubt it.

In those early days of the century the Doubleday business was the wonder of the publishing worlds. How could any business progress at such a rate? No great amount of capital was supposed to be available and yet it kept branching out. Success was no doubt the explanation of success. Rivals and gossips used to say that Doubleday was backed by the Rockefeller millions, that "John D." himself was greatly interested in the firm, that the Doubledays, husband and wife, had been playing golf with the old man and that he had been carried away by their schemes, their enthusiasms. All guff, I fancy. Doubleday's capital may or may not have been large, but he had what no amount of capital could have secured, flair, the habit of picking the right men as his associates, and the gift of inspiring loyalty.

And in the meantime *Sister Carrie* was almost dead. Dreiser wrote nothing for years. It is true that Heinemann brought the book out in London in the Dollar Library, but it was in a much cut down form. In New York a lesser publisher, B. W. Dodge, took it over and tried to galvanise it into life; he did not succeed. Perhaps if it had not had the praise of Arnold Bennett,[1] of Frank Harris and of a few other English men of letters, and if James Huneker and Mencken, its admirers, had not again and again reminded their worlds of its existence, it would have died altogether. I

[1] When *The Financier* came out, Bennett described it as "a most powerful and masterly work". That was in a letter; I cannot find that he praised it in print. Authors—George Meredith was a case in point—will often praise a book in a letter but will refuse to have that letter quoted in print. The Meredithian instance was curious. When I was on the eve of publishing Frank Harris's *Montes the Matador* and was anxious to get any useful publicity for it, Harris showed me a letter George Meredith had written to him, a letter in which the novelist had spoken in the highest terms of the author of *Elder Conklin* as the English master of the art of short-story writing. I wrote therefore to Mr. Meredith asking permission to quote it in advance-paragraphs and advertisements. Such praise from the Master if known would have helped Harris enormously at that stage of his career. But Mr. Meredith refused: "Frank Harris is one of the men who can stand on their merits. It would be absurd for me to appear as an indicator to them in his case. I cannot consent to have my privately expressed opinion serve as an advertisement . . ." Odd! Meredith had himself failed of early recognition just because the men who admired him were slow in giving him publicly and effectively the praise they gave him in conversation and in their letters. He had been a "reader" to a publisher and must have known well enough how much a few sentences from his pen would help the younger man who, however well known he was to the worlds of politics and letters, was almost unknown to that greater world on whose acclamation a writer's commercial success must depend. It was the reiterated praise of a few insistent critics who at a fairly advanced period of Meredith's own career won him circulation.

know that when I myself went back to America in 1906 I was proud to find an extract from a letter of mine to Dreiser proclaiming the book's merit printed as a puff on the jacket of the Dodge edition. But *Sister Carrie* came to no considerable public until Harper published it years later.[1] If Frank Norris had had his way, if Doubleday had published it as he wished and had given it the full prestige of the firm's name and backing; if I had taken Norris's repeated advice and had produced it in its entirety in England and with enthusiasm—well, a great reputation would have been built five years sooner than it was, and perhaps the whole course of American literary history might have been altered. . . .

What I remember most vividly in that early Dreiser story is Frank Norris's generous enthusiasm for the book of his protégé, his insistence on its merit. Praise from the man who was to write *The Octopus* was praise indeed.

I did not actually meet Dreiser until ten years after my talk with Norris, although we exchanged several letters. After the almost-failure of *Sister Carrie* he retreated for a time into himself. I paid my second visit to America in 1906 and went again every year thereafter until, and including, 1913. One of Dreiser's letters, written from the *Delineator* office on May 27, 1910, is almost cheerful: "our health keeps the even tenor of its way, our prosperity sometimes appears to have a slightly faded complexion, but at other times appears to be very pale and rosey [*sic*]. I think it varies with the weather." He and Mrs. Dreiser were "dreaming" of coming to London. "If I do not get over

[1] I have written this sentence and it must stand, but I cannot reconcile it with a fact that I have just recovered from a re-reading of the Dreiserian correspondence. There was evidently a Grosset and Dunlap edition at some time before May 4, 1912, for Dreiser refers to it in a letter to me from New York written on that day. It could hardly have come out after the Harper edition which appeared in the early spring of 1911. He wrote to me from Rome on Feb. 21 of that year that Harper's were "bringing out *Sister Carrie* this month". But Grosset and Dunlap were not in the habit of printing small editions. To be included in their cheap reprint series was to be sure of a great circulation.

there pretty soon, however, I think I will make up my mind
not to go at all, because I have become so fixed and settled
in my ways that stirring around would be a hardship." He
continues: "I was really greatly shocked personally when I
read of King Edward's illness and death. From various
articles and scraps of personal information that have come
my way I had come to think of him as a really remarkable
person with a charming broad-minded point of view and it
seems a pity that he had to be removed. As a matter of fact
English affairs are interesting and clearer and more intelligent to me than American problems although I am right
here on the ground. I am, as you know, always strong for
the British because of the profound admiration I have for
their intellectual leadership. If I had means I would live
in England, but not having them I will stay in New York
and hope that Grant Richards, Gilbert Christie[1] and
W. J. Locke, and a few others may occasionally come my
way."

In the autumn of 1911, immediately after my arrival in
New York, Dreiser and I met at once. He was now, as
he would say, once more in fairly good shape and working, and had just published a book, *Jennie Gerhardt,* which
proved to be a success. Harper's had brought it out. People
were taking its author seriously.

Evidently I had informed him of my arrival in New York,
for on November 12 (a Saturday) he writes to me on the
note-paper of my hotel, the Knickerbocker:

MY DEAR RICHARDS:

I called, as witness. My house number is 3609 Broad-
way. My phone number is 1980 Anderson. Welcome to
America. I am leaving you an inscribed copy of *Jennie
Gerhardt.* For the rest of this afternoon and evening my

---

[1] "A wholesale chemist by trade—or profession—(I don't know what
they call it in London) but by mental qualification he is a gentleman
and a scholar. Actually, he is very fascinating—familiar with literature,
art, science, a traveller and a cosmopolitan". (Extract from the same
letter).

phone number will be 408-Party R. Tompkinsville. You
can get me there or tomorrow morning at my house.

I hope if you are interviewed you will say something
definite about me and Jennie. It seems almost impossible
to make my fellow Americans understand that I am alive.
I am thinking of moving to London. Once there I will get
at least an equal run with Robert Hichens and Arnold
Bennett over here. My best wishes.

THEODORE DREISER

Promptly I rang him up and arranged to go to breakfast
on the following morning. I took it for granted that, in spite
of his second paragraph, I should find him in good spirits,
crescent, satisfied with his prospects. He was not satisfied.
He was in the lowest spirits. What was wrong, I asked—for
he entered at once into friendly, unreserved, intimate talk.
Everything was wrong. Yes, *Jennie Gerhardt* was being
talked about, was being fairly successful—but ... Well, he
had intended to follow it with the first volume of an ambitious trilogy which would trace the career of a character
based on Yerkes, the genius and millionaire.

"Yes, you wrote me something about that. Go to it!
Jennie Gerhardt has succeeded; all you have to do is to get
ahead and write the first part—perhaps it's already
written?"

"No, it is not written, and I dare say it won't ever be
written."

"Why?"

"Money—finance. ... Yerkes was a millionaire. His
playground was Europe and he worked there too. I can't go
on with my man's story unless I go to Europe, travel in the
places he travelled in, live the kind of life he lived, see the
kind of people whom he rubbed shoulders with, eat the
same food, know the same type of woman—" He paused.

"Well. What's preventing you?"

"Money—money, of course. How in God's name can I
do these things without money? Travelling as an ordinary

tourist with a few spare dollars in my pocket would be useless——"

"Yes, I see something in that. But you look here as if you had money. You must have money coming from the sale of your book. When the question's put to them, Harper will surely give you a big enough advance on the next——"

"No, I don't think so." He shook his head despairingly. "They have an option on the book anyway, I fancy."

I looked at him with amazement. Here he was with, as I thought, the ball at his feet, and he couldn't get away with it. Surely the matter of an advance could be arranged. . . .

Well, the long and the short of it was that I asked enough questions to get to the bottom of the difficulty. Of course he had over-estimated the amount of money that he would require for a visit to Europe. I corrected his figures. I thought he could have his desired six months out of New York, travel comfortably and see London, Paris, Rome, Monte Carlo . . . if his time was well mapped out, if he would stop with me in England as long as would be useful, and if he avoided the more obvious pitfalls of the travelling American—yes, he would be able to do these things and, in a sufficient sense, to travel in Yerkes's footsteps, so to speak, if he had three hundred pounds—say fifteen hundred dollars.

"I haven't the slightest chance of getting fifteen hundred dollars."

I stood up the better to impress my novelist:

"I'll find them for you—will cause you to have them any-how—if you'll do what I tell you."

"I'll do anything you tell me, Richards."

"Then, to begin with, write this very day to Harpers to send six copies of *Jennie Gerhardt* to me at the Knicker-bocker, my hotel, at once. Yes, six. I'll want 'em all. Let me see, the Century Company have at least five principals. I want one for each and——"

"The Century Company—where do they come in? They won't touch *me*."

"They shall—and will. If not Harper, then the **Century** people. That's my programme. One or other of them shall provide your money. Look on it as a certainty. I'll go down to Union Square to the Century the first thing in the morning——" and then I proceeded to explain to him what I was proposing to do and how little there would be left for him to do. He agreed to all I suggested, promised to follow my instructions exactly. But he did not profess to have any hope.

He must however have been cheered by a column and a half review by Frederic Blount Warren that appeared on **the** following day in the *Morning Telegraph*, for he took the trouble to cut it out and post it to me at my hotel. It was a laudatory review. It ended: "He ought to choose a bigger theme than the story of a kept woman."

The Century Company were friends of mine. Very pleasant people. I had known their older literary advisers. I had known Chichester, the President. Now I knew well Frank H. Scott who succeeded him, and W. W. Ellsworth, the Vice-President, and I was on good terms with Douglas Z. Doty, their Editor. I had made Chichester's acquaintance years before—in 1901—soon after *The Helmet of Navarre* appeared and sold into six figures. It was at the time that the Bobbs-Merrill people had burst into ordinary publishing and had "boosted" *When Knighthood was in Flower* into a huge, an unheard-of, sale. I had congratulated Chichester on the way *The Helmet* was still going. "It must make **you** feel very comfortable," I said. "It makes me feel very uncomfortable," he replied. "Why? A best-seller!" "Yes, we've got a best-seller this season, but what will happen next year? These big sellers are unhealthy. I can't sleep at night for wondering what we shall do to keep up our turn-over if next season we don't have luck of the same kind." But of course this conversation had happened ten years before. Now, in that autumn of 1911, the Century's business seemed to me rather in need of luck. Sound enough, but getting a little old-fashioned. . . .

But to come back to Dreiser—I hurried down town next morning to the Century office and asked to see Mr. Scott. "Mr. Scott," I said, "you'll be losing a chance of securing the best American author ever if you don't listen to me——"

"That's a tall order! Who is he?"

"Theodore Dreiser. Did you ever hear of him? Ever read anything of his?"

"No, never. I'm told he's 'risky' in his writing, and that he's a difficult fellow too."

"Believe me, that's all rot. He's not 'risky' and, properly handled, he's not difficult. All he wants is intelligent handling."

"Yes, I dare say, but he's presumably got that with Harper."

The conversation continued. If I ever did justice to myself I did so then. The other men were called in to conference. I explained frankly the Dreiser position; I expounded my theory of Dreiser: I went over the Dreiser history. I made each one of them undertake to carry home with him that very day the new Dreiser novel. They were to read it immediately and I would turn up at ten o'clock in a couple of days and learn whether they didn't consider the Dreiser proposition an interesting one, whether they were not sure that Dreiser as author was worth going after for all the Company was worth. I told them that I did not suppose Harper would be so foolish as to let him go as far as the books were concerned on which they had an option, but that it was always possible that they would stick to the terms of their agreement and not see their way to provide the absolutely essential fifteen hundred dollars. If they would supply the money, then well and good. If, on the other hand, they wouldn't, then Dreiser would come to the Century Company as soon as he was free *if* the Century Company would put up fifteen hundred dollars now as payment for three articles for the *Century Magazine* on Europe from the point of view of a hundred per cent. American, articles which they could, if they chose, after magazine publication, bring out in fuller form as a travel book. In addition, the Century people must also put up another fifteen hundred dollars as an advance against novels that Dreiser would write when he had fulfilled the terms of the Harper contract. (Dreiser had not said anything to me about this second fifteen hundred but I thought I had better make things safe—presumably he would have to leave money behind to keep his home going.)

My enthusiasm, to say nothing of my cheek—for it was cheek, butting in like this on someone else's business—won the first battle. By the time I'd finished talking I had those rather unexcitable Century people all hit up about Dreiser, of whom, mind you, up to that day not one of them had read a line.

Two days passed and I was back again at the appointed hour and was received in full conclave.

Yes, the Century Company would do what I wanted.

I have before me, jotted down in pencil on a sheet of Century Company notepaper, the "Terms provisionally arranged (and abandoned) for Dreiser Nov. 10, 1911".

I rushed off to my novelist and there and then made him sit down and write to Harpers—or perhaps he went straightway to see them: I have forgotten which. Anyhow, he told them that to carry out his contract with them satisfactorily an advance was necessary—of course he gave the reasons—and that if they couldn't see their way to make it he would have to accept the offer of immediate cash from another New York house which had sufficient confidence in his work to give him fifteen hundred dollars in advance of royalties on the novel or novels he might write when his Harper contract had been carried through.

The Harper people, as I remember it, did not think twice about it. I was sure they wouldn't. I did not know the men at that time in charge of the business, but I knew they were unusually capable. They put up the money. And the Century Company put up their fifteen hundred dollars in advance for their three magazine articles; and within a few hours it was arranged that when I returned to London Dreiser would go with me, that he would use the Century's dollars for the journey and the European tour, and that the Harper advance he would leave behind for the purposes of his household.

The Century Company gave him a send-off party and we, Dreiser and I, departed for Fishguard in the *Mauretania*. Of his journey and of how he fared in England and on the Continent of Europe he has told in *A Traveller at Forty*. It is a narrative in which he allowed himself considerable latitude. A work of art rather than of correct and veracious observation. Before it came out, a couple of years later, he described the book to an interviewer of the *New York Times* (November 30, 1913). Here is most of that interview:

AN AUTHOR "PERSONALLY CONDUCTED"

Theodore Dreiser tells how Europe became Literary Material for Him

"For a whole book to be written around the personality of a man, that man must have a truly remarkable character," said Theodore Dreiser to the interviewer who had been sent to ask him about his first non-fiction work, *A Traveller at Forty*.

"No; you wrong me," laughed Mr. Dreiser. "*A Traveller at Forty* is by no means written around myself, but around the personality of the extraordinary Englishman I call Barfleur. Without him the book would never have been written. I have always been fortunate in having within reach people who believed in me and who insisted that I must write.

"This was the case with my first book, *Sister Carrie*. An intimate friend of mine kept ding-donging into me that I must write a novel. He was the city editor of a newspaper. We were both hard-worked men, and lived together. He would not take no for an answer. So, eventually, *Sister Carrie* was written.

"In the case of my latest book, Barfleur invented it, told me I was to write it, arranged for an American and an English publisher, and then what was the most difficult of all, made it possible for me to see the people and things I was to describe.

"If I had had unlimited time, I might have rambled through England and the Continent and got a series of impressions of some value, but without Barfleur's sympathetic guidance how could I have seen the real color of life that I was seeking to observe?

"Barfleur and I have seen something of the world. I know America, which, by the way, does not interest Barfleur. He knows Europe. We both look upon life from a similar viewpoint. He also is fascinated by the color of life.

"Whenever he told me to go to see a certain thing or placed me in touch with some human condition, I invariably found it worth while. I did make a few of what the tourists call 'side trips', which interested me. . . . But many of the characteristic and charming people I met on these travels I should never have seen at all had it not been for the foresight and wisdom of Barfleur.

"Barfleur telephoned me in New York one day that he would breakfast with me the next morning. He arrived late. He is magnificent, with a gleaming monocle, and behind it a shrewd inquisitive eye. He is also masterful. He unfolded his plan, not as a proposition that I might accept or decline, but as an elaborate series of instruction that I was expected to obey. As I am not at all managerial myself, there was no argument. If I had been asked to assent, I should have assented.

"Those who may read *A Traveller at Forty* may feel that Barfleur is an important figure in it, but no one can quite appreciate how nearly every door I entered was opened to me by Barfleur. . . .

"Barfleur is an English gentleman who, I believe, wishes that he was not so conservative as he is. What I am grateful for is his tactful consideration for my moods as I, at 40, first came in contact with Europe, and especially his beloved England.

"He took me for a few days to his place in the country. There again he was not only showing me something admirable and typical of England, but he made everything easy, smooth, orderly for me personally, just as he did on the ship.

"One day his two sons took me for a walk to such an English village, on the banks of the Thames, as the untravelled American dreams of. The inns were the inns we read about. The houses were thatched. The stone walls were mossy. It was lovely, but very sad.

"Of course Barfleur had an uncle who was an Oxford don. And so I came to see the university whose very name means so much to the world. Even without the uncle I should have had the book on Oxford that Barfleur put in my hands. . . .

"Later, Barfleur let me take part in an English Christmas. Not the sentimental convention of the story books, but a genuine festivity with good cheer and a live Santa Claus. . . .

"Barfleur is a wonderful man. We were constantly meeting people that he knew, not only in England, but in France and Italy. One of the most delightful invitations I ever received . . . was, I am sure, instigated by Barfleur.

"He arranged my whole programme—Paris, the Riviera, Holland. Of course, he was entirely at home in Paris. The first morning in Paris was typical. I was to walk in the nearby Tuileries alone. Then we were to go to a certain bootmaker's who was to make me a pair of shoes for later walking trips. Then a few visits to haberdashers. After that, the bookstalls on the banks of the Seine, the churches of St. Etienne-du-Mont, Notre Dame, the Sainte Chapelle; Foyot's for lunch, and so forth and so on. Now could anything be a better introduction to Paris than a morning walk alone in the Tuileries? The scene of taste, lightness, magnificence—these gardens give it. We would be hampered in expressing so much charm and beauty because we do not permit in America the public use of the nude in our parks in this way.

"Along the Seine I kept recalling Balzac. Barfleur was fuller of allusion, from Rousseau to George Moore.

"At Monte Carlo Barfleur looked after our credentials, and was careful that we stopped at exactly the right hotel. His kinsman, Sir Scorp, who had joined our party, also had ideas as to the most desirable restaurants and other sights, but in a contest with the experienced and capable Barfleur he always lost out.

"On our way to Eze I exclaimed with delight at seeing a real barefoot goose-girl. Barfleur beamed at me through his monocle. 'Trust me.' he said. 'I provide goose-girls, monuments to Caesar, fountains, shepherds, everything!'

"My visit to Rome was made delightful by Barfleur's mother, who was spending the winter there. With infinite enthusiasm and graciousness, she took care that I saw what would most interest me. Although intensely conservative, she had an acute interest in life, and was a wonderfully industrious social mentor. . . .

"Barfleur made *A Traveller at Forty* possible. But, of course, it is by no means the story of Barfleur's life. That would indeed make a book!"

Let me be frank: in the Dreiser chronicle I was Barfleur; Sir Scorp was no kinsman of mine but Sir Hugh Lane, a great friend, a collector, an expert. I have written of him in a novel called *Caviare!*

One turns to the last pages of *A Traveller at Forty* and one finds its author beset with misgiving. He presents me, on his return to Paris from Germany and Holland, as having a new programme for his interest, amusement and education. We were to return to my home in England that he might see the Thames Valley in the later days of spring; we were to have a week's walk in the Thomas Hardy country. It is not unlikely. "I put up my hand in serious opposition," says Dreiser. "Money is a matter of prime consideration with me. I've got to buckle down to work at once at anything that will make me ready money. I think in all seriousness I had best drop the writing end of the literary profession for a while, anyway, and return to the editorial desk."

No wonder geniality and romance did, as he says, fade from my eyes; no wonder my face did become unduly severe. Here had our author been spending six months accumulating actually essential material and he was wanting to rush back to some editorial desk . . . ! Perhaps, but from luck rather than from calculation, he was right. Even a short time longer spent in Europe might have imperilled that Americanism that has done so much to make him what he is. And, more, it might have still further weakened his self-confidence. "My outlook," he said to me then, "outside the talent you are inclined to praise, is not very encouraging. It is not at all sure that the public will manifest the slightest interest in me from now on." About that he was wrong—and I was sure of it. We fell then to discussing the day of his departure and the boat that he should take. Money was now "a prime consideration" in my eyes too. I had said he should get back to New York on his initial fifteen hundred dollars—and he should, unless he exceeded the six months. On that basis there was no margin for him to return on a smart boat. Besides, he had already travelled in the *Mauretania.* Now he should have a longish journey and should rest and digest.

Ultimately it was decided that Dreiser should return from London by Atlantic Transport, and, since the decision involved a great deal of argument and interference on my part, he reconciled himself to it with reluctance and some small resentment. We passed then, as we sat that night in Madame Gerny's Bar, to a discussion of his German experiences. A few days had made him very German in his sympathies and his beliefs. The Germans were the Cocks of the Walk. Of course there would be war, and equally of course Germany would destroy France, would go through France as a knife goes through butter. Yes . . . yes, and then they'd conquer England. He had no doubt of that. But, later—well, later, their pride would be their downfall, for they would vainly shatter themselves against the power of America. . . .

Within but a few days I had cause to be glad indeed that I had so obstinately resisted Dreiser's wish to return in a smart boat, for that boat, he had decided, was to be the *Titanic*. "The third day we were out news came by wireless that the *Titanic* had sunk after collision with an iceberg in mid-ocean," Dreiser wrote in his book; he had, apparently, forgotten that but for me he would have been on board.

A Traveller at Forty did not appear without creaks. Perhaps it is enough to say that I have exchanged a bare half-dozen words with its author since I read its manuscript. Dreiser was a difficult man. He would tell the truth as he saw it—but he very often saw truth where it was not. For instance, when he first reached London I took him to lunch at the Carlton Grill Room, my favourite place in those days. As we descended the stairs from the Palm Court Dreiser looked round and, missing the garish splendour, the ornate vulgarities of the American hotels he had most admired, he seems to have stored up a few reproachful and resentful reflections to use in his articles—invidious comparisons, shall I call them? A few months later the Century Company sent me a proof. Good heavens! If the article had appeared without alteration in the English edition of their magazine, the Carlton would have been able to soak them and Werner Laurie, the English publisher of the magazine, good and hard! Libel! Talk about fair criticism! . . . I cabled frantically and was just in time to stop the circulation of the offending pages; but whether, as in the case of the famous Kaiser interview, the Century Company chartered a tug and sent them out to sea that they might be dumped in deepest water, I do not know.

But I do know that when in November 1912 I arrived as usual in New York, I had before I landed a desperate letter from Doty of the Century Company. Dreiser had sent in the manuscript of the book: it was of stupendous length: a million words or so and—well, he (Doty) thought I ought to read it at once. (Fancy a million words: the length of a dozen novels!) He feared I should not like what Dreiser had written about me and my friends.

For the first week of my visit, after my hard day's work was done and when I ought to have turned out my light, I lay in bed and read and read at that hand-written manuscript. It made extraordinarily good reading, but what would have happened to me if Dreiser's frank descriptions of my friends to whom I had introduced him, and to whose homes I had been allowed to take him as a guest, had been permitted to stand, I tremble to think! To the reflections on my own character and morality I attached no particular importance, but where others were concerned I had to think and to act. Reticence on any matter and Theodore Dreiser were as far apart as the poles. As I read I discovered that George Moore at his frankest was, compared with Dreiser, the essence of discretion. No confidence was sacred, no actual, or imagined, secret respected. Luckily Doty allowed me, encouraged me even, to cut and cut. I did. And yet I left a lot I did not like. In the long run I myself imported a small edition of the book rather than let some other house publish it in England. I did not exactly repeat the Double-day-*Sister Carrie* trick, but I certainly was not very zealous in pushing the book. I could not be.

MY BELIEF IN DREISER

On the whole I do not regret *A Traveller at Forty*. And in the course of time Dreiser has more than fulfilled my belief in him, my belief in him both as a writer and as a potential best-seller which in Paris he had thought so exaggerated.

By the way, Charles Hanson Towne wrote an amusing skit, *A Traveller—and Sporty*, in the *New York Tribune* of Feb. 26, 1914.

XVI

MORE DREISER

I HAVE never allowed my interest in *Sister Carrie*, and Dreiser's early work in general, to slumber, but I have continued to prefer the first book. I used to recommend it as often as in later years I have recommended a very different story, Norman Douglas's *South Wind*. In 1910, the year before I met Dreiser, I lent *Sister Carrie*, with Frank Norris's *Shanghaied*, to John Masefield. Returning them, he wrote from Great Hampden that he thought the Norris book "poor", but that in his opinion *Sister Carrie* was "very complete, a wonderful piece of work, but no vision in it, all superficial observation of life, wonderfully put together". I did not, I do not, agree with the Poet Laureate.

I will run the risk here of overdoing my Dreiser memories by correcting two or three errors into which Miss Dudley has fallen in her *Dreiser and the Land of the Free*—she is writing of me:

"After Heinemann's success with *Sister Carrie* and Norris's praise, he had sought him out in New York." The facts are that Heinemann did not have, and did not deserve to have, any success worth mentioning with the little book that was all that remained of *Sister Carrie* by the time it had been cut down with the idea of making it more suitable to the English market; and my searching Dreiser out in New York, while in the last resort attributable to Norris's praise, followed on that praise after ten years. In fact I had neglected the light—but then it should be added that the novelist was not very findable until he had published *Jennie Gerhardt* and was living in New York.

"Perhaps it delighted him to know a prodigy from the people scorned by our polite society." No. I knew nothing of Dreiser being scorned by the polite society of America. Things don't present themselves in that way to the visiting Englishman. I knew nothing of Dreiser's social standing.

"One morning in the month of the debut of *Jennie Gerhardt* this personage appeared for breakfast and proposed England, the Riviera, Rome and Paris, and a book of notes to be published on his return. Dreiser's answer was, "If it can be arranged'. Richards arranged it with an advance on the travel book from the Century Company." Rather a perversion of the facts. I had no idea of proposing that Dreiser should visit England when I sat at breakfast with him in his comfortable flat. That proposal came later when he had told me of his embarrassments and of the impossibility of his carrying out his immediate literary plans unless somehow or other it could be arranged that he should "go to Europe". It was then that I applied myself to a consideration of ways and means and invented the scheme into which I invited the Century Company to come. Dreiser's response was not so much "If it can be arranged" as ". . . It can't be arranged". He just would not believe it could be pulled off.

"There were two actress friends of Richards who gave them their perfumed time." I knew only one of these ladies. Having admired her from afar as a comedian, I had been more than pleased to find Miss Sarah Brooke was a passenger on the *Lusitania* on which I had sailed *to* America that autumn. It was she who used so delightfully to say in Henry Arthur Jones's *The Liars* "Where *did* I dine last night?" My pleasure was naturally increased when I found Miss Brooke on the returning boat. She introduced me to the second lady, Miss Malvina Longfellow, an American actress who, later, made some success in silent films. Neither lady gave us as much of her "perfumed time" as I should have liked, nor, incidentally, can I sing coon or any other songs. I wish I could.

Curiously, I find that one of the first contacts I arranged for Dreiser in England was with Masefield.

On December 30, 1911, Dreiser, having for the time seen enough of the English country—I had taken him straight from the *Mauretania* to Cookham Dean, where I then lived, and where he shivered for the greater part of a month while he absorbed the English rural scene—was stopping at the Capitol Hotel in Regent Street, a building which had its place in late Victorian social history. Standing where British Columbia House now stands, it had had, under the name of the Continental, a great reputation for a generation or two as the place in which soiled doves (a favourite Victorian phrase) congregated after the closing of the Empire and the Alhambra. As a scene it was incomparable. During the day and at dinner-time nothing, as far as I know, was to be said against the hotel's respectability. It was a rather noble edifice in the Nash tradition—actually a Nash building, I suppose—and the rooms had space and dignity, the smoking-room, dark, impressive and yet gay in some Whistlerian manner, being one of the most attractive in London, although it seemed to me that nobody except myself and my friends ever entered it.

At about eleven the hotel would wake up, and the two restaurant floors were crowded with little tables, at most of which sat attractive, provocative, well-dressed young women, each of whom had been allotted a table at which, unless she were "resting", she could be found night after night. The noble staircase, too, would be crowded with the comings and goings of these inviting beauties and with the young men and old who had come to seek them out and make their choice. An orderly scene withal, and one that should have been drawn or painted by Rops.

The day came, however, when the conscience of the country woke to this iniquity in its midst and the Continental had to mend its ways. It was swept and garnished morally and actually, and it became first the Chatham and then, under Oddenino, the Capitol. Very respectable people occupied its bedrooms: one of the rich Singers had a floor, I believe, and Sir Edward Carson, as he then was, made it his London headquarters. No place could be more convenient. I lived there on and off for six months myself when, in 1911, my children spent a spring and summer at St. Cloud, in Paris and at Douarnenez.

It was natural therefore that, seeking a central, suitable and economical hotel, I should plant my American novelist at the Capitol. On December 30 then he writes to me about his immediate plans: "Friday lunch will be all right for John Masefield, but not Friday dinner; on that day I am dining with Mr. and Mrs. Griffiths, the American Consul-General and his wife. . . . I am reserving Thursday evening for Mrs. Leverson [The Sphinx].[1] . . . Next Sunday, the 7th January [1912], I visit W. J. Locke in the country."

That penultimate day of the year was not a day of rejoicing in the Dreiser stable. If there was one paper in which a welcome for *Jennie Gerhardt* might have been looked for with some assurance it was the London *Nation*, but our hopes were dashed. A long but very grudging review: "No, Mr. Dreiser is not an artist, but he has knowledge and comprehension, and amid the fictional fireworks of so many American story-tellers, his honest Teutonic lamp shines with the steady glow of mental integrity and unbiassed truth-seeking. We respect him, but yearn to inject a little quicksilver into his organism. . . . Mr. Dreiser fails to fuse his carefully selected materials in the true artist's crucible of feeling. It is an interesting failure, and one, we are inclined to believe, that has its genesis in American civilization. . . ."

New Year's Day found Dreiser at the Midland Hotel, Manchester, from which he writes a note of greeting, adding, "I am very comfortable at this writing". It was careless of me to send him to the Midland. He should have stopped at an hotel less conscious in its absorption of the transatlantic hotel habit. . . . But anyhow England was not to keep him

[1] See *Memories of a Misspent Youth*, by Grant Richards, 1932.

long. When he had finished with Manchester I had induced
him to go to Canterbury and thence, for the sake of likeness
and contrast, to Amiens, and there I joined him. In the
second week in January we arrived in Paris. On January 15
I have left him there (at the Normandy Hotel in the rue de
l'Echelle) for he writes to complain that he "can't find the
list of restaurants we visited Saturday night. You started
to make them out at Marguery's, but went to sleep instead,
I think. Please send at once. Or an account of our day
Saturday. I can't think where we went after we left Fer-
guson's[1] studio. . . . I miss you much. . . . I don't find Meg
Villier's address."[2]

Next day's communication is not so cheerful. He had
heard from his American publishers:

> Thanks for the letters. They have gone to their des-
> tination. A letter from Harpers by mail—very disappoint-
> ing. It was dated Jan. 4. The Royalty accounts hadn't
> been made up yet but wouldn't exceed 10,000 he thought,
> yet on Nov. 22nd he told me (or Nov. 20th rather) that
> there was due me at that time $800 or thereabouts—the
> first 3,000 at 10 and the balance at 15. He also said there
> were orders in sight aggregating 10,000. It would look
> as though they had never gone beyond those orders and
> yet there has been a real gob-fest critically. I have more
> stuff from America to-day. Can you understand that.
>
> If I were you I wouldn't be so concerned about me. I
> am not going to be a best seller or even a half seller. My
> satisfaction is to be purely critical if even that. Critical
> approval won't make a sale and critical indifference won't
> hinder one. I haven't the drag on the public—that's all.
>
> However, I'm enjoying Paris and life can be lived in
> many ways. Since my book isn't going to sell I want to

[1] J. D. Fergusson is meant.
[2] Miss Meg Villars is meant—Meg Villars, who has written novels—
The Broken Laugh was one of them; I published it—who knows her world
and who, happily, still shines as a journalist in that Paris on the stages
of which she has so gracefully danced.

return to America with as much money as I can. It is just possible that The Financier will do a little better.

Duneko[1] is greatly depressed over my interest in you—notwithstanding my unprofitable character. He still insists his house can do as well as any other, but I am writing him to-day a few more plain facts.

TH. D.

Don't build any financial hopes on me. You see what happens.

But he is mercurial and his mind is always on his work. I had told him of the way in which I made a practice of treating the noxious creatures who in Paris, at least in those days, were constantly sidling up to you and offering to show you what is best worth seeing in the Louvre . . . or to conduct you to some house where . . . and he had asked me to write it down for his own edification and perhaps for that of his readers. "You forgot your advice to guides and the sad facts concerning what their mothers might think.[2] Am having a fine time," he writes two days later. And the next day he sends me W. B. Trites's address, Trites being a beginning American novelist in whom he is interested and whom he thinks it will be profitable for me to cultivate. Trites had written *Life* and was many years later to write *The Gypsy*. In this note appears for the first time the name of the original of the character with whom he was to make such play in *A Traveller at Forty*. Dreiser and I had planned a visit to the Riviera: "By all means persuade Sir Hugh Lane to come. I like him very much. Raphail,[3] whom I also like, says that we must stop at Avignon and that he would like to go along." When the time came we did not stop at Avignon. That papal city would not have been agreeable in January, and besides I, being human and disliking any interference either with my own plans or with my American prodigy, no doubt

---

[1] Read "Duneka".
[2] See *A Traveller at Forty*, by Theodore Dreiser, p. 242.
[3] John N. Raphael, the journalist, he means. I had introduced him to Dreiser.

resented the Raphaelesque interference with my plans. Moreover, we had no time to spare and I had no reason to suppose that Yerkes had paused in Avignon.

On January 23 I am going again to Paris from London and, hearing this, Dreiser says he will abandon his plans to see the Gobelins Tapestry works, Fontainebleau and Malmaison for any other scheme I may have. But two new characters have appeared on the London scene. W. W. Ellsworth of the Century Company has arrived in England, not so much to see what this new author of theirs is doing as to whip up business, to secure English books; to get something out of George Moore for the *Century Magazine*, and generally to improve himself and his knowledge of art and the world. And for another reason: America at the moment was much interested in Morgan Shuster, who was on his way back from Persia. Ellsworth was keen to secure his story for the *Century* before anyone else could get it. Dreiser and I were told to call on him at his hotel and to do our best to induce him to wait Ellsworth's arrival.

Ellsworth had brought with him from his America Abraham Flexner, brother of Simon and already well enough known on his own account as a playwright and as a social investigator. Flexner had been sent over by John D. Rockefeller Junior's Bureau of Social Hygiene to investigate the conditions under which prostitution was carried on in Europe and to embody the results of his researches in a tome, a similar tome on Prostitution in New York having recently been published for the same Bureau by the Century Company. Now for some reason or other Ellsworth had conceived the idea that I knew Paris inside out, that I knew every side of it, that I talked the language like a native, that the chiefs of the Sureté were my very good friends, and that, in consequence, if I could be roped in my assistance would be invaluable to Flexner and that, as far as Paris was concerned, his work would be half done. Pure fancy, of course. But anyhow the pundit was duly introduced to me and we were both conveyed to the Carlton grill, where over a suitable lunch it was proposed to me that I should abandon my proper business for a month or so, be taken by Flexner to Paris, have all my expenses paid out of the Rockefeller pocket and should help in the good work.

"And what is to happen to my business?" I asked. "I'm a publisher, not a social investigator; and anyhow prostitution seems a rather grimy subject."

"Oh, that's all right," I was assured. "Compute what you'll suffer in your business owing to your absence and the Bureau will compensate you—of course: that goes without saying."

But I didn't see myself in the rôle and although, when Hugh Lane and I went to Paris to join Dreiser, Ellsworth and Flexner trailing along with me, I had no other connection with the mission than the fact that, having published the New York book, I was in due course to publish the European. It might sell. All the same I could not help feeling that I was assisting at a vastly important sociological investigation and I stalked the deck of the Calais boat with dignified steps and felt there was an innate fitness in our having a private cabin and half a bottle of champagne to ward off sea-sickness.

We arrived in Paris. Dreiser, who had succeeded in running down Morgan Shuster, had made his report, and we sallied out to dinner. Flexner was wasting no time. He was on the job from the word Go! If I couldn't help him as an accredited assistant, I might possibly put him wise to that side of the gay Paris which the young visitor to Paris cannot altogether avoid, however much he may be devoted to Giotto and Jean Goujon, Watteau, Manet and the natural beauties of the Bois de Boulogne. Surely, Ellsworth said, I could at least convey the investigator to the neighbourhood of that gilded shore on which so many healthy young Americans had been wrecked.

Well, I had heard of a few places, so I took them through the Place de la Trinité, up the rue Blanche into the Place Blanche, and then into Palmyr's Bar, a small and reasonably select establishment presided over by a red-haired lady of a certain age and of rather opulent charms who held in the vicious life of Paris a very distinct place of her own. I do not know Palmyr's real name, but she had been introduced to me as the lady in whose arms the painter, Toulouse-Lautrec, died. Then, she had functioned in a milieu definitely feminine, but, now that her charms had faded, she had transferred her interests to a circle just as definitely masculine. It was interesting to see the skill with which she controlled her curious establishment. In the hours which she could spend away from her specialised business she bred bull-dogs at her home in the country, and she would prefer to sit and talk about her success in that canine field to any gossip about her past. In fact, she was always willing to neglect her job for a chance to talk about her dogs. I took Ernest Belfort Bax to see her one night, and he became so interested in her mingled perversity and domesticity that, dear old man, he would, I believe, have stayed on her banquette chattering till the hour of closing had I not told him, with quite sufficient truth, that the place might at any moment be raided by the police. It was curious to discover that some of the most emancipated inhabitants of that Devil's acre which is Montmartre would have done almost anything rather than be seen taking their refreshment *chez* Palmyr. There are prejudices even in the Place Pigalle. I have watched a young daughter of joy burst into hysterical tears when she realised to what bar her admirer had brought her. The older women were less particular.

On this Dreiserian evening, however, we were there to dine as a preliminary to a night of investigation into the lighter side of that vice which Dr. Flexner was in Europe to study. We were experiencing the more domestic side of the bar, for Madame used to provide for her eccentric clients a very simple and inexpensive meal. I forget how much it cost in those pre-War days. Three or four shillings perhaps, with wine on a rather more expensive scale. Parisian figures would turn up at that dinner. I have seen Madame Emilienne d'Alençon there, for instance, and other great lights, male and female, of that French world which amused itself and amused others. We would eat our *pot-au-feu*, our fried whiting and our chicken and cheese and behave ourselves with admirable discretion—and indeed admirable discretion would be the note of the evening and would not give place to gaiety and the side issues of perversity until the night was well advanced and mixed drinks had had their cheering effect. The atmosphere of such a place is faithfully reproduced in the untranslatable novels of Monsieur Francis Carco to which at a later date Ronald Firbank was to introduce me. Asking if I had read *Jésus-la-Caille*, and finding that I had not even heard of it, he insisted on running from St. Martin's Street to Hachette's that he might bring me a copy without delay. Its argot made it hard reading.

From Palmyr's we went to the Abbaye de Thélème and Dr. Flexner was shown the lighter side of the subject about which he was to write so important a tome. By the way, his very horrifying work, although treated respectfully, did not, in spite of its title, do anything much in the way of selling. Both I myself and The Bureau of Social Hygiene made a great mistake in that we did not produce a huge edition at a very low price for the use of the American Expeditionary Force. Its members would have taken it seriously; it would have done an immense amount of good and have prevented a great deal of misery. I did think of it, but too late. I even produced the big edition, but its printers found the difficulties of production in war-time too great for them: I had been beguiled by a specious agent into entrusting it to a firm across the water, which I was assured had both machines and paper at its disposal and would turn out thousands of copies before I should have finished preparing the ground for their sale—and then weeks and months followed one another and my book had hardly arrived in London before the Expeditionary Force was on the way home. A great pity. It was a cut down version too, a version specially designed to enlighten the youths of America and of Great Britain as to the risks they might be running and the singularly meretricious nature of the insincere delights to which they might succumb. . . .

Dreiser and Paris got on very well together and he might have been left to the pleasures of that one-time happy city had it not been necessary to go on with his programme. We pushed on to the south, travelling by that too fast day train that I might show him a France in which woods and pasture would gradually give way to limestone and vine, and in which one exchanged the Seine and the Loing for the Saône and the Rhone, and grape-famous slopes of the Côtes d'Or for olive-trees and the little hills and castles of Provence. I thought it would be good for both of us and for Hugh Lane, who was now of the party, to spend a few days at Agay, at the water-side Grand Hotel d'Agay, under the first spurs of the Estérels, where there would be no world to vex or to entice us. But Lane, ascetic by profession, had a heart that yearned for the green tables of Nice and Monte Carlo, and my idea of a brief rural holiday was rudely shaken within twenty-four hours by a demand from my companions that they should at once be conveyed to the neighbourhood of pleasure cities. We compromised. We would not go to Monte Carlo but to Cap Martin and, with Lane feebly protesting that we should spend all our money on cabs, we took shelter at the Riva Bella Hotel at the root of Cap Martin.

It was a fine time that we had during the fortnight that Lane, Dreiser and I spent at Agay and Cap Martin. It proved, certainly, one of the pleasantest holidays of my life. Dreiser was at his simple Indianapolitan best; Lane at his most capricious. These two men quarrelled like playful puppies, feeling for one another's weak spots, exploding into smiles and laughter, showing intolerance of one another's tastes and prejudices. . . . We did not really look as tripperishly respectable as the camera has made us. I have a particular dislike of my own jaunty air and my wing-collar. Did one wear wing-collars with lounge-suits in those days? I suppose so, or I should not have worn one. And had there been a temporary respite in the turning-up of their trouser-ends? Twenty-two years ago! Men's clothes have not changed so much after all.

But the novelist had soon wrung from the Riviera all that it had of value for him and he passed on to Rome, from which (at the Continental Hotel) he wrote on February 10, 1912, protesting that my estimate of his likely expenses was all wrong, but that "otherwise Rome is very fine". In two days he is more specific: "Rome interests me greatly historically. I don't think anything of it as a city, but as a collection of ruins and art objects it cannot be surpassed." He adds his opinion about my mother's "pessimism"—for she is stopping in the same hotel—and proclaims that my family, outside of myself, is too easily put out: "I may talk pessimism, but I never cease to fight forward." Then he tells me that he has "had a leter from A. P. Watt wanting to be my agent", and finishes with a reference to Mencken's power. On the 16th of February he is tiring of Rome, like Sam Lewis the "financier" who, having fled to Rome from the trente-et-quarante table at Monte Carlo in order that his London bankers might have a little rest, returned incontinently to Monte Carlo with the remark, "You can 'ave Rome". Dreiser's comment is: "I don't care much for this noble village of Rome, so I am going to leave it earlier than I expected. . . . I like the ancient remains, but they are endless and it would take a lifetime to decipher them. Outside of these, Rome is nothing—an eighth-rate city." He has not forgotten his London friends: "I am glad Miss [Sarah] Brooke has succeeded and that Wish Wynne[1] is properly appreciated by her manager. I had a card from [Hugh] Lane warning me against the ruins by moonlight and urging me to see Mancini[2] who is working by day at Frascati. I don't think I shall." There is talk about someone wanting

[1] A music-hall artist whom my cousin, young Grant Allen, had insisted that he should see; she came out later as an actress and played in Arnold Bennett's *The Great Adventure*.

[2] The Italian painter whose work John Sargent so greatly admired.

the dramatic rights of *Jennie Gerhardt*. Finally: "If anyone ever says anything to me about Rome after this I'll bang 'em in the eye." But he adds a postscript: "I did like Pisa more than I can say."

All the same, Dreiser lingers on in Rome. He is still there on February 21, and does not plan to leave until the 26th. On the 21st he says: "Had your letter about the Century Company, which seems somewhat like a dream, but it may come true. I don't see what I can say except thanks." I have no idea to what this refers. Two days later he has heard from Harper: "The exact sales of *Jennie* up to Jan. 1st (I have no earlier figures) were 7,720. I have no notice of sales since then. A letter from Duneka shows him in a very cheerful frame of mind, however, and it argues that they are not absolutely despairing. They are bringing out *Sister Carrie* this month. . . . Rome has interested me on the Pre-Christian and mediaeval sides. I have never seen finer gardens anywhere. The old sections are depressingly filthy and run down however. . . . I leave Monday morning at 8.50 and am quite glad. I've had enough."

My next Dreiserian news from Rome is in a letter, dated February 24, from W. W. Ellsworth, who has "the pleasant task of taking care of four ladies". About his author he says: "Dreiser is seeing the Pope this morning. I told him he would need to fold three handkerchiefs at once[1] . . . I looked him up immediately and he lunched with me that day and dined us the next. Oscar Browning was among his guests— a nice old boy who seems to love you."

Dreiser writes to me on the following day: "Ellsworth blew in here the other day and insisted that I must go to Venice, so I am varying my plans sufficiently to include Venice—say two days. My present itinerary is as follows: Monday—Feb. 26th. Spello and Assisi and possibly Perugio—seeing that it is only 30 minutes away. I may stay all night there. Tuesday, 27th, leave for Florence and remain there until March

[1] An allusion to Dreiser's habit, as he sits and talks, of folding his handkerchief into small squares and then of unfolding it.

4th or 5th. . . . About March 9 I shall be in Milan for 1 day and March 11 in Frankfort, Germany. I am stopping there because my father was born at Mayence only 25 miles away and I want to see for myself what sort of country he came from. On the 12th or 13th I shall be in Berlin. . . . I ran into a man by the name of Conybeare who has been showing me considerable and introducing me round. Also I have seen the Pope—a rather doleful old man. . . . I understand from one letter from New York that Erwan J. Ridgeway has fallen out with the Butterick Company and quit. I may go back there"—so already his spirit was becoming weaker and his feet colder. Why in the name of wonder should he contemplate taking his talent back to that machine? By the way, let me explain something about Dreiser's itinerary. In so far as it was influenced by me it showed my own preferences. I did not myself suggest Venice because I had never been—and have never been—there, and also because I had been warned by A. E. Housman that it was very cold until May. It was true that Dreiser had a fine fur coat, but he was not careful of his health and I did not want to have to rush out and nurse him through pneumonia! Spello was very much an idea of my own. I have no reason to think that Yerkes ever visited the place, but it was one of the towns which my father insisted on setting out to see because, I suppose, of its connection with the Roman history which he knew so well. He had failed to reach it, but I succeeded and have insisted that all my friends who were going to Assisi should travel those few extra miles. . . . Dreiser tells me from the Palace Hotel, Perugia, on February 28, that he is "glad" he stopped at Spello and Assisi; "I think Spello the better of the two. This place [Perugia] is the strangest I have ever been in. It has all the spirit of an Ohio manufacturing town combined with a mediaeval appearance. The women are as smart as those of Paris—and all on a mountain top."

On March 5 Dreiser has arrived at the Royal Danielli in Venice: "Nothing could be finer than Venice. I could not stop to describe it, but rise to remark that I had the advantage of a full glittering moon and a warm summer breeze as an introduction at 10 p.m." No other letter of importance came until March 17 (from Zehlendorf, a suburb of Berlin) and that is mainly about business and his plans. He is annoyed that a certain New York publisher did not return him "the triplicate copy of *Idylls of the Poor*" and reproaches me for "talking very lightly of Amsterdam, Rotterdam, The Hague, Brussels, Bruges and Ghent, Paris, a walking tour of a week in England, etc., etc. I really don't know how much time you expect me to spend, for you furnish no itinerary. . . . I ought to be in America and at work by April 15th or I will not get *The Financier* done by fall. Then there is this other book [*A Traveller at Forty*] which is going to be long —very—and delightful to write. And there is still another novel for 1913 to do. Dear God!" He thanks me for "a general tendency to straighten me out and cheer me up" and adds: "like Hugh Lane I find myself getting as mad as hell at times and still, nevertheless and notwithstanding being hauled about at your convenience. You are at once a nemesis and stoic and quite the most interesting man I have ever known. But you do play the game with too high a hand— really you do—and you have at once a conscience and none. I am feeling much better."

Thereafter a tragical sartorial episode. My tailors, Hill Brothers, then of Bond Street, had made Dreiser a suit. By the 20th of March it was not unnatural that this young man in Berlin should begin to think of Spring suitings. "The suit they made me fits me so well that I think they shall make me another of such dark material as you may select to the same measure. Will it be asking too much of you to stop in there and select a cloth which you think will be suitable. . . . Have them make it at once." I must have sent him an indication of what I had chosen. A telegram from Zehlendorf on March 27: "Cloth too thick double breasted never July August New York." And then a letter on the same day: "All North America is terribly hot in July and August and I have to be there—lighter please and built for summer. The quality of the cloth is excellent. Don't try to keep me now. I will come back another time and we will go into Russia. I owe you much for a wise interpretation of my various needs and in spite of my temperamental divagations I think (I know) you understand that I put you first among those who have come near in a world that never comes very near at its very best." Then from Amsterdam on April 1: ". . . I will not arrive in Paris before the 6th. . . . Holland is charming— entirely so. I have nothing but praise for the natural artistry of life here. . . . Sorry about the suit, but if I find it too heavy shall put it aside and wear it next winter." I too was sorry about the suit. It never occurred to my simple and economical soul that one bought suits for the immediate season only. I am in the habit of keeping them from season to season. . . .

Finally, as far as Europe is concerned, a telegram from Amsterdam saying that Dreiser will be leaving London for America on April 11th. I have already told that the boat in which he wished to sail was the *Titanic*. Dreiser did better on the boat which I induced him to take.

From America I do not seem to have an addition to my Dreiserian budget until May 4, 1912, from Saint Paul Hotel, New York. He plunges into interest: "On investigation I find that Harpers have sold exactly 12,717 copies of *Jennie Gerhardt* to date and 1,026 copies of the new edition of *Sister Carrie*. This can be verified from the books of Doubleday Page and Co., B. W. Dodge and Co., Grosset and Dunlap and Harper and Brothers. I am glad I did not leave on the *Titanic*. I am now soundly at work again and making some progress. . . . I am profoundly glad that I am on my home ground and out of your clutches. . . . Lunched with Doty to-day."

The *New York Times* Literary Section for June 23, 1912, has a long interview with Dreiser by Montrose J. Moses. America had taken its time to discover that its novelist had returned. Here are some passages:

"To Theodore Dreiser *Jenny Gerhardt* is an accomplishment of the past. He declares that he will never write another book like it; that such a type of woman no longer appeals artistically to him. . . . Seated in a rocking chair, which moved back and forth whenever we were travelling fastest, he every now and then emphasised a point with his goldrimmed glasses, in between whiles folding his handkerchief four times in length and then rolling it into a tight ball to clinch an argument. Above average height, with a decided stoop, he is altogether a serious looking personage. If seen on the street, he may be quickly identified by a characteristic stride, which is such an excellent excuse for a man to let his mind wander in the busy thoroughfares. Slow but sure of speech, Mr. Dreiser is modern in taste and poetic in feeling. . . . 'You may think it strange that I am avoiding New York as the locale of *The Financier*', he averred. 'I haven't struck the city of cities yet, but I have a novel stored away for it. I'm going to write about it some day. But now I'm crazy about Chicago with its great personality. The only reason my book is to be in three volumes is that 500,000 words couldn't conveniently be put into one.' . . . 'Maybe I sound disloyal, but Jenny's temperament does not appeal to me any longer. I found, however, when I came to finish it, that I had to be true to the first part of the book—in other words, to the character —rather than to my personal likes. That is why I didn't shift the key. Structurally the book is sound, I believe. But in the new novel, the note of the plot will come from the man, and man shall be the centre of the next three or four novels. It would have to be a most remarkable woman for me to write a book about one after Jenny! Possibly that is because I know more about women now.' "

Thereafter recriminations, which sadly reminded me that in the previous November, just seven months before, on the occasion of our first meeting, Dreiser, seated in his room at 3609 Broadway, had warned me that I should be sorry if I persisted in my wish to befriend and assist him or, if you will, to thrust my assistance upon him: "There's something strange in my make up. I quarrel with my friends, I'm too suspicious. . . ." Anyhow, since seeing him off to America in the Spring of 1912 I have met him only once, and that for no more than a few minutes and in circumstances which, perhaps, reflect little credit either on my sense or my sensibility. It was in the late Autumn of 1912, that Autumn in which I had struggled with his manuscript and had been dismayed. Hearing that I was in New York and on the point of returning to England, Dreiser wrote to me suggesting that we should meet before I sailed. I replied, I believe, to the effect that I could think of nothing about which we had to talk, but that—well, if he liked to come to the Knickerbocker he would find me between 2.30 and 3.45 just before I went down to my boat. Re-reading his letter, twenty-two years later, I feel that it deserved a more understanding reply. Well, he came, was shown to my narrow room, and after some salutation we each waited, like nervous dogs, for the other to begin, I folding my clothes and putting them away, he leaning back in his chair, interminably folding and unfolding his handkerchief. In effect, I believe, we neither of us spoke and, after a space, he departed. Defending myself, let me add that my own particular quarrel with what he had written was one which from its very nature I was unable to point out to him or to discuss. . . . Something in his manuscript.

Yet, I turn with pleasure to page 37 of *A Traveller at Forty*:

"As I think of it now I can never be quite sufficiently grateful to Barfleur for a certain affectionate, thoughtful, sympathetic regard for my every possible mood on this occasion. This was my first trip to this England of which, of course, he was intensely proud. He was so humanly anxious that I should not miss any of its charms or, if need be, defects. He wanted me to be able to judge it fairly and humanly and to see the eventual result sieved through my temperament. The soul of attention; the soul of courtesy; patient, long-suffering, humane, gentle. How I have tried the patience of that man at times! An iron mood he has on occasion; a stoic one, always. Gentle, even, smiling, living a rule and a standard. Every thought of him produces a grateful smile. Yet he has his defects—plenty of them. Here he was at my elbow, all the way to London, momentarily suggesting that I should not miss the point, whatever the point might be, at the moment. He was helpful, really interested, and above all and at all times warmly human";

and again to page 60:

"Barfleur in many respects, I wish to repeat here, is one of the most delightful persons in the world. He is a sort of Beau Brummel with literary, artistic and gormandising leanings. He loves order and refinement, of course,—things in their proper ways and places—as he loves life. I suspect him at times of being somewhat of a martinet in home and office matters; but I am by no means sure that I am not doing him a grave injustice. A more even, complaisant, well-mannered and stoical soul, who manages to get his way in some fashion or other, if it takes him years to do it, I never met. He surely has the patience of fate and, I think, the true charity of a great heart";

and I read the words he inscribed in the copy of *Jennie Gerhardt* that he gave me:

"To Grant Richards who would have been the publisher of this in England if it could possibly have been arranged. With the esteem and good will of Theodore Dreiser. N.Y. Nov. 4, 1911";

and, being sentimental by nature, I even read with some emotion the motto he found on one of *Hovell's Crackers* and passed to me at our Berkshire Christmas dinner:

> Our work shall still be better for our love,
> And still our love be sweeter for our work.—*Anon.*

Finally, I cannot resist the temptation of adding that my own copy of *A Traveller at Forty* has the following inscription: "To the Victim! This first copy is presented with mixed feelings and deep emotion by the Editor, D.Z.D. November 1913." D.Z.D. = Douglas Z. Doty.

XVII

ARNOLD BENNETT AND H. G. WELLS–MRS. GEORGE
STEEVENS–A GLIMPSE OF CECIL RHODES–WILLIAM
WATSON AND JOHN DAVIDSON

ARNOLD BENNETT I have had on my list: *Fame and Fiction: an Enquiry into Certain Popularities*, by E. A. Bennett–the unfamiliar initials show that it was very early in his career–in 1901. I always urge authors to use on their title-pages one Christian name rather than several initials. Bennett was wise about such technical subtleties, but evidently this one came to him late in the day. The practice of H. D. Traill, of H. G. Wells, of T. W. H. Crosland, would seem to contradict my theory, but I remain convinced that a book should, if possible, be set out as being by a man with as simple a name as his parents have provided. And this theory is not only true of books: you can parallel your Andrew Lang, your Thomas Hardy, your Herbert Spencer, your Grant Allen, your Hugh Walpole with Stanley Baldwin, Joseph Chamberlain, Jesse Collings, John Bright, Gordon Selfridge.

I never knew Bennett well. It would have been better for me if I had. He must have been good and constantly stimulating company. *Fame and Fiction* was one of the least important of his books, interesting indeed, especially from the "shop" point of view, but now only of value to Bennett fans as showing the development of his mind and of the increase in number of the contacts that came to him as he grew in literary stature. It was founded, I take it, on the experience he gained in the days he was helping Lewis Hind with the *Academy*. At an earlier date he had worked on a jolly little paper, *Woman*, from 1893 to 1900, first as assistant-editor and then as editor; indeed he occupied that chair for four or five years. He gave it a liveliness that made me a regular reader.

I imagine that it was not so easy to find publishers for Bennett's books in his early years or he would hardly have gone to Nutt to publish one of his earlier experiments in the fiction which he wrote under the influence of the French authors whom he studied with so much assiduity. That was *Sacred and Profane Love*—in 1905. It was very rare for Nutt to publish a novel, and he was hardly a regular enough advertiser to compel some kind of critical attention to the one or two that he did. I suppose the ordinary publisher, although *The Grand Babylon Hotel* (1902), *Anna of the Five Towns* and *The Great Man* had all had a fair success, was nervous of Bennett's experiments in a new manner. It is difficult now to believe that such fears existed at the beginning of the present century.

Recovering now in my memory the relations I had with E. A. Bennett and reading through a small sheaf of letters which I had from him, I cannot help feeling that I was very much lacking in foresight in not doing more than I did to show him my appreciation of his work in those early days. I see that I did not lack encouragement. One cannot have an eye on every corner of the literary and journalistic world. In short, I had not time—and I certainly had not capital. Besides, Arnold Bennett was always a rather elusive figure, and he, too, was extremely busy. The letters I had from him cover one year. The first is dated April 11, 1901; the last, April 15, 1902. Their theme is *Fame and Fiction* almost entirely, and all are written from Trinity Hall Farm, Hockliffe, Bedfordshire.

In the first letter Bennett inquires the fate of "the MS. novel which I sent you three months ago on behalf of an anonymous friend", and adds that he understands from Mr. Metcalfe[1] that the question of his own book, *Fame and Fiction*, was now settled—"I will let you have the complete copy

---

[1] Cranstoun Metcalfe, the essayist, to whom so many men of the new century owe encouragement.

by the 1st May." Two days later he is obliged to me for my letter returning the MS. novel. "I do not hope for a wide popularity for the book, and sent it to you because you seem to me to have a way of selling books that some other publishers fail to sell. But I think the novel should cover expenses." I wish I could remember what that novel was. The next day comes the sub-title for *Fame and Fiction—An Inquiry into Certain Modern Popularities*. "If you would prefer to substitute 'reputations' for 'popularities', pray do so, in the catalogue. Or if you have any alternative suggestions, I shall be glad to have them." A very reasonable E. A. Bennett indeed.

There is then a hiatus of more than three months. I had been to America, and, returning, had evidently written to Bennett about *The Octopus*: he will keep an eye open for it. I had, it appears, an approach to the modern house organ. "Your *The Reader* is a very appetising production." But the chief object of his letter is to suggest that I should send my "productions in belles lettres and fiction" to *Hearth and Home*: "I could be of service to you and to literature. This paper has a large circulation among a wealthy class. I do a weekly signed article in it." On August 1 he thanks me for an advance copy of *Fame and Fiction*: "It makes a very presentable book—but you do all your books well. The only thing I don't like about it . . . is the quadruple line of rails running along the tops of the pages." There was at that time a craze for such "decoration".

On September 11 my note about Frank Norris has borne fruit: "You drew my attention to *The Octopus* recently. I have just read it. It is a superb piece of work. I have reviewed it enthusiastically in the *Academy* and I hope my article will get itself printed as I wrote it." A brief letter on December 12 shows how close an eye Bennett kept on the journalism of literature and reveals him as a collector of his own books in their various forms: "In a very amiable review in the N[ew] Y[ork] *Mail and Express* I see that *Fame and Fiction* has been issued by E. P. Dutton & Co. in New York. I expect this is the English edition, but as it will probably have a new title-page and binding, I shall take it as a favour if you will put yourself to the trouble of procuring me a copy from Messrs. Dutton."

With the 9th January, 1902, Bennett writes to ask that I will send him "by return, for the purposes of an article, a list of all the novels which you propose to include in your new French fiction series, which has begun with *Salammbo*". This batch of letters, which have been growing more and more cordial, but which as far as I know were not paralleled by any meetings between Bennett and myself, closes with a letter which I had entirely forgotten until to-day:

15 April 1902

DEAR MR. RICHARDS,

Many thanks for your letter. The result of *Fame and Fiction* is not absolutely dazzling, but another book ought to go better. It is impossible for me to disguise my admiration of you as an enterprising publisher. You are the one publisher in London that I know of, and I know a few, who has the courage of his convictions.

Yours sincerely

E. A. BENNETT

My forgetfulness of such a letter shows that I entirely underestimated the Bennett of those days, for I cannot have had many such tributes. I can quite believe that he was generally underestimated until *The Old Wives' Tale* came to bowl everyone over!

Bennett and Wells; Wells and Bennett. They came a few years ago—especially in the war years—to be thought of as brothers in literature and publicity. I myself thought of them as I used in an earlier day to think of Sickert and Steer in another sphere. I had a great wish to publish Wells, to be his publisher-in-ordinary. I put a proposal to him to that end, but he would have none of it in the form in which I presented it and, very soon, he was beyond my means. But I am convinced that I recognised the power in what he had

210

written—in the stories he wrote for the old *Pall Mall Budget*, for instance—much earlier than any of my rivals did. There was in Wells's case no period of literary struggle, of experiment. He arrived more or less full-fledged. From the beginning his work was finished, wrought by a craftsman who had little to learn. Again, for one reason and another, he had much of the best critical opinion, much of the most persuasive anyhow, with him almost from the start. W. E. Henley's young men, for instance. True, it was I who introduced him to G. W. Steevens, but he wrote stories, as I have said, for the *Pall Mall Budget* and his work was not unknown on the *Gazette*.[1] Here, for example, is one of his earliest pieces of political journalism—from the *Gazette* of October 28, 1895:

OCC. PROSE

Now, when the sheep were separated from the goats, there stood a little band apart. And I looked, and behold they were Somerset House clerks. And after the sheep had gone to their heaven, and the goats to their own place, these clerks were sent back to Somerset House, and put each of them in a little waiting-room by himself to wait. And each sat there many ages. Then at last, after many ages were accomplished, one arose and said, "When is my judgment coming?" And he went out by a little baize-covered door into a passage, and so came to One at a pigeon-hole, and him he asked whether he should go to Heaven or Hell. And he who sat at the pigeon-hole regarded him evilly, and at first would not answer him, and then he told him roughly to go to Room 13 and enquire of those he should find there. So he went through many passages like unto a maze, and came unto Room 13, and there devils tormented him a space. And after they had

---

[1] H. G. Wells sent me in the Autumn of 1895, a letter in which, after thanking me for "writing up a reputation for" him, he gives a brief account of his life and achievement up to that date. It is given in full in *Memories of a Misspent Youth*.

tormented him they thrust him out and sent him to Room 47, where was One, deaf, who wrote the date of his death incorrectly in a book, and would not hear him explain, and charged him thereon half-a-crown, and passed him on to Room 10. And so he passed, weeping and wailing, from room to room, through thousands of rooms, and infinitudes of passages, for epochs and æons, until at last One told him that there in Room G he should find his abiding place. And he saw before him a door marked G, and he entered therein. And lo! it was the waiting-room where he had been in the beginning. Then he fell on his face and all the clerks in the waiting-rooms cried out with an exceeding bitter cry, saying that they were damned. And a voice sounded, and it said, "Any one but a Somerset House Clerk had found that out, ages ago". And so it was with them for ever and ever.

Just as applicable to-day as it was forty years ago! To Wells, when I asked permission to print it here, it came as a surprise: "Are you sure it is by me? I completely forget it! It reads libellous." He asked me how I had got it. My habit of cutting things out. In this case I dated the cutting and, evidently having satisfied myself either by reference to "H.G." himself or through some one on the *Gazette* of its authorship, I inscribed it as coming from his pen. There is no possibility of my having made a mistake. "I am dropping all journalism now," Wells wrote to me on November 6, 1895, so this particular example of the *Pall Mall's* "Occ. Prose" must have been one of his last essays in the craft until he blossomed out as a national and super-journalist in the War. Apparently the journalist Wells of 1895 was on the road to becoming a prose David Low.

Yes, I was early with my Wells enthusiasm. I induced him to contribute to the 1895 issue of *Phil May's Winter Annual*, where he figures with Richard Pryce, Walter Raymond, Violet Hunt and A. B. Walkley. And in 1896 J. S. Cotton allowed me to review in the *Academy* that early novel, *The*

Island of Doctor Moreau, and not only to review it but to sign my review—which was something to be proud of in those days, for the *Academy* was a nursery of young talent. But, as I say, from the publishing point of view I stalked Wells in vain. And after all, as he had already been published by Heinemann and by Methuen, I was not surprised. I will print here two letters I had from him about *The Argonauts of the Air* (the *Phil May* story), for they show him to be exact and businesslike in a way that few writers are business-like, and they show how modest may be the early financial demands of great men! The first is in answer to my enquiry as to whether he could let me have a story:

LYNTON, MAYBURY ROAD,
WOKING,
June 15th [1895]

DEAR SIR,

I have no story in hand of the length you specify, but I will get one done before July 7th. Seven guineas would I think be a fair price—what do you think?—two guineas a thousand.

Yrs very faithfully
H. G. WELLS

The second is from the same address three weeks later:

DEAR SIR,

I've just discovered to-day is the 7th—I hope you'll give me this one day's grace.

I'm sorry I've not had time to have this story type-written, but I think it is all right.

Don't be dispirited when you read it if the story does not seem to jump in the earlier two thousand words of it. I've made that go quietly in order to enhance the wobbling flight and smash of the flying apparatus at the end of it.

With apologies for sending you the rough MS.

Believe me
Very faithfully yrs
H. G. WELLS

Wells's regret that his work is not typewritten and that it is in a "rough" state is amusing in view of the fact that a Wells manuscript is now one of the rarest things in the world. One came up for auction—a short story, *Æpyornis Island*—and was bought at not much less than a thousand pounds by Gabriel Wells, the American dealer. It should in fairness be added that it was sold for a charity and that Mr. Gabriel Wells is a kindly man, but still . . .

Writing of H. G. Wells reminds me of the Henley group and, in particular, of George Steevens, and then of E. B. Iwan-Müller, a brilliant writer, a witty talker and, politically, I believe, one of the most powerful journalists of the Salisbury period—his chief work was that of leader-writer on the *Daily Telegraph*. There was talk in 1898 of my sharing a flat with Iwan-Müller, under the sheltering wing of Mrs. Steevens. It fell through, however, if for no other reason than that Mrs. Steevens's idea of what I could afford and the facts were at the opposite ends of the scale. And yet heaven knows that for what she was prepared to do for me her suggested five guineas a week was modest enough in all conscience. Her table groaned always with good things; no imported meat ever entered her kitchen; her greengrocers sent her fruit and vegetables at the beginning of their seasons as a matter of course. I remember that when she gave her guests champagne, it was the best champagne, and that it was always served in jugs in the centre of which was a hollow receptacle for ice—a practice I should not encourage nowadays! If, while I remained her lodger, I should chance to have guests, well, their meals would be thrown in!

Dear Mrs. George! But, my word, she was eccentric! I have known no man or woman more capable of inventing a story or of embroidering the truth. If it was on the strength of her evidence that Dilke was thrown to the wolves, I can only say he wasn't very fairly treated. When I knew her and delighted in her society she was already of considerable age. It was, say, thirty-five years ago. Personally, I am not convinced that she is dead to-day. I don't see how she could die. She had too much vitality, and the idea of arranging a mock funeral and so shedding most of her troubles is just the kind of mystification that would have appealed to her ingenious brain. I think myself she is a sort of feminine and Scotch equivalent to the Wandering Jew, or, she might prefer me to say, a sort of female counterpart of the "mysterious" Comte de Saint-Germain. She did me good and harm with impartial hand and I think of her with affection. I even published a volume of short stories for her—*A Motley Crew*. It did not sell. I am told that the most striking of the tales therein printed was autobiographical. Certainly it was a transcript of her account of an achievement of which she sometimes boasted.

Because I was willing to publish that book—which was not likely to pay and never in fact did so; because I was a great friend; and because she held that she and her husband owed me so much for introducing him to Alfred Harmsworth and so securing him his job on the *Daily Mail*, it was promised that I should publish his story of the Egyptian campaign, the book which became *With Kitchener to Khartoum*. But Blackwood had printed much of Steevens's work and his acquaintance with Mrs. Steevens was of old standing, so that when the manuscript was ready she handed it over to him, just as if I and the promise to me had never existed. That was her way. Had I been more business-like and secured a contract when the promise was made, I should have trebled, quadrupled, my business capital, for *With Kitchener to Khartoum* was one of the first of the modern "best sellers". However, we did not quarrel, and a little later, having invented out of my own head the detailed plot of a South African story of Roman and modern times rather of the Rider Haggard sort and having told it to Steevens, he or she suggested that as its working out required some classical scholarship he should collaborate with me. We began. I wrote the first chapter and he then took up the tale. That we were seriously engaged on it was announced in the paragraphs of the

Athenæum devoted to literary news of importance, and we started regularly to confer—until the South African War called him. There was talk of Quiller-Couch taking up the work where we had laid it down, but it came to nothing, although I think that he in his turn did do a little work on the manuscript. I still have it somewhere. I recall that I had a lot of trouble in extricating it from among the papers which were left in the charge of Mr. Stewart, Mrs. Steevens's solicitor brother.

After George's death in Ladysmith Mrs. Steevens, poor lady, became more herself than ever. Going down one week-end to stop with her at Merton Abbey[1] I found that she had set up a man-servant. "Jim—come here!" she called when, having announced me, he was retiring to his own quarters. "Jim, this is Mr. Grant Richards, one of Mr. Steevens's oldest and best friends. You are to take particular care of him." Then she turned to me: "George died in Jim's arms, Grant——"

Later, I found Jim unpacking my things: "So you knew Mr. Steevens well, Jim? Did you serve right through the campaign?"

"Lor bless you, Sir, I never set eyes on the gentleman as far as I know. That's only Mrs. Steevens's way!"

But—a little reluctantly perhaps, for I feel as if I could fill a book with the doings of Christine Steevens—to return to Iwan-Müller. I found the other day among my letters a note that he wrote me in June 1902. I had written to him for advice or assistance in connection with the fact that a brother-in-law of mine who had been gold-mining in Western America was going out to South Africa in the hope that it would give him better opportunities. Iwan-Müller knew South Africa well, or at least he knew its rulers, and he replied discouragingly: "Rhodes told me almost the last time I saw him, that everyone going to the Rand now must be content to pay 19/10½ for every 'sov' he digs up."

[1] See *Memories of a Misspent Youth*, by Grant Richards, 1932.

I myself often saw Rhodes in the days when I worked with Stead, for when he was in London he was a pretty frequent visitor to the Sanctum, but I can recall nothing about him which is worth recording, save that to me, little more than a youth, he seemed to bulk unusually, to give the impression of physical size and of rude health, to be a sort of mid-Victorian squire in his gait and manner or, perhaps, even more, to resemble a Roman pro-consul.

It is my pride that I have known intimately and have published an unusual number of poets. Some of them remained with me; some of them I carelessly let go; some of them went. At the end of my second year I am able to advertise, among others, Laurence Binyon's *Porphyrion*—Binyon had been a pupil of my father—Walter Leaf's *Versions from Hafiz*,[1] Laurence Housman's *Spikenard*, Katharine Tynan's *The Wind in the Trees*. It was not until the autumn that I achieved the satisfaction of adding *A Shropshire Lad* to my list, and not until the new century that I issued my first John Davidson, *Self's the Man*. For William Watson I never published until well into the new century, and then it was a mere pamphlet on the Irish Question. Why Watson, with whom I was on very happy and intimate terms—he almost made my rooms in Barton Street and my flat in Chelsea his homes—began gradually to fade from the market-place I have never been able to account for. His work was there and procurable. It had nothing specious or meretricious about it. Perhaps the poetry of the men from whom he was in direct succession was growing a little out of fashion. I don't know. One seems now to hear as much as one ever did of Wordsworth and of Tennyson. Watson's subjects were national or eternal. It was seldom he wrote occasional verse or on trivial themes. He carried himself with dignity as if conscious of a high destiny. It is, however, true that he has little or nothing in common with the young poets of the post-war period, or

---

[1] Many years later I published two other books by the learned Chairman of the Westminster Bank: two series of *Little Poems from the Greek*.

the poets who are to-day providing us with something craggy to break our minds upon. Then he was ill and, when he recovered, it seemed that he had in some way passed from the world that had known and acclaimed him. Certainly he passed from my world: I have hardly seen him since those days. Almost certainly he will "come back" to popular favour. The sooner the better.

John Davidson was a very different type of man—and poet. While he lived he let no one forget him. He was a fighter, and if he had in a way the same kind of bee in his bonnet that Grant Allen had and thought himself "a man forbid", a poet whom no one would allow to do his best, well, perhaps it was not altogether so unnatural a delusion for a man of his confidence and temperament.

As far as England was concerned Davidson was at that time a John Lane, a Bodley Head, man. He had published books in his native Scotland, where he was a schoolmaster of no particular importance, but it was not until John Lane, or Le Gallienne for him, had recognised the poet's worth that he really became known. His *Fleet Street Eclogues* did the trick. After that he was, for a while, the vogue. (Many of John Lane's poets were for a while the vogue!) But there was and is much, much more in Davidson's work than that phrase suggests, and no one who has read the *Ballad of a Nun* is likely to forget it or to neglect for long the other poetry of its writer.

I did not myself go hunting for Davidson. I had known him pretty well from his first arrival in London, but it was, I believe, John Lane who had introduced me to him and I looked on him as a Lane poet whom it wouldn't be decent to attempt to seduce from the Bodley Head list. But one day Davidson wrote offering me his play *Self's the Man* and I was glad to respond to his approach. He asked twenty pounds on account of royalties! I paid that small sum, but, may I add? the sale of the play did not justify even so small an advance. In fact with me only two of Davidson's books covered the out-of-pocket expenses of their production: out of *Fleet*

Street and other Poems I made about fifteen pounds, and out of *Holiday* twenty—in each case without reckoning anything for office expenses. Commercially, poetry was already on the wane when *Self's the Man* appeared, and there were few exceptions to the rule. I use the phrase "may I add?" because I am, unfortunately, forbidden by his wishes from saying much, anything like as much as I should like, about my friend or his life. Before he went to his sea grave Davidson wrote that, as his literary executor, I was to discourage chatter, that I was even to frown upon any idea of a biography. An awkward injunction in these days of "critical and biographical studies", of the pulling aside of every curtain, the abandonment of every reticence.[1] Alas! here in England at least few people have shown any great wish to devote attention either critical or biographical to this poet out of Scotland. There are honourable exceptions: Edward Thompson, who induced me to permit a selection of Davidson's poems to appear in Benn's sixpenny *Augustan Books of Modern Poetry*, is one of them. He wrote me on November 22, 1927, that he had "always had a grateful memory of your help." There have been, too, one or more books in America on Davidson's work, and one at least in Germany. I can only remember one essay in England which did the poet anything like justice—a paper in the *Fortnightly Review* by Filson Young, which did in fact secure Davidson's approval. Then there was an unsigned and shorter article (from the pen of T. Earle Welby) in the *Saturday Review* of July 23, 1927; Morley Roberts also wrote with interest and appreciation of Davidson in *John o' London's Weekly* as recently as September 30, 1933; and "Mimnermus", in an article on Davidson in the *Freethinker* of June 24, 1934, claims that "George Foote, fighting bravely in the cause of Freedom, was heartened by his encouragement and that of George Meredith and Gerald Massey".

[1] "No word except of my writing is ever to appear in any book of mine as long as the copyright endures.

"No one is to write my life now or at any time; but let all men study and discuss in private and in public my poems and plays, especially my Testaments and Tragedies."—Extract from John Davidson's will.

Davidson was a recluse—not so much from choice, perhaps, as from the fact that he had too little money to meet his friends on what he considered an equal footing. To him more than to any other man I have known, a small purse was a constant, if hidden, source of discomfort; but that discomfort did not prevent his shouldering the ordinary domestic burdens that come to a man and his carrying out all his duties scrupulously. There was in Davidson nothing of the Bohemian habit: his rebellion was all of the spirit and of the imagination. He was a cross between Khubla Khan and a bank-manager rather than a Villon or a Verlaine.

When I first made Grant Allen and Davidson known to each other, Grant Allen looked at the poet: "You're a Galloway Pict, Mr. Davidson?"

Davidson assented: "But who told you so? You have friends in the North who know me?" Instantly he was uncomfortable lest my uncle's too great acquaintance with his origins might place him at some disadvantage in this England which he never grew quite to understand. But Grant Allen put him at his ease. My uncle was a biologist and he had trained himself to tell the stock from which a man came after one glance at the structure of his head.

It must not be thought that Davidson was a snob. He had nothing of the snob in his composition. He asked of the world that it should consider him for his work and not for the money in his banking account or the outward appearance of his life. He shrank in that sense from observation, although he was as glad as any other writer to secure such friendship and such literary appreciation as he could value. One of the first books of his that I published received from James Douglas, who had succeeded Le Gallienne on the *Star*, an enthusiastic, almost a hysterical, welcome, such as Douglas used to give to the books he liked. Knowing that Davidson was always hoping that each new book of his would bring him the recognition he was convinced was his due and that, yes, he was hungry for fit appreciation, I hurried to his home by an office messenger a copy of the *Star* that I had read over my lunch. He reproached me. It had been good and thoughtful of me to send the paper to him more quickly than the post could bring it, but—well, he pointed out that his home was not of the kind at which he would feel comfortable in entertaining his friends or receiving their messengers. . . . For one brief week Davidson achieved, no doubt as a matter of policy, a bedroom and a sittingroom in St. James's Place. How he revelled in it!

Soon after he came to London it seemed likely that Davidson would succeed and that he would make for himself as a poet, a critic, an essayist, such a place that he would be able to live in honour and comfort. It was not to be. He had too sturdy and uncompromising a character and he did not care to make easy friends. In his later life indeed I cannot think that he had other intimate friends than two, Max Beerbohm and myself. By that time he had secured a small, an inadequate, Civil List pension. Seventy-five pounds a year, I think it was. It was paid quarterly and on the day on which he received it he would ask either Beerbohm or me to dinner. He asked us in turn. The invited guest would arrive at the Grosvenor Club at the corner of Dover Street, Piccadilly, and having been given a glass of sherry he would be taken, on foot if it were fine, in a cab if it were wet, to the Trocadero, where a table would be waiting the poet's arrival and where he had already indicated that he was to be served with neither the five-shilling nor the seven-and-sixpenny meal, but with the best, which cost half a guinea. A bottle of very good, almost superlative, claret would be the wine, and after dinner would be coffee and old brandy—not the most expensive of the cognacs, not that one whose price per glass would indecently affront a guest (for it was the Trocadero habit to have the wine waiter stick in front of you the several bottles, each bearing a large and priced label), but one which would properly complete the meal of which we had partaken. Then we would smoke largish cigars from the cabinet of the Grosvenor Club, for even on this day of the nation's quarterly appreciation of his worth, Davidson retained respect for the shillings in his pocket and he knew that a club cigar would cost less than those supplied by the restaurant's head-waiter.

There in the Trocadero we would sit and talk. Davidson would mellow, would cast off all doubts as to the future, would be certain of a great success, and he would give you the feeling that for the moment he loved the world for your sake. And indeed those evenings were the occasions when the world became attractive in his eyes, rosy—and that not because his stomach lusted after rich food and good wine but because they were for the moment the symbols, the outward signs, of the comfort, the luxury, he knew he deserved. That meal, four times a year, at the Trocadero, was his one concession to extravagance. But at a certain hour the clock would strike. He knew too well the time at which the last train would leave Victoria for Streatham and, when it approached, nothing would induce him to linger. No: he would take his hat and his stick from the cloakroom attendant and, thanking you for the pleasure your company had given him, he would summon a hansom, tip the commissionaire and rattle away down Piccadilly.

I have always been proud that John Davidson honoured me with his friendship. As a fellow-worker he was untiring. For a considerable period before his death he read manuscripts for me and I have never known a man more scrupulous in the performance of his duties. Never did he fail me.

That he knew Beerbohm and me better than others did not mean that he had not other friends. He knew them less well and confided in them less whole-heartedly. Bernard Shaw was one of them; he had reason to be grateful to Shaw. John Lane, his first serious publisher, was evidently another. You must understand that Davidson's assumptions for himself were always magnificent, that he felt he had great claims on humanity, and yet that he felt he was, in his own words, a Man Forbid. One attempt to assist him comes to light in a letter written to John Lane by Shaw on March 23, 1910. Lane had evidently been busying himself in securing a continuation of Davidson's pension to his widow and had put a petition on foot. Here is what Shaw says:

IO ADELPHI TERRACE
LONDON, W.C.

DEAR LANE,

I return the petition, signed. If the attempt to get a pension fails, it might be possible to scrape some money by a benefit performance of a play which Davidson wrote a few years before he died. I asked him to try his hand at a modern play, and to put all his ideas into it and do just what he liked with it; but as he could not afford the time, I advanced him a sum of money on account of whatever fees he might make by it subsequently. This unfortunately spoilt the whole affair; for instead of doing what I wanted him to do, and really letting himself rip to his heart's content, he conceived himself bound for my sake to try and make the play popular. The result of this was that he made it impossible. It was not popular enough for a popular theatre; and it was not advanced enough for a coterie theatre; and so nothing came of it. I believe he improved on the MS he sent me: no doubt Mrs. Davidson has got it somewhere. I do not advise you to stir this matter up unless the application for a pension be refused, because though the anxiety of actors to get some work to do makes it easy enough to shark up a benefit matinee, it is extremely troublesome to get it managed and put through in such a way as to secure any pecuniary results; so I should regard it as a last resort. All the same you had better know about the existence of the play.

Yours faithfully
G. BERNARD SHAW [1]

Yes, Davidson constantly deplored the fact that the conditions of the commercial theatre of those days made it impossible for him to do his best work and Shaw, out of his own abundance, evidently determined to put him to the

[1] I owe the opportunity of copying this letter to Messrs. Dulau and Co.

test, to grubstake him. I never read the play. It has been destroyed.

I have a second letter from Shaw about Davidson. A German lady wished to write about Davidson and his work and applied to me for certain information which I did not have and about which I had to ask Shaw, who replied from Adelphi Terrace on June 23, 1927:

DEAR GRANT RICHARDS,

Tell the German lady that Davidson had nothing whatever to do with Nietzsche or his philosophy. His speciality was an attempt to raise modern materialism to the level of high poetry and eclipse Lucretius. He told me he could not afford to write the great drama he had in his head on this subject because it would make no money and he had to drudge at journalism to support himself and his people. I asked him how long it would take him to write the poem, and how much he could earn by journalism in that time. He said six months and £250. I handed him £250, to be repaid out of half his royalties (if any) on the poem. He took the money, and gratefully resolved that he would enrich me for my generosity. So instead of writing the great poem he wrote what he thought would be a popular melodrama with millions in it. I believe I have a copy of this abortion somewhere.

When he realised that he had done me no good, and thrown away his chance, he killed himself. At all events that was the next I heard of him, poor fellow.

In short, he died of poverty.

Ever

G. BERNARD SHAW

The excellence of the Shavian memory would almost make me a vegetarian.

There is much more that I could write of Davidson. Some day I must reconsider the inhibition he put upon me and see exactly to what extent it was intended to bind me. Mrs. Davidson says she trusts to my discretion. The matter is a little complicated by the fact that my poor friend's will was never properly executed. He did not realise that he must have his signature witnessed. However, it has served.

In appearance Davidson was short but distinguished. The drawing by Will Rothenstein in the *Yellow Book* (and in his *Men and Memories*) did him justice. For many years he wore a wig that he might not be handicapped by the appearance of age, and he dressed as might any respectable citizen who had the prejudices of his suburb and of his family to consider. But his mind was a furnace. One odd peculiarity he had, a distrust of Irishmen. "Grant Richards, man, never trust an Irishman," he said to me as we lay on the heather over Cadgwith Cove not long before he died.

At the beginning of January, 1924, several Davidson first editions were sold at the Anderson Art Galleries in New York for rather more than the prices at which they were published. The manuscripts fetched higher prices. Thus the manuscript of *A Ballad of a Nun* went for forty dollars, and the manuscript of *Ballads and Songs*, with the exception of that poem, for sixty-two dollars—sums quite disproportionate to their importance in the literary history of their decade.

XVIII

MASEFIELD–GALSWORTHY–THOMAS BURKE–
ALEC WAUGH

IT was *The West Wind*, a poem that I read in the *Nation*, which first drew my attention to the work of John Masefield. Immediately, I wrote to its author, care of the editor, to say how much I had admired his lines and how much I should like to have the opportunity of publishing a book of his poems, if he had such a book in contemplation. *Salt Water Ballads*, published in November, 1902, was the result. It was the first book from Masefield's hand and it attracted immediate, if not considerable, attention. I believe I invented the title, and if that is so I am not very proud, for it seemed, as did the binding, deliberately to invite for the book comparison with *Barrack Room Ballads*.

Of the first edition of *Salt Water Ballads* five hundred copies were printed and the story is told in the trade that owing to a fire that took place in the warehouse of Leighton, Son and Hodge, the binders, the book was soon unprocurable. I believe this story of the fire to be an invention. My ledgers of that period in no way support it. The copies printed, with the exception of a small number, are all accounted for as normal sales and review copies. The first binding was three hundred. In the first part of 1903 a further hundred and fifty were bound; and a further fifty were bound at a later date. I have, but see no reason for giving, the details of the sales. Anyhow, the book became very much of a collector's item, one copy selling, I believe, for twenty-eight pounds, the original price being but five shillings. A few bound copies *may* have been burnt in the Leighton fire and so have given rise to the tale. It no doubt seemed necessary to account for a book of which over four hundred copies had been sold becoming so scarce and so valuable. Some copies in the later bindings were done up in a different cloth and that of course would have enhanced the value of the first issue.

In the *Spectator* of April 4, 1931, that same "Amicus", whose description of the appearance of A. E. Housman I have quoted, discusses John Masefield and falls into error. He describes him as having "crashed into celebrity" with *The Everlasting Mercy* in 1912. "One week he was a young literary journalist who wrote reviews for the papers and was vaguely known to be familiar with the sea. . . ." "Amicus" is at fault. Masefield did not do so much reviewing that he was identified with that kind of work, and he was by no means "vaguely known as familiar with the sea". The sea poems in his two books and a number of articles and stories about sea life that he contributed to the *Manchester Guardian* —in fact he seemed for some years to be a regular *Guardian* man—had given him a poetical and sea reputation far in advance of any slight fame he had earned as the owner of a fine literary taste. The sea articles I reprinted under the title of *A Tarpaulin Muster* in 1907, but no sooner had the agreement been signed than Masefield began, quite unnecessarily, to be nervous about the excellent, the unique, material the book was to contain. His slight distaste for it continued, for on December 21, 1911, writing from 30 Maida Hill West, he tells me that I should be well advised to leave out two-thirds of it and to print about a third "all of the sea"; and in a postscript he returns to the subject: "Looking through the *Muster* I see about 100 pages of tolerable stuff. The rest, Ach Gott!" Well, I did not, and do not, agree with him; and anyhow the stuff would never have got into the *Manchester Guardian* if it had not been very good.

That same "Amicus", by the way, seems to see our contemporary poets in military terms. He says of Masefield: ". . . the surroundings of his early manhood, which saw him, at various times, as apprentice on a sailing-ship, a bartender, and a New York journalist. In view of all this he might be expected to show traces, in his appearance, of the tough adventurer. Not a bit of it . . . Mr. Masefield resembles Mr. A. E. Housman in having a partly military, partly academic appearance; he might be a retired colonel of sappers of the kind that has a different smile and dabbles in archæology." I wonder.

I did several Masefield books, but in the end I lacked courage—which in a publisher is often synonymous with capital. Thus I published *The Tragedy of Nan and Other Plays* (of which "Amicus", casting an eye over Masefield's work, seems never even to have heard) and two novels, *Captain Margaret* and *Multitude and Solitude;* and he edited for me, and wrote introductions for, several volumes in a little parchment-covered series that I misnamed The Chapbooks —*Lyrists of the Restoration, Essays Moral and Polite, 1660-1714, The Poems of Robert Herrick* and *Lyrics of Ben Jonson and of Beaumont and Fletcher*—and a two-volume edition of *The Voyages of Captain William Dampier.*

To my shame, in 1909 I developed cold feet. I was offered *The Tragedy of Pompey the Great.* I dilly-dallied with it until its author had no further patience and asked me to send the manuscript back to him. I had no excuse. I admired the play intensely, and the two extracts which are given under the titles *The Chief Centurions* and *Philip Sings* in *The Collected Poems* have sung in my ears ever since I first read them in the manuscript. Here is the shorter of the two:

> Though we are ringed with spears, though the last hope is gone,
> Romans stand firm, the Roman dead look on.
> Before our sparks of life blow back to him who gave,
> Burn clear, brave hearts, and light our pathway to the grave.

To tell the truth, I had allowed my ledgers to influence me. It was a folly. No publisher worthy of his job, if he has any money left in his banking account, will, if he can help it, allow an author whose work he respects and admires to go elsewhere. In the long run things will come right—and even if they don't—well, he will have the happiness and satisfaction of having been true to his own taste and of having on his shelves good books of which he is proud rather than rubbish which he has acquired in the mistaken belief that he knows what the public wants. In the Masefield case I was the more to blame as it was no literary adviser who counselled me to do without the luxury of *Pompey the Great*. The truth is that the novels *Captain Margaret* and *Multitude and Solitude* had not had the kind of success which pays the rent and the salaries of the staff and all the other expenses of a publisher's office. I think I may say that Masefield entered on the experiment of novel-writing at my suggestion. If it was not mine, then it was that of C. F. Cazenove, his agent. We used to conspire together, Cazenove and I, and as a result of our conspiracies the two novels came into being. I should have had the third, *The Street of To-Day*, but cold feet interfered in that case too. I had an option on it which I did not choose to exercise.

As a result of my lack of courage (or capital) Dents added to their reputation, Sidgwick and Jackson secured an ornament to their list, and William Heinemann made a fortune—for quite soon John Masefield scored with both barrels: he became a best-seller as a poet *and* as a novelist, and the publishers alone know how many copies have been sold of his books on the War and on literature in general.

Shed no tears on my behalf, reader. . . . Not this time anyway. On this occasion it was all my own fault.

To go back to Masefield himself. In an article of a page and a half by Ashley Gibson in the *Bookman* of April 1909 I have further evidence that he was well enough known before *The Everlasting Mercy* appeared in the *English Review*. The *Bookman* was not in the habit of bestowing its pages on unknown writers, however meritorious. The article is also interesting for its facts: "It was on the training ship H.M.S. *Conway* that Mr. Masefield first heard some of the best sea stories in . . . *A Mainsail Haul*. The man who told them to him was an old sailor of the name of Wallace Blair, an instructor in seamanship, and a type that has now passed away among sailor-men. He was of the sort 'whose hair—

so the legend says—was rope-yarn, whose fingers were so many marline spikes, and whose blood was good "Stockhollum" tar'. His kind old mind was full of coloured threads, each thread a bright tangle of romance." Mr. Gibson has much to say about the poet's life in New York and elsewhere, but that is a period which I believe has assumed an unnatural importance in a consideration of the circumstances that have made him what he is, and, for the present at least, I see no sufficient reason for repeating what is generally known of it, or for adding my little contributions. Certainly the *Weekly Dispatch* printed on April 2, 1916, a sort of poem which a Philadelphia paper had recently discovered in Yonkers, New York, and which may have some slight autobiographical interest, but I should do no one the slightest service by disinterring it, and anyhow the law of copyright would prevent me, for Masefield is very properly jealous of his rights. However, to the curious in such things I will indicate the existence, in the *Evening Standard* of May 8, 1913, of a letter in which one W. H. Browning, who is described as an old "shellback", falls foul of the terminology and the technical details of *Dauber*. I do not know whether he was right. And there is a column in the *Evening News* of February 19, 1912, in which one artist in words salutes another: Arthur Machen writes of *The Everlasting Mercy* as "the one literary production of the year 1911 that has in it the real and abiding stuff of letters; it was the true book of the year, because, in my judgment, it is also the book of many years, of all succeeding years in which true poetry will be loved and honoured. . . ."

Another interesting fact about the Poet Laureate is that he has been his own publisher in that he has issued from his own house, 13 Well Walk, Hampstead, several of his own books. I have, for instance, before me a leaflet in which, beginning "Dear Richards" (the name alone being in his handwriting) he announces that the following books "by myself will be issued during the next three months, to subscribers only. 1. *Sonnets and Poems*. 2. *The Locked Chest* and *The Sweeps of Ninety-Eight*, two plays in prose. 3. *Good Friday*, a play in verse. 4. *Personal Recollections of John M. Synge*. The cost of the set of four volumes will be one guinea net. The edition will be strictly limited to 200 sets. Yours sincerely, John Masefield", the signature being in his own autograph. I bought the set and treasured it. It did not make me Synge-conscious. John M. Synge was one of my mistakes: it appears from a letter I recently read that I refused one of his early books!

It was always a matter of regret to me that *Salt Water Ballads* passed into the hands of Elkin Mathews, for Masefield, although I was commissioning him to write other books at the time and although we were in the most cordial relations and discussing many projects some of which matured and some of which came to nothing, would not allow me to reprint it. On December 12 [1906] he wrote me from Hill Crest, Boar's Hill, Oxford, regretting that he had kept me so long without an answer, "But I have been producing a play and haven't had a moment". He thanks me for taking "such an interest in *S. W. B.*" but he hasn't decided yet what to do about the book; "much will depend on events during the next few days, but I do not think that in any case I shall be able to let you have the book". Cazenove, his agent, and I puzzled over his obduracy with regard to this book which had been his first and for the launching of which I had been responsible. That he should have preferred to place *all* his work with other publishers I should have been able to understand, but that he should refuse me permission to reprint *Salt Water Ballads* while letting me have almost everything else he was writing I could not understand.

I sat one day in the early years of the century in a Cornish garden reading the *Spectator* and found that its critic of fiction had discovered a new novelist in the person of one John Galsworthy. He wrote of the book in such terms that I sent at once to London for it. It was *The Man of Property*. I had not read many of its chapters before realising that Heinemann had another winner and one who did not depend on

231

some accidental or meretricious quality for his success, and that the older tradition of English fiction was to renew itself in this new writer. Of course, as it turned out, Galsworthy was not a new writer: he had written other books under the signature of "John Sinjohn". They had attracted no attention. When I think of *The Man of Property* I think always of J. C. Snaith's *Broke of Covenden,* a success too in its way but a book that never became the fashion. It should be looked at again. People talked about this new man Galsworthy all through the succeeding months. Who was he? What sort of a man was he? I was told that he was immensely rich, that his family had made a fortune in the copper trade, but that John Galsworthy himself cared nothing for fortunes and preferred to live modestly and to write. I never had the curiosity to discover what truth there was, if any, in this piece of gossip. The further suggestion that he was a recluse, averse from the society of his fellows, was certainly untrue. My friend Lancelot J. Bathurst, a partner in the publishing firm of Alston Rivers, had been at Oxford with him, at New College, and they had seen a good deal of one another. They had been in the habit of going racing together, and that fact at once disposes of the legend that Galsworthy had never seen a racecourse until he had to get up the subject for one of his books. Soon after he became well known as a novelist Galsworthy achieved a fresh fame as a dramatist. At the first night of *The Silver Box* I found myself seated behind A. B. Walkley, who turned to me after the end of the first act: "Grant Richards, who is this man? They say he's written a novel . . ."

Walkley was visibly impressed.

My own acquaintance with Galsworthy was not intimate but it was pleasant. He dined with me on occasion. On one evening John Masefield was also of the party and we discussed and almost decided upon the starting of a new quarterly, something less precious than *The Yellow Book* and more widely representative. We did go so far as to fix its title—*The Peacock*. Nothing came of it.

JOHN GALSWORTHY AND A CRITIC

Absurd little things are apt to stick in one's mind about the personalities of the men whom one does not know well. I can never forget that John Galsworthy, in spite of his conservatism of interest and his sense of tradition, and in spite too of his rather aloof appreciation of the good things of this world, smoked, actually smoked, while he drank his port!

Galsworthy had a heart. I think it was his pre-eminent quality. Knowing he was publishing his books with Heinemann and with Duckworth, who had published his first essays in fiction, I do not think that I should have suggested his giving me a book, but he himself brought me *A Commentary*. No doubt he was influenced by the fact that after a reverse I was building up a fresh list. It was not one of his best books but it was characteristic. A book of sketches rather than of short stories, it was full of the sense of pity that informs all his work. In this connection I wonder if anyone has kept record of a letter he wrote to the *Saturday Review* of the 25th September 1915:

MANATON, DEVON

16 September 1915

SIR,

In an article on my novel, *The Freelands*, your reviewer pens the following description of me: "He is a fanatic with a very palpable axe to grind." I do not know whether this is fair criticism, but I do know that anyone with personal knowledge of me will laugh at seeing the word "fanatic" applied to one so hopelessly moderate as myself. Your reviewer further says: "In all Mr. Galsworthy's novels and plays may be traced the revolutionary." With his good leave I, who ought to know my own mind, say that he is much mistaken. If there be a coherent gist to my novels and plays, it is certainly not incitement to social revolution; it is deprecation of extravagance, and the plea, however negatively or indirectly made, for more toleration and understanding between man and man. Out of that comes the only revolution worth having. So far as I know, Sir, this is the only axe I have to grind.

I have never asked for space to reply to a criticism before, and I apologise for doing so now.

Yours truly,

JOHN GALSWORTHY

It is well for England and for humanity that success came soon to John Galsworthy, and that it enabled him to give always of his best, and in a sense to round off, to complete, his work. That success came in more forms than one. His reputation was international. The admiration he evoked in America was enormous. Copies of the first editions of his early books went in the auction rooms at huge prices. That was before the slump.

As an example of the way in which the bottom dropped out of the American market in rare modern books and in the manuscripts and letters of modern authors whom the curious fashion in such things had chosen for exploitation, a provincial bookseller told me this year of a book of Galsworthy's which he had bought at auction as a commission for an American customer who had cabled his instructions. "Don't talk to me about rare 'moderns,' my dear fellow. The end came almost in a night. I arrived home one evening well satisfied with having secured at auction a good copy of"— I forget which book it was—"for a hundred and seventy pounds. I just added the usual commission to the price and sent the book off to New York. Before it could get there the slump came—I mean the general slump, of course—and in less than a month the book was back in my shop. My customer wrote that he was sorry but that he certainly couldn't hope ever to be able to pay for it and that he thought it was more honest to return it. He was broke, like so many of his fellow countrymen, and I suppose he reckoned that the book was worth more to me than a debt I could not hope to recover. So it was—in a way. But I couldn't get rid of the damned thing at anything approaching a decent price.

I hung on to it for years and then sold it not long ago for seven pounds—and glad to have the money. I can tell you the rapidity with which that American bubble burst jolly near smashed some of us!" I had heard the same thing elsewhere.

Just now I mentioned my friend C. F. Cazenove, the literary agent. Some year or two before his death he asked me to remember that he had a young chap in his office who he was sure would one day ring the bell. "I have him marked down for you," he said. "No, you needn't bother about him just yet. He isn't ripe. But he'll do something. You might remember his name—Thomas Burke."

Cazenove—to the great regret of everyone who knew him —died untimely, as did his partner in The Literary Agency of London, the amiable G. H. Perris. But his young assistant did not forget that he was to address himself to me, and after a while I met Burke and he followed up our meeting with a letter. Now Burke has one ineradicable vice: he does not date his communications. But in that letter from the Agency, after mentioning my interest in his work, he adds that he is sending me "the enclosed", but the absence of date makes it impossible for me even to hazard a guess as to what "the enclosed" might have been. (A dated letter of Burke's would be a collector's piece of some value: I have only seen one and that goes no further than providing the day of the month!) At some period, I believe, he produced an anthology or something of the kind, but I do not think it was that; whatever it was I fancy that my lack of interest damped Burke's belief in me as his destined publisher. Next I heard.that he was working in a publishing office—Allen and Unwin's, I think—and it was not until some time had passed that he came in bringing with him a sheaf of typewritten manuscript bearing the title *Limehouse Nights*. I thanked him and he went away and I, remembering my promise to Cazenove, took the packet home to Cookham Dean where I then lived, intending to give it my immediate attention. But it was war-time, and although it sat for weeks on my desk so that it might be ready to my hand, it was a long time before I had an opportunity of tackling it.

There came a night when my wife, as it was getting late and she had finished whatever she was doing at the moment, suggested that it was time to go to bed. I looked up from my work and asked her to wait a few minutes—"Here, my dear, read one of these short stories. The man's worrying me to decide about 'em. They ought to be good—but then short stories never are any use in book form. Still, do read one and tell me what you think of it"; and I returned to my task.

In a few minutes I had finished what I had to do and turned round from my desk: "Ready?"

My wife did not reply. That did not surprise me: she was reading and when she was so engaged she was usually deaf to interruption. But—but she was crying. Tears were coursing down her cheeks. . . . I waited—for I could see that of the story she was reading only a couple of pages were left. When she had finished she turned to me: "—one of the saddest and most beautiful tales I've ever read. If the others are like it you've got one of the books of your life. But don't wait—read the story now. I'll read another in the meantime."

I did as I was bid. Indeed we both of us, before we did close up for the night, decided that *Limehouse Nights* was the real stuff. . . . "But I don't know about publishing these, dear. They're what you'd call 'difficult', these tales. I don't want to get myself into trouble."

"If you don't publish that book I'll never read another manuscript for you as long as I live. . . ."

During the following day we completed our reading and, apart from my doubt as to what the public and the authorities would stand, we had made up our minds. Thomas Burke was in his kind a master. . . .

Next morning I took the manuscript back to town and devoted my mind to the problem that it presented. That it was extremely well worth publishing I had not a pennyworth of doubt, that it justified its frankness, and that its "rawness" was inherent in the material as its author saw it. But the authorities were at that time far more alert, more touchy, than they are now. Feeling ran high against frankness in fiction. D. H. Lawrence's *The Rainbow* had only recently been suppressed. But, although I went through the motions of turning the affair over in my mind, I had really made it up quite firmly. *Limehouse Nights* and Thomas Burke were too good to let go. I must get some support, however, and I bethought myself of the manager of my bank, J. D. Wightman, a man who might be willing to read the typewritten sheets, who was interested in books and yet who could be trusted to give a common-sense verdict rather than a literary appreciation. I wanted to be able to say that I had gone outside bookish circles for advice should there be any trouble after publication. . . .

So Wightman read and his opinion was definitely in favour of going ahead. Yes, he would allow that Burke had gone further than many people would be willing to follow him, but, essentially, the stuff was true; it was ugly but not obscene; it convinced one of the author's honesty of purpose; moreover, such things were and therefore they could be written of. Then I took the "strongest" stories to my manager and tried them on him. He shook his head. . . . **Of course** *Limehouse Nights* went to the printer. The next thing was to try to place it in America.

Now there is nothing in common between *Plays Pleasant and Unpleasant* and Burke's book, but the American reaction was identical in both cases. My best friends told me I should be ashamed to have printed such a book and that I was a fool not to realise that I ought not to expect them even to consider it seriously—"and we never thought that books of that kind were in your line; we thought you cared for finer stuff". In the long run, however, I did secure New York publication. Robert M. McBride "blew in"—the phrase is just—and asked what I had to sell and I handed him the proofs of *Limehouse Nights* with an injunction that he had better not read them in bed at night unless his nerves were very strong. The next day he bought it. It was a lucky purchase.

America took very happily to Mr. Burke's book and he became very much in demand as a writer of short stories of a similar kind in the magazines of the country. No one, I believe, took the view of my censorious publishing friends. Over here things looked for a while as if trouble was pending. Arnold Bennett told Burke that the possibility of securing a conviction was being seriously discussed at headquarters, and that he himself feared the worst. Personally, having once taken the risk and having grown even fonder of the book, I refused to be worried. Not so the author. Being of a more temperamental and more nervous nature he would not rest until I had agreed—for a consideration, I had better frankly confess—to cancel the clause in our contract which would have made him financially responsible for the costs of defending any action brought against me as the book's publisher and for the payment of any losses or financial penalties incurred. For some reason I was indifferent to these risks and to the further risks of being held by the Court to be guilty of uttering an obscene libel. We should have had some witnesses and some active friends on our side if the matter had been taken into court. Copies had been sent to G. B. S., to Arnold Bennett, to Eden Phillpotts and to George Moore. They had all, except the last, written to Burke in the book's praise, and George Moore could only say that it was "out of his key" and that he did not feel that he "could give a competent opinion on it".

The one dated letter that I have from Burke is of April 17, 1917, sending me the manuscript of *Twinkletoes*, the short novel on the same kind of theme as those of *Limehouse Nights* which I had encouraged him to tackle. Publishers are like that—even the best of them: write poems and they want you to try your hand at short stories; write short stories and they will have you try your hand at a novel. In this last they are by no means disinterested: collections of short stories are not generally the stuff out of which publishers make big money. It is the novel that sells into big figures. There are exceptions of course: Rudyard Kipling's books, for instance. Burke, however, had yielded to my suggestion. In delivering the manuscript of *Twinkletoes* he confessed himself as "feeling utterly sick with it" and says that he "will be sorry to hear from you when you have read it. But you have been warned.... The short story is my job. The effect, as you will see, is the same as if you had put the side-drummer on to deputise for first fiddle." I did *not* see; nor have I ever seen: I liked *Twinkletoes* and if of the two books I prefer *Limehouse Nights* I do not feel that the fact bears out Burke's contention. The method and the matter of the first book were new. It had at the time the advantage of being a unique experiment. Burke anyhow never had a sufficient belief in his own talent. Besides, he has further proved himself as a novelist since.

After *Limehouse Nights* had captured America McBride cabled to me one day saying that D. W. Griffith wanted the film rights and, I believe, that he offered five hundred pounds. I told Burke and he was all for an immediate acceptance. We heard less in those days about cinema people paying huge sums to authors and five hundred pounds did sound like money. Luckily, however, the control of the matter rested with me and I refused to part with the rights for a sum which I knew in my own mind Griffith would be willing greatly to increase. Burke left the office dissatisfied, but I was right. We got a thousand pounds. Personally I believe we could have got more and would have waited, but in the face of Burke's anxiety I could not persist. As far as I know, *Broken Blossoms*, which I did not see, was the sole fruit of that contract.

It is worth mentioning here that Burke had not found it so very easy to find a publisher for his first book. He told me that he had offered it to either eleven or twelve houses. One had told him that he would like to bring it out but that it would surely offend the huge connection which looked to this particular house to bring out texts and works of miscellaneous devotions, high-brow, religious and uplift stuff generally—"You know what it is, old fellow: I just can't afford it." Heinemann was willing to accept it straight away, but he would have as a condition in the contract that he could if he chose hold it back till the War was over—"It's too damned depressing for these days, Burke. We want cheering up. Your stuff, fine though it is, would make people even more miserable than they are." Other publishers thought it too shocking, or refused it with no further explanation than that they didn't like it.

There was in the early 'twenties a good deal of talk about the possibility of increasing the number of potential book-buyers. I had been hammering at the subject in the *Times Literary Supplement* in the half column that at that time I wrote every week, a little gossip in which as a publisher I advertised my own wares. Burke had noticed this, and one day he sent me the proof of an advertisement he had himself written which was to appear in the *Publishers' Circular* as a whole-page pronouncement from Jonathan Cape's office. Burke said he did so that I might see "a specimen of my advertising writing", but, he added, its authorship must not be disclosed. It is one of the best pieces of writing in its kind that has appeared. I am allowed now to print it as an example of trade propaganda, and I am allowed too to give the name of its author:

AN AUTHOR TO A BOOKSELLER

It is time, I think, that we authors recognised and celebrated the bookseller. We talk much about publishers, in words sometimes fair and sometimes stormy. We lunch with them and dine with them and exchange cigars with them. But towards the bookseller we maintain a frigid indifference.

Yet the bookseller, far more than the publisher, is the controller of our welfare. Our sales are in his hands. He can kill the eager youngling with a wave of his hand. Only through the bookkseller can the author get what even the most aloof artist desires—circulation.

Perhaps this indifference of the author to the bookseller explains the somewhat languid interest which some book-sellers take in their business. One often feels, particularly in small provincial towns, that he doesn't want to sell books. He stocks his shop, and then waits for customers to come in and demand and insist on having books, instead of going out and creating that demand.

This is to be deplored, for bookselling is the major part of the mechanics of books. When the publisher has found the MS., has spent money on giving it an attractive format, and much more money on making its existence known to the public, then, at that point, the real work of advertising begins, and it rests with the bookseller.

The publisher cannot reach the purchaser; he can only in a general way tell him that the book is to be had. It is for the bookseller to take up the campaign with advertising of his own; and the very best advertising is that which the bookseller can most effectively employ—advertising by word of mouth.

He can, if he chooses, in his particular town create and foster the book-buying habit. He can *make* book-buyers, and can increase the number of potential book-buyers. He should not count alone on the publisher's publicity; he should add his own to it and make book-buying easy and not, as it is to-day, a matter often of delay and difficulty.

Wherefore, while expressing here one author's gratitude to the bookseller for past efforts, I, speaking in all humility, and with a lively sense of favours to come, would ask him to do more.

I would ask him to get to know the people of his town and their tastes. I would ask him to conduct a book cam-paign in his town. I would ask him to circularise all sorts and conditions of residents. I would ask him to make his shop not merely a shop, but a pleasant rendezvous. And when he has made a new customer, I would ask him to note that customer's preferences; and when a new book appears which he thinks impinges on that customer's taste, to *send* him the book. Not wait until the customer comes to look at it, but send it to him for leisurely inspection. Let him have the book in his house and under his hand, and he will almost certainly buy it.

And, for that circularising, we, of Jonathan Cape's office, will gladly write, and print if desired, for any book-seller who cares to ask us and to tell us roughly the book-taste of his town, an attractive book-leaflet about himself and his shop.

I was unhappy when my business relations with Thomas Burke came to an end. I believed in him from that night at Cookham Dean when I read his first story. I always wished that I could inspire him with my own belief in the fortunes of his star.

During the War many publishers kept themselves alive by selling at prices very much higher than they would have taken before that catastrophe the huge stocks of normally unsaleable novels which had accumulated in their cellars and in their binders' warehouses. Some did so by their cleverness in selecting the kind of thing wanted by the soldiers and the public in that nerve-racked world. I was unfortunate in not having very large stocks to unload, but I was pretty suc-cessful in judging what would sell—perhaps my own taste was the deciding factor in my choice. In 1916 I had *Lime-house Nights*; in the following year I had Alec Waugh's *The Loom of Youth*.

The Loom came to me by chance rather than by calcula-tion. It came to me as a result of S. P. B. Mais's never-failing interest in the work of his pupils. (He was a schoolmaster in those pre-B.B.C. days.) It happened in this way. A pub-lisher, you must understand, never rests except when he sleeps, and even then he generally dreams of sales and of travellers and of his difficulties. It was August but I was not at rest. Once again I was in a Cornish cliff garden and once again I was reading a review in the *Spectator*. The critic was writing about a book John Murray had lately published, *A Public School in War-time*, and something in what he wrote made me wish to make the acquaintance of the book's author. I wrote to him and had a reply from Sherborne in which I was told that he was on the eve of starting on a walking tour round the Cornish coast. The very thing. He must stop for a meal as he passed my cottage. A telegram was despatched. Unfortunately it went to some other Sherborne (or Sherburn) and he and I did not meet until the autumn. Then he came with his wife to stop with us at Cookham Dean. Mais talked at large and enthusiastically, as was his wont, and I remember that on the evening of their arrival I was, before dinner, labouring an old point, that the good publisher should be willing to give some sort of examination to a manuscript however uncompromising it might look——

"Petre, let's send him Alec's book," Mrs. Mais broke in.

Petre thought not. He said it was too long, that too many publishers had turned it down, that they ought to have compassion on me. . . . He was talking lightly.

But I was not so easily put off once a manuscript had been mentioned: "Tell me about it, though. Who's Alec?"

"One of my pupils at Sherborne. It's a book about a public school. Attacks the whole system. Gives it hell. Long, very. Difficult to read in its present shape. You'd better leave it alone."

"Yes, but what's his name? 'Alec' isn't enough."

"Waugh—Alec Waugh. He's the son of Arthur Waugh, the man at Chapman and Hall's as a matter of fact. Oh, it's 'written' all right. It's promising. But no one wants it."

"Well then do as Mrs. Mais suggests and send it to me. It can't do me any harm."

"I haven't got it now. I've just handed it over to Thomas Seccombe."

"That's all right, then. I know Seccombe. I like him. He'll let me see it." And so the matter was left.

243

Seccombe duly sent me the manuscript and, reading it, I saw at once that, if published, it might altogether miss its market, might never catch the attention of the reviewers, unless in some way I could strike a provocative note at the moment of its birth. I knew Mais would help as much as he could; I knew Seccombe could help considerably: he said he would; he liked the book. And then I had a brain-wave. Seccombe had the respect of editors. His name carried weight in academical circles. He should write a provocative introduction. Introductions are almost always out of place in novels but here was a special book in which an introduction with Thomas Seccombe's name at the end of it was bound to attract the attention of literary editors. . . . It would go out for review and, considering the fact that youth from all the public schools of the country was now going through the furnace and that the subject was of crying importance, the critics would surely be told to hurry up with their opinions. And they did. . . . "A Wayfarer" in his weekly column of notes in the *Nation* of September 15, 1917, did as much for it as anyone (a note in the right place is better for attracting attention than almost any review):

"I have read few books that have interested me more than Mr. Waugh's *Loom of Youth*. It is in one respect an almost miraculous production. Here is a boy of eighteen who diaries his school life, reproduces its talk and atmosphere, and builds up a merciless memorial of its evils and shortcomings. It is a most straightforward account; it cannot have been invented, and yet I thought it sufficiently delicate. Read it with *Tom Brown's Schooldays* in your mind, and see how, in spite of his romantic affection for his old master, Hughes could not but trace the early growth of the evil which this boy of eighteen, with his soul full of his subject, probes to its root. It seems to me that it is a revolutionary work—if only the parents of England will read it, and having read, act on it. If they do the one without the other, it is on their conscience that they risk the ruin of their children's characters and mind. So I urge them to do the one and the other."

And now Alec has written *The Balliols!* A day or so after this last was published I walked with E. S. P. Haynes over Hampstead Heath and through Ken Wood to call on Mr. and Mrs. Arthur Waugh, the parents of the boy who had been so great a prodigy. We drank sherry and talked of the unanimously enthusiastic reviews the new book was having that morning—it was a Sunday and the papers were full of it—and we talked of Evelyn Waugh's successes, and of *A Shropshire Lad* and of Heinemann and of Spencer Blackett and of Austin Dobson and of poor Edmund Gosse; and when we left Arthur Waugh came to the door and repeated what he had said to me half an hour before: "Now don't forget that Alec was saying the last time I saw him that he could not imagine an author being happier with his publisher than he was with you. He said you were always so sympathetic and so full of enthusiasm." I liked that.

The truth is that I have always had something of an affection for Alec Waugh. You cannot know a boy of eighteen and be responsible in a large degree for launching him in the world of letters without forming for him either an attachment—or a considerable dislike. Alec signed his agreement with me and after a time departed overseas. I knew his father and mother; I had known his father for twenty years. These were anxious hours. No son of mine was old enough for that ordeal, and in a way I felt that I stood by Arthur Waugh's side. Anything might happen to his son. He had vanished into the mist of war. What should we hear? . . . Mercifully we heard quickly. Alec had been in action and was missing. Mercifully? Yes, I think so. The immediate suspense was over. And then, almost at once, the news came that he had been captured by the Germans. Soon his father knew he was a prisoner. After that we could be fairly easy. Out of those prison-camp experiences came a book, *The Prisoners of Mainz*. Alec's agreement with me would naturally bring it to me for publication. His father said it would be a happiness for him to be its publisher. I gave way. I should have felt that I wanted the book if I had been in his place.

I am, however, not quite sure that Arthur Waugh did me justice in his *One Man's Road*, a book of reminiscences which I warmly recommend. He is writing of Alec: "Some time before Christmas [1915] he began *The Loom of Youth* ... he carried the task through within a period of six weeks. ... My own position in the matter was not an easy one. From the day when he sent me the first chapter, I felt that I could not publish the book, seeing that I knew so many of the people portrayed; and yet I was convinced that the story was an honest one, while it never occurred to me that any intelligent reader would fail to appreciate that it was absolutely permeated by enthusiasm for the school. I must confess that I was rather amazed to read some of the letters which accompanied the refusals of one after another of my colleagues and rivals to have anything to say to my son's first novel. Once or twice I was sorely tempted to change my mind and recommend the book to my own board. Its chances of success seemed so obvious; the risk, at the worst, so small. But, without a little editing, my conscience could not shoulder the burden. And Alec was at one with me in this. 'The thing is clearly unmarketable', he said, a little bitterly; 'it had better be put away and forgotten'." But *The Loom* had more vitality than that: "Now, it happened that among the professors at Camberley was our old friend Thomas Seccombe, and one morning Seccombe received a letter from a literary friend in London, who had read the manuscript of *The Loom of Youth* for one of the recusant publishing firms, and remembered its refusal with reluctance. This friend had seen Alec's name in the Sandhurst list, and suggested that Seccombe might keep an eye on him. He also gave him some account of the precocious school story. So one day, at the end of a lecture, Seccombe asked an embarrassed cadet to remain and report to him, and then and there accused him of his secret authorship. He asked him to recover the manuscript from its cupboard at home; he read it, and thought well enough of its sincerity to send it to Mr. Grant Richards, with a word of keen recommendation." What I quarrel with is the next few sentences: "With the kindliest good nature, considering everything except his own advantage, Seccombe undertook to do all that he was asked, and Alec was, not unnaturally, ready enough to set his signature to an agreement binding him to offer his next two books to the publisher who had had the courage to adventure where so many of his rivals had held back. 'I am afraid', wrote Alec, 'this news will not be too welcome at Underhill; but for the moment I can only think of my own delight'." Am I unduly sensitive or is there a suggestion that the agreement to which Alec set his signature was one that he was forced by circumstances to sign, but that he regretted signing and ought not to have signed? If so, I can only say that his father thanked me for publishing his son's book, and that he read the proposed agreement before it was signed and approved it.

On April 29, 1917, Alec wrote to me:

ROYAL MILITARY COLLEGE
CAMBERLEY, SURREY

DEAR MR. RICHARDS,

Thank you very much but I am afraid I am absolutely full up for the first three days of the week. Will you be in on Tuesday if I come round? Have you read *Mendel* yet? Mark Gertler's big picture "the Merry go round" is on show now. He is Mendel. I have just read Mr. Seccombe's preface and am awfully pleased with it. It makes me feel hopeful about the book financially.

I am awfully sorry I can't come. I wish I could.

Yours v. sincerely
ALEC WAUGH

P.S.—I have been gazetted to the Machine Gun Corps.

247

XIX

RONALD FIRBANK–MRS. LEVERSON–THE SITWELLS–THE
POWYS BROTHERS

HOW Ronald Firbank first appeared on my horizon I
cannot now recall. Did he sway and wave his fragile
body up my St. Martin's Street stairs, carrying the typescript
of *Vainglory* in his hand, or did he send it to me by post? I
think he must have come himself, for otherwise I do not suppose I should have read far into even so slight a manuscript.
I must have had some personal motive. Firbank's personality would have supplied it. His was not a figure that you
could easily forget–and yet, as far as the beginning is concerned at least, I have allowed much to fade. I am not going
to attempt to estimate the value of Firbank's queer talent
here or ever, but I have never been quite sure in my secret
mind that he really deserved the appreciation that he secured
both here and in America–but especially in America. No
line that Firbank wrote was like the work of any other writer.
One thing I do remember and that is that I felt that *Vainglory* was intensely individual and also not a little mad. Its
perversity and that of its several successors did not strike me
particularly. Perhaps I hardly noticed it. Certainly those of
my friends who had read any of the books would rally me for
my blindness and simplicity. It is true that now and again I
was brought up suddenly by some ambiguous phrase in one
of the stories, and that I suspected that a schoolboy naughtiness had gone to the coining of the names of some of his
characters. Then I would say to Firbank: "Come, this won't
do, you know: you must alter this phrase and this name";
but when I did he would look so shocked or would answer

me so ingenuously that I had great difficulty in persisting. Perhaps even I did not persist. I felt about Firbank that like a child he could take liberties, and that I, as one of his elders, must not take them seriously. It was just his way.

Vainglory when I had read it through had some curious fascination for me. I took it for granted that the extraordinary punctuation or lack of punctuation was a mere carelessness of an uninstructed copyist, and that the printer would, if the book came to be produced, follow the usual custom and supply the deficiencies and correct the errors of the author. But first I refused the book. Firbank came down to see me about it and undulated shyly about the room. What was the matter with his story? Surely it was better than most stories. He had attempted to do something like Beardsley had done in the illustrations to *The Rape of the Lock*. Was I an admirer of Beardsley? Did I like Felicien Rops' work? So I knew Beardsley ...! Surely I would bring his child into the world. I could not be so unkind as to turn it from my door. It was my impression that the book was so slight and so unusual that there was little chance of it selling more than a few copies. Well, he would of course like it to sell, but it wouldn't matter so very much if it didn't. But it would matter to me. Yes, he supposed it would. Supposing he paid for the cost of production, would that make any difference? He was not rich; really he was very poor although perhaps I didn't think so. It didn't do to look poor; besides he loved clothes. And he waved himself a little more sinuously. How much would it cost to produce his book in a small edition, but beautifully—yes, beautifully?

I felt as if I were dealing with a child.

And after a while we came to terms and Firbank waved himself down my stairs. But first he had promised to bring me a little Rops painting of a girl. It was so charmingly corrupt. Could it not go on the wrapper of *Vainglory?* And as a frontispiece too? Well, he would bring it to me tomorrow. Colour printing was expensive? He was very poor, "but we can talk of that to-morrow. I am so happy you are going to do my book, so happy...."

Although I say it who shouldn't, I did make a very attractive, if simple-looking, book of *Vainglory*—but no, Rops' young woman does debar me from the use of the word "simple"! Firbank was delighted with the result. I think now that his ideal was to have a thing look very simple and unadorned and yet to be in very fact as corrupt and as depraved as art could make it. I was hardly his accomplice. Perhaps I was his dupe.

Ronald Firbank was the most nervous man I had had dealings with, and in some ways he was both cunning and suspicious. But he had a curious wayward charm which, however, slowly lessened even in the short period of our association. I could never be sure of his age. His face and his figure too in some way seemed, toward the end, to be going the same way as did the picture of Dorian Gray. Or was it fancy on my part?

His nervousness? He had a definite reason for nervousness in those war years: he had an idea, very unlikely on the face of it, that he would be roped in for the army. A less reasonable fear was that someone with whom he was in more or less daily contact had acquired a mastery over him and his soul and that if he were not careful he would be destroyed. Poor Firbank had dealings with wizards, crystal-gazers, astrologers and soothsayers, and it was an acolyte or practitioner of those sciences who in some unholy way was to finish him off. I struggled to the best of my ability with this notion. After a year or less it died down of itself, but not before he had suffered considerably. He was during that period a man who either actually or metaphorically was always looking over his shoulder lest his persecutor should steal up behind him....

One day he came to me and said, as if he expected me to be astonished, that on the previous morning, before leaving me, he had had a strong impulse to ask me to lunch.

"But why? Why didn't you ask me? I couldn't have come, but I should have appreciated the gesture."

"Would you have come? Would you really have come?" He waved himself about the room. I waited for some fresh pronouncement.

"Will you come to lunch with me to-day? To the Savoy? I want to go to the Savoy. Will you come?"

"Yes, of course I will. But I hope it's to the Grill Room you're going. I don't like the restaurant at lunch. I don't want music."

He looked disappointed. "Are you sure?" There was a pause, and then: "Very well, we will go to the Grill Room."

We started out in a taxi. As we passed the Cecil he looked at me seriously: "Are you sure you couldn't stand the music? It's very good. It would be so kind of vou to go to the restaurant."

There was nothing for it but assent. We entered and were given a table in the middle of the large room. The maître d'hôtel tendered the carte.

"You must have what you like—everything you like. I shall only have strawberries and Chablis. But I insist that you have all you want. I eat nothing but strawberries."

"Chablis is good. I approve of that, my dear Firbank. But I'm afraid strawberries wouldn't stay my hunger. You see I live in the country and breakfast early." I looked at the menu of the lunch of the day. "I'll have smoked salmon, and khebab, and then I'll have strawberries."

Firbank was satisfied. After a minute, however, he became restless, looking about him as if he feared something untoward would happen: "Would you mind if we changed our table? I can't stand this table. I want to be on the balcony."

"But you've ordered your meal here. . . ."

"I don't care—I can't stop here; I can't stop. I won't. The waiter must find us"; and before I could let anyone know of our intention we were half-way across the room and, in a moment, were seated on the balcony behind a pillar. The waiter did not find us, and soon Firbank was querulously demanding attention. . . . When at last the knot was unravelled and when, after we had drunk a double cocktail apiece, the food and the wine did arrive, Firbank regarded the wine-waiter with ire. "I don't want Chablis now. You have spoilt my pleasure in the idea of Chablis. I won't have Chablis. Give it away. Bring me a bottle of ——" and he named the most fashionable and costly brand of Champagne. We were by now attracting a deal of attention. . . .

Some months later he appealed—yes, that is the word—to me to lunch with him again. But would I mind the Café Royal. He liked the Café Royal. Was I sure I wouldn't mind? At that time the Café Royal had a very mixed clientele. Firbank evidently had a vogue of his own in that gilded saloon, the domino room or café itself. Our entry was much observed. We found a table. Cocktails of course. No, the ordinary lunch wasn't good enough for us. While our special food was being cooked we sat and looked on at the curious medley of painters, young officers, models and daughters of joy. C. R. W. Nevinson drifted by, nodding to me as he passed. He returned: "You haven't seen John, have you—Augustus John? I'm lunching with him here."

I had not. He stood for a minute and I introduced him to Firbank. "I don't like that fellow," my host said, as Nevinson left us; "I think he's sinister."

In a few minutes Nevinson, who had been roaming about like a lost spirit, returned: "I don't think John's coming. Can I have my lunch at your table, Grant?"

I assented with rather a poor grace, indicating that Firbank, as my host, was really the man to ask. After all, I was in a difficulty, since my host had said he didn't like Nevinson. Nor did Firbank help. He glared. I said something that implied that Nevinson had been a soldier, that he had been invalided out and that he was not anxious to return to any kind of battlefield now or at any time. Firbank's face brightened. Evidently the painter was a fellow sufferer fearing the same enemy. Nevinson must have a cocktail. The waiter must bring double martinis for all three of us. Nevinson must be his guest. . . . Painter and writer became as thick as thieves, bosom friends in the twinkling of an eye.

Left alone with Nevinson for a minute, I told him who Firbank was, indicating that he was a possible patron as he was interested in the arts. Later, Firbank insisted on knowing where his guest was going. To the New English Art Club show. Could he come too? "Yes, do go," I broke in, "and buy one of Nevinson's paintings." Firbank looked, unsteadily, at his watch. Good God! Was it really half-past three? He must get to Coutts' to cash a cheque. He'd break the door down with a hatchet rather than be balked. I had time to tell Nevinson to look after him a bit. "He's got to get back to Oxford," I added, for Firbank was then living in Oxford, occupying, I believe, a whole large house at the bottom of the High, where he hoped that the military authorities had lost sight of him.

A day or two afterwards I saw Nevinson. What had happened?

"Well, I took him to a party in the Temple after he'd failed to get into Coutts' and we'd looked at the Show. He got tighter and tighter, proclaiming all the time that he must catch the 6.5 to Oxford. . . . But he wouldn't start. You told me to look after him so I thought I'd better see that he did catch the train. I got a cab and pushed him into it and, while I was telling the driver where to go and to hurry, Firbank opened the door and got out on the other side. Then, looking at us, he smiled jauntily and remarked that he could very well look after himself, that anyhow he'd changed his mind about Oxford and that he was going to see St. Paul's. That's the last I saw of him."

I was not myself at the luncheon at the large, round corner table at the Junior Carlton Club when, having entertained Osbert and Sacheverell Sitwell, Firbank got under the table at the end of the meal rather than face the head-waiter, but I had been invited and the story was told to me afterwards as a solemn fact and as an example of what I had missed. Firbank's behaviour on another occasion does not lead me to doubt its truth. I had received a formal invitation from him to luncheon—again at the Junior Carlton. We were to be a party. The only man to turn up, however, was Michel Sevier, the young Russian painter, who with his amiability is a host in himself. We started with cocktails of course—double cocktails. The same large corner table had been reserved for us upstairs. There was a magnum of an old Champagne at its side. Sedate and more mature members saw us come in, I thought, with a certain distaste—and that reminds me: On leaving home that morning I had told my wife that I was lunching with Firbank and could not lunch with her, although she was to be in town. Forgetting this, she turned up at the office at one o'clock. Firbank had come to fetch me. I introduced them, and, later, went down with her to the door. Women generally do not like men with the peculiarities of manner and bearing that my novelist affected, and she was not an exception: "Your Firbank may be all the reviewers say he is, but I don't like the idea of your lunching with him. Well, it can't be helped: don't stop too long over the meal; I'll look for you on the 4.50 train." The fact that I was to walk and lunch with so strange a creature did really distress her.

To go back to Pall Mall. Yes, the crusted members of the Club did look towards our corner with a certain resentment. I formed an idea of the reason. Here was this young fellow, whom they didn't like the look of any way, both outraging their ideas of the right ways to behave and drinking up all their best wines. . . . As the meal approached its end a rare vintage port made its appearance. I believe it too was no ordinary bottle but a magnum. I am not sure. I don't myself drink port after champagne for choice, and did little more than sip at my glass, and after a while we went down to the smoking room. The brandy of the Junior Carlton is very good. The waiter brought us double portions. Soon, having smoked a large cigar, I went out to the fresh air of Pall Mall and walked towards Waterloo Place. By the time I reached the Carlton Hotel I began to feel a little sleepy; I felt that I had better postpone my return to the office. No, no, I wasn't drunk: I have never been drunk—not what you'd call drunk;

the nearest I was to it was in December 1895 when, lured by its classic name, I drank a whole bottle of Falerno all by myself in a cellar-restaurant in the Corso and did not thereafter walk too straightly to the Pincian, where I slept the afternoon away on a seat. Well, on this occasion too I went to sleep. Indeed I went to sleep in the little drawing-room just inside the Carlton door. I slept there for hours. Indeed I slept until the attendants, who knew me, made a noise in order to wake me up. I looked at my watch. It was after six. I caught the 6.50. And I had promised to meet my wife by the 4.50! There was a certain coolness at Cookham Dean. . . . It must have seemed to my wife that her worst fears were realised.

I am afraid that Firbank could never make up his mind that he liked me. On one occasion he told me that he had meant to bring with him that day a jade elephant which he greatly liked and which he wished to give me as a mascot. He promised that I should have it on his next visit. Now it happened that I was anxious to have an elephant, and if it were jade it would be so much the better, so when he did next come I asked him quizzically if he had remembered my quadruped. He writhed; I had never seen him more annoyed. "I am taking great care of the elephant for you. You shall certainly have it." I heard no more about it.

All the same, my relations with Firbank were invariably cordial. We never differed, although he was unable to reconcile the fact that the five hundred copies I used to print of his books were, even after allowing for fifty copies going out for review and for free copies, more than sufficient to meet the demand. In spite of his having slowly attained a small but precious reputation, of its having become fashionable in certain circles to discuss his improprieties, and of young and high-brow reviewers often bestowing upon him too warm if rather equivocal praise, the various books sold in single copies rather than in dozens. Even after America discovered him five hundred copies of a book sufficed. I am told that smart young hostesses in New York would give parties at which each guest would be presented with a copy of the same Firbank book and that one who could discover most improprieties therein after an hour's reading would get a prize. Indeed American adulation almost ended my relations with Firbank. That tall and solid imp of mischief, Carl Van Vechten, wrote an article about him in one of the New York dailies, in which in detail, and with an apparently serious pen, he described how on mail days the traffic would be suspended owing to the crowds of people who were trying to get to the Holliday Bookshop in order to make sure of their copies of the new Firbank out of that week's consignment, And so on. . . .Firbank took it all at the foot of the letter, and it took me a long time to convince him that all together the Holliday Bookshop importation of that particular book had hardly exceeded a score or so of copies. I wrote to Van Vechten, whose *Peter Whiffle* I had had a great deal of pleasure in publishing, and remonstrated with him. Of course it didn't cure him of his joke. And Firbank wrote to him and received a reply to the effect that if he would go to New York many thousands would flock to his lectures and many scores would meet him at the pier. And, Van Vechten added, if he would but publish his books in America he would sell thousands and thousands and thousands. . . .

It had happened indeed that for a year or two before this American publishers had been writing to me or dropping in and asking for a set of Firbank books to be sent to them in order that they might consider issuing them in New York. This occurred several times. Then invariably they would write from America and declare their great admiration for the books, but—well, they wouldn't "dare". . . .Dare what? *I* couldn't see it. Van Vechten's advocacy, however, made a difference: Firbank offered his next story to Brentano and it did sell many more in America alone than I had succeeded in selling of any one of his books in the two countries. By then, of course, the ground had been well prepared. . . . It was not unnatural that the sale should increase. But it annoyed me, especially as Brentano's London house published it here.

However, Firbank came back to me. He came up my stairs a little sheepishly. Might he return? Would I publish his next story? My books were so very much more distinguished in their appearance than the American had been. He professed contrition; he felt, he said, "like a lamb returned to the fold". He did not add that he had been doing his best to get C. S. Evans of Heinemann's interested in his work! I discovered that fact from a clue in Dulau's catalogue. One of the Firbank letters they have for sale is to Evans: he asks him to consider *Sorrow in Sunlight* which he describes as "purposely a little 'primitive', rather like a Gauguin in painting—extremely gay".[1]

One other anecdote: I had suggested to Firbank that he should follow the Rops of *Vainglory* with similar decorations by painters of distinction on and in each of its successors. He agreed: in one case a drawing by Augustus John was used; Albert Rutherston, Albert Buhrer, and C. R. W. Nevinson were pressed into service. In the case of Nevinson I suggested—it was not long after the Café Royal episode— that as he knew Nevinson he should take the proofs of the story up to Steele's Studios and discuss the matter with the painter. He assented, but by the time he had reached the Sir Richard Steele public-house all his courage had oozed away. He was too shy to ring the bell. Ultimately he flung the packet through an open window and took to his heels. Nevinson told me he found it on his bed.

I have remarked that the young intelligentsia did Firbank more than justice. The practice continued. Here is the *New Statesman* of August 24, 1929, about *Concerning the Eccentricities of Cardinal Pirelli*: "In a universe crowded with tallent, uncomfortably overflowing with brilliance, his was not a gift which can be entirely ignored." The whole article should be sought for by the Firbank fan. And there was

[1] I realise at this moment that it may not have been C. S. Evans and Heinemann, but Mr. A. W. Evans of Elkin Mathews.

Arnold Bennett in the *Evening Standard* of September 19, 1929: "For a dozen years I have been hearing, from the young, of the work of Ronald Firbank; and during all that time I refrained from reading him because of a suspicion in my wrong-head that he belonged to the confraternity of the precious. I gathered that he was in revolt against current ideals of imaginative literature, and I like and sympathise with literary rebels—but on the sole condition that they are not precious. I admit that I have listened to praise of him from young men who had done good things themselves and whose opinions, therefore, I valued. ... The whole thing" [he is discussing *Caprice*] "is lit with the refracting light that never was on sea or land. It is a lark, a joke, a satire, accomplished in a manner rather distinguished, mainly by dialogue and in brief paragraphs. It is brief, but it is homogeneous. It can be read easily, and without shame or humiliation. Whether it is worth reading I cannot quite decide, even in the privacy of my wrong-head. I have a notion that it isn't. ... At the same time, I should not be surprised if the Firbank cult grew. I can foresee young men and maidens at large in King's Road, Chelsea, stating plainly to the uninstructed that Firbank is the sole modern author worthy of attention from the elect. However, I am not of the elect, and never shall be. And I should regard Firbank more seriously if he showed strong imaginative power. He does not show it. To me he is an elegant weakling."

Both these critics were writing rather after the fair: Firbank had been some time dead. Later still, on May 11 of this very year, Harold Nicolson wrote of him in connection with a posthumous work, *The Artificial Princess*, for which Coleridge Kennard wrote an introduction ("Anything which can tempt Sir Coleridge into print had fulfilled its function," Mr. Nicolson says. The phrase reminds me of how "The Sphinx" loved her Coleridge Kennard!): "Ronald Firbank is an arresting figure. Most people who were born before 1900 belong to a bygone age. The odd thing about Ronald Firbank was that he belonged to two bygone ages. Emotionally he belonged to the Beardsley period, whereas intellectually he belonged to the Sitwell period. . . . Firbank possessed a talent at the same time undulating and incisive. Being a shy man with acute instincts, he indulged in innuendo. It was not the demure innuendo of Samuel Butler, nor yet the hearty innuendo of Norman Douglas; it was a baroque type of innuendo. He dealt in porcelain hints. The timidity inseparable from such epicene gigglings has discouraged me from becoming an admirer of Ronald Firbank. Yet, in his own medium, he was almost a supreme artist. . . . A certain immortality always attaches to writers who are inspired by one period and forecast another. Ronald Firbank, even to-day, is regarded in America as one of our important literary figures. I question whether such a reputation will prove durable. As a specimen of all that is most delicate and witty in Ronald Firbank this *Artificial Princess* could scarcely be surpassed. Yet would any serious reader, however fascinated he may momentarily be by the cachinnations of Ronald Firbank, contend that he is anything more than a literary curiosity? Had he lived longer he would certainly have written something of lasting value; his talent, however variable, was authentic and unexpectedly wise; yet he died while still in his experimental period; he achieved several brilliant improvisations on the theme of Beardsley in plus-fours; and brilliance is an evanescent quality." I myself should have been much surprised if Firbank had written something of lasting value. The Nicolson tribute is generous. Let me quote again from that *New Statesman* review: "Firbank's satirical portraits are too spiteful to be always very amusing; but when a distinguished diplomat and essayist tried to turn the tables and gave us his version of 'Lambert Orme', we were left with the impression that, in the various encounters he narrated, it was the diplomat, and not the novelist, who had always had the worst of it. The diplomat was brilliant and talented, but Firbank had an additional, undefinable spark. . . ." One knows one's Firbank better when one has read Harold Nicolson's admirable reconstruction in *Some People*.

AUTHOR HUNTING

Not long ago Charles Graves, who is generally right, described the Hon. Evan Morgan as having been Firbank's greatest friend. I wonder. Certainly a Firbank of the middle period was to have been dedicated to Evan Morgan. He heard of it and called at my office to protest. He was very angry, and he was angrier still when I told him that I had no power to interfere, Firbank was free to dedicate his little story to anyone he pleased except perhaps the King, the Queen and the Prince of Wales, and that all I could do was to promise to represent his views to the author, who would no doubt attach great importance to them. Evan Morgan went away threatening to invoke the law. Indeed he did invoke the law in the person of an Officer of the Court, his solicitor, who threatened—well, I don't quite remember what he did threaten. Was it an application for an injunction? I did tell Firbank what a hornet's nest he was raising. Naturally I added that he could do what he pleased. He would, he said: it pleased him to keep the dedication. He would keep it. It was well perhaps that before the book went to press he thought better of his resolve. The dedication was taken out. What would have happened if he had remained obdurate? I wonder. . . .

I have just written of "The Sphinx" (Mrs. Ernest Leverson)[1] and of the Sitwells. "The Sphinx", having done what she could to save Oscar Wilde from the penalties of his own folly and having helped him in all ways in her power, turned her attention after a while to the appreciation and the assistance of the other artists in letters whose work she liked. Her conversation, and her anxiety to do something or other to help them on, had in them much that was like inspiration to the young men who had achieved insufficient public recognition. There came a day when she would have it that I must publish the books of Osbert and Sacheverell Sitwell. I, who had heard of them as rebels bent on revolutionizing the arts they practised and busily engaged in attempting to influence the appreciation of the arts they admired, had not found

[1] See *Memories of a Misspent Youth*, by Grant Richards, 1932.

them easy reading and, while wishing to meet them, had been sure that I should find them arrogant and altogether too successful to wish to have a publisher found for them. However, once Mrs. Leverson had expressed her wishes it was difficult to evade them. She willed; her friends obeyed. The manuscript of Sacheverell's *The 101 Harlequins* arrived at my office, and thereafter on every second or third day I should be rung up by Mrs. Leverson, or bidden by letter to ring up, to say whether I would publish. Of course I would publish, and there began then for me an association with the two brothers which was one of the most agreeable of my career. Far from being arrogant, I found them listening and even docile about such matters as those trade affairs which I presumably understood and of which they must necessarily be ignorant. And appreciative. Model authors. I wish I had been as model a publisher. And their books had their growing public. When in 1923 I went to America, I took with me proofs of Sacheverell's *Southern Baroque Art*. Publishers over there were rather afraid of it; it was a big book. Yes, they had heard of the Sitwells, but it would be better to begin with something a little less costly, less ambitious, than this book of architectural criticism. Luckily the name caught Alfred Knopf's attention. Might he see it? I went to him and he turned the proofs over. In a minute he looked up: "What's your price for five hundred sheets?" I told him. He agreed. I have known two other publishers as quick in their decisions. Once I arrived in Boston in time for breakfast and carrying in my bag five books of which I wished to dispose of rights or editions. At ten I had an appointment with Ferris Greenslet of Houghton, Mifflin. Before he took me out to lunch he had bought all five of them. George Doran was the other speedy publisher. Once he thought well of your taste, he would, if it were humanly possible, give immediate attention to anything you believed that he would like. In this way I sold him James Agate's first novel, *Responsibility*. He bought it on the morning after he received the proofs, was as enthusiastic about it as I was myself, and even (I believe) paid for it a fair sum in advance of royalties. The same thing happened in the case of Huntley Robertson's *Through John's Eyes*, a book that deserved a success but which, alas! did not achieve it. There too Doran was enthusiastic and immediate in his acceptance. And he was generous in spirit. If he liked a book and it proved commercially a failure, he never reproached you or his own judgment. It was the fault of the public. . . . "Better luck next time: Anyhow it was a good book." Generally American publishers are slow, so slow, in coming to a decision, and often, almost promising a favourable verdict, they insist on taking proofs or manuscript back to America that they may get the formal approval of their partners. They will cable in eight days. In such cases you too often get a written refusal in three weeks! Frankly, I think that with few exceptions the American publisher is less adventurous than his English brother. He seems to depend more on the made reputation—or he used to do so.

To go back to the Sitwells. They would drop into the office with suggestions and would always radiate good humour. Their visits had a tonic effect. Mrs. Leverson certainly did me a good turn when she caused them to come to me, and luckily I believe that I was not unuseful to them. Another man for whom she would have me publish was Coleridge Kennard. I did his *Level Crossings* and his *Suhaïl*. I feel about Coleridge Kennard as Harold Nicolson does: it is Kennard's duty to write more.

"Max", too, was of the Leverson circle, as was Aubrey Beardsley, and Somerset Maugham, whose photograph stood on her mantelpiece to the end. "Max" and Maugham must both of them have understood her, have been appreciative of her gifts, and particularly of that sudden wit which was hers, and they must have been kindly to her weaknesses. Poor lady, the sun shone when she was carried to her end, but the air struck cold to our hearts when the furnace doors opened to receive her. She had played her part valiantly and with infinite wit.

I did not publish the first book of the Sitwells. But first

books have always been rather a habit of mine. Thus, I published *The Philosophy of the Marquise* for Mrs. Belloc-Lowndes, and its successor which was anonymous. I published too the first novel by Cecil Roberts, *The Chelsea Cherub*—a story greatly different in mood and technique from the many that have followed it. Some day his admirers should insist on its being made available again. It will have value as indicating his rapid development. I also published the first novel of Sir Philip Gibbs, the first two of Warwick Deeping, and the first two of Edward C. Booth.

Looking back I recall how much of my good fortune came from America. One day in a New York paper I read of a book *Ebony and Ivory*, by Llewelyn Powys. It attracted my attention the more in that Dreiser had written an introduction for it. I sent for it, and was greatly impressed. It did not sell, but it was a fine book, short, but of the true stuff. Thereafter I fell into correspondence with its author, one of an extraordinarily gifted family, Somerset or Dorset. Of Llewelyn's work I also issued *Black Laughter* and *Thirteen Worthies*. For his brother, John Cowper Powys, I published that long and sombre novel, *Ducdame*. Its author wrote me a letter of extraordinary kindness and appreciation. I wish I could quote it here, but alas! I pasted it into a copy of the first American edition (John Cowper Powys lived, lectured and first published in America) and left the book lying on a chest in my sitting-room. It vanished. Such things happen, and they happen the more often when your friends know that you have a rooted objection to lending books . . . for when the book has been "borrowed" you have no clue to the "borrower". Llewelyn Powys wrote to me from America urging me to travel into Dorset to make the acquaintance of a third brother, T. F. Powys. I meant to do so, but did not. Had I done so I might possibly have been the publisher of *Mr. Weston's Good Wine*, which is to me one of the wonder books of its decade. Philip Sainsbury gave me a copy and I read it with an awful joy. Vlaminck, with a touch of Greco, translated into English narrative prose. As it was Dorset in its scene I recommended it to my mother. She told me that she would have given much to forget that she had read it. Wonderful men, those Powys brothers. How is it that America has had so great an attraction for two of them? I saw Llewelyn when I went to New York in 1923. His curly hair and bright eyes seemed to have an irresistible fascination for women, old and young, but the circle in which he moved had too much mutual admiration about it. Deeply I hope that he is now back in Dorset for good and that he will be more careful of his health. His malady has been of service to him in that it sent him to Switzerland (read *Skin for Skin*) and to Lake Elmenteita (read *Ebony and Ivory*), but there are risks one should not take.

XX

SUGGESTIONS FOR AN ANTHOLOGY—A. E. HOUSMAN'S
LAST POEMS

IF there had been space I should have liked to devote one
of these last chapters to some indication of the kind of
anthology I should make if I were to set to work to construct
one for my own pleasure and for the entertainment of my
friends. It would contain much that is amusing, and room
would certainly be found for Dr. Johnson's *On the Death of
Mr. Robert Levet:*

> Condem'd to Hope's delusive mine,
>   As on we toil from day to day,
> By sudden blasts or slow decline
>   Our social comforts drop away. . . .

Hilaire Belloc's work would find a place too:

> Napoleon hoped that all the world would fall beneath his sway.
> He failed in his ambition; and where is he to-day?
> Neither the nations of the East nor the nations of the West
> Have thought the thing Napoleon thought was to their interest.

I do hope that I am correct in my attribution. For years I
have been going about quoting

> How odd
> Of God
> To choose
> The Jews

and, despite the fact that in *The Week End Book* it was given
to W. N. Ewer, I continued in the belief that Belloc was its
author and that the name of Ewer, which I honour for other
things, had been attached to it by editorial slip or printer's
error. Why? Heaven knows. Sheer folly. I have it from

Mr. Ewer's own lips that he wrote it, and, as my meeting
him (at Paul Willert's wedding) was entirely unexpected,
it is something of a coincidence that I had spent part of a
sleepless half-hour of that very morning wondering whether
I ought not to summon up energy to write either to Belloc
whom I know or to Ewer whom I did not know for the truth.
Belloc is not the poem's author and there is an end of that
question in my mind; but he did write the ingenious

> When I am dead
> I hope it may be said,
> "His sins were scarlet,
> But his books were read."

I wish I had published a book by Hilaire Belloc. No, not
his fiction so much—although I like his novels—but such a
book as *The Path to Rome* or one of his histories. I should
have done so if I had had the necessary capital.

Another poem I should include is the anonymous and
miserable *A Portrait* (*After Pope*), which appeared in the
Spectator of April 12, 1913:

> O when a Wife at last begins to see
> Her Husband's not the man he seemed to be,
> Brave, tender, chivalrous, heroic, pure,
> But half a tyrant, half an epicure;
> Sharp-tongued if thwarted in his slightest whim,
> As if the world were all arranged for him;
> In converse commonplace, in habits gross,
> Luxurious, idle, querulous, morose;—
> As this blurred portrait proves itself the Real,
> Effacing, flouting, her adored Ideal,
> What wonder if, in dear defeat of hope,
> She turns an atheist or a misanthrope;
> Arraigns the Powers that mocked her maiden prayer
> And e'en in motherhood finds fresh despair;
> Still, as she feels her own poor life undone,
> Fears to revive the Father in the Son;
> With wistful terror scans the baby face
> And dreads to read th' hereditary grace;
> Marks his sweet eyes, those eyes of heavenly blue,
> Which seem to say, "If false, then nothing's true,"
> Then murmurs, "Gracious God, will *he* be traitor too?"
> ————————
> Who but must weep if such a Wife there be?
> Who would not shudder if his own were she?

I do hope that after this lapse of twenty-one years the author will not resent my quoting it here without permission. It was not signed and indeed the Editor added a footnote complaining that the writer had omitted to enclose his name and appealing to him to make good his omission. I do not think the name did ever appear. I should like even now to know it.

Then I should give space to John Masefield's *The Chief Centurions* and *Philip Sings* and John Davidson's *Ballad of a Nun* and something of William Watson's and Sir Ian Hamilton's *Ballad of Hadji*; and I should do my best to induce A. E. Housman to make an exception for the third time to his rule of never allowing anything from *A Shropshire Lad* to appear in an anthology in order that I might include *Is my team ploughing?* and I should be miserable indeed if I could not induce him to permit the printing of two or three poems from *Last Poems*. Here my trouble would arise from the difficulty of choosing, for I have in my heart that *Last Poems* is even a better book than *A Shropshire Lad*.

Yes, the greatest moment in my life as a publisher was when I opened the sheaf of manuscript that was *Last Poems*, the manuscript that is now in the Fitzwilliam Museum at Cambridge. I will go further and say that no publisher alive has had a greater thrill. *A Shropshire Lad* had been published in 1896; it came into my list in 1898, and there was never a week thereafter and seldom even a day that one person or another—sometimes a bookseller's "collector", sometimes someone whom I met at a party—did not ask me when it would have a successor. American publishers, as I have written, would often open their conversations with such an enquiry. Certainly my own curiosity on the subject was greater than that of anyone else. But I soon learned not to give it rein. At the beginning, when I did ask I used to be told that it was by no means certain that there would ever be a successor, even that it was unlikely. I arrived at a feeling that it was a subject that I had better leave alone. I was able to feel sure in my own mind that if new poems there were

I should hear of them as soon as, if not sooner than, anyone else. In fact, the subject was one to be avoided. And yet I was not able altogether to avoid it, for now and again my travellers would bring me stories to the effect that book-sellers had told them with conviction that a new book of poems was ready for the printer, perhaps, even, in the print-er's hands. I would pass the stories on to Housman without comment. Of course there was no truth in them. At the end of 1920, however, there seemed to be some hope of a new deliverance. Housman must have asked me—verbally and more or less casually, I think—how long it would take to produce such a collection of poems as *A Shropshire Lad* if a manuscript was placed in my hands. And I must have jumped to conclusions, for on January 6, 1921, I received this letter:

TRINITY COLLEGE,

CAMBRIDGE,

5 *Jan.* 1921

MY DEAR RICHARDS,

"My new book" does not exist, and possibly never may. Neither your traveller nor anybody else must be told that it is even contemplated. What I asked you was a question inspired by an unusually bright and sanguine mood, which has not at present been justified. . . .

Yours sincerely

A. E. HOUSMAN

And so the matter rested until—

In April 1922 Housman told me (by letter) that he would be having a book ready for the Autumn.

In the meantime the fact that such a volume was in prepa-ration or contemplation was to be kept a secret.

Later, we came to discuss the matter more particularly, and Housman must have given me some information about the likely length. He writes to me on the 22nd of April, 1922:

MY DEAR RICHARDS,

The end of September, as far as I can judge would suit me quite well for publication. The size of page should at any rate not be more than in the Riccardi edition,[1] if so much. The poems should not be run on, as originally in *A Shropshire Lad*, but each should start on a fresh page.

If, as I rather gather from what you say, printers no longer print from MS., then I should be obliged if you did the typewriting, though it will not be more legible than the hand I write literature in.

The Oxford Dictionary defines *reach* as "to stretch out continuously, to extend", and quotes "how high reacheth the house" (1526) and "the portico reaches along the whole front" (1687). Perhaps your friends are baffled by the subjunctive mood, and think it ought to be *reaches;* but see Psalm 138. 6, "*Though* the Lord *be* high, yet hath he respect unto the lowly".[2]

When you next print *A Shropshire Lad* I want to make 2 alterations.

Yours sincerely

A. E. HOUSMAN

My object being to produce a book as unaffected in appearance as had been its predecessor, I experimented with specimen pages at The Riverside Press in Edinburgh, and on April 30 Housman wrote to me that the page I had sent to him for his approval "looks all right to my untutored eye". That specimen page did not exhibit any of the text of *Last Poems;* it is unlikely—although I cannot be sure of dates—that the manuscript could have reached me so early. However, I do know that printed slips of the whole were in the author's hands in August, if not July.

A few days after I had first heard of the manuscript's existence I was alarmed by a paragraph in *John o' London's Weekly* into believing that someone had got wind of the

---

[1] A reference to the Riccardi limited edition of *A Shropshire Lad* which Philip Lee Warner had induced me, and I had induced Housman, to permit.

[2] This paragraph is evidently in answer to the unnecessary question of an admirer of *A Shropshire Lad* as to the meaning of the line "And straight though reach the track", in the thirty-sixth poem in that book.

book I had in store for the Autumn. I wrote in apprehension to Housman who replied on the 9th of May, 1922: "There is no leakage. . . . The only person besides you whom I have told is sure to be equally trustworthy, and is not in touch with journalists. . . ." His letter also made clear that I had misread *John o' London's Weekly*.

I had but one regret—the book's title. I remonstrated with its author. He replied that there was nothing in that title to make a volume of posthumous poems impossible. The likelihood of such a collection can be estimated by anyone who reads the note with which *Last Poems* is introduced.

I believe that the manuscript came into my hands on a Friday: I took it home with me to the country at Cookham Dean, where Housman had so often been our visitor, and I showed the packet to my wife. It had not been opened. Indeed I refrained from opening it until the evening, when I cut the string, and turned the pages. Then, for the first and last time in my career, without, I am certain, any idea of being theatrical, but with a feeling that here was an occasion, *the* occasion of my life, I began to read the poems aloud. Their effect on me, and I think on my hearers, was instantaneous. I cannot, I will not, attempt to describe it. As each poem was read and returned to the envelope I became encompassed by the sad, haunting, tragic air that the book has and I felt uplifted into ecstasy by its beauty. . . .

The packet went back to St. Martin's Street; the poems were typewritten by my secretary, Miss Hemmerde; on September 11 a printing order for four thousand copies was sent to The Riverside Press, and on October 19 the book was published. The number of copies in the first edition was decided upon with reference to the number that the "trade" had ordered. I wanted to make certain that everyone who was sufficiently intelligent could get one on the day of publication. There was no attempt to create an artificial value for the copies of that first edition. On the contrary in fact. My first intention was to print five thousand. The booksellers discouraged me. Housman had suggested ten thousand. At the end of the year the number printed had reached twenty-one thousand.

No special edition, "numbered and signed by the author", or anything of that kind, was ever even contemplated. It was suggested to me by the trade that some such issue would be very profitable. I knew my author. I should have thought it unsuitable in any case, but I was sure that the very idea of a limited edition would annoy him and that he would have nothing whatever to do with it. The appearance of the book was not heralded by any fanfare of trumpets; indeed the first announcement to the "trade" and to the public was made on September 21, 1922, in my regular advertisement in the *Times Literary Supplement*. It was modestly and briefly worded:

> Early in October I shall publish a new book by A. E. Housman. It will be entitled "Last Poems" (5/–).

Two days after the appearance of *Last Poems* I reached my fiftieth birthday. In celebration of the two close events I induced the author to come to London and he, my wife and I dined at the Carlton Restaurant. The menu bore no special relation to the occasion, but Housman is himself so learned and famous a gourmet[1] that I do not try when I order a meal for him to give him something that he might not have thought of ordering for himself. I forget the dishes on this occasion, however, save that they include a saddle of hare done in a manner at which at that time Monsieur Escoffier's successor excelled.

I have sat even recently at the tables of educated people and have heard poetry mentioned and have made my own contribution to the conversation by speaking of A. E. Housman and of *A Shropshire Lad* and *Last Poems*, and have been asked to repeat the names since they were fresh to my hearers. How can such things be?

[1] Did not Frédéric of the Tour d'Argent invent the *barbue a la Housman* in his honour?

XXI

THE TWO *KAI LUNGS* – BRUCE BAIRNSFATHER – *THE RAGGED TROUSERED PHILANTHROPISTS*–NEVILLE CARDUS–*THE SANDS OF PLEASURE*–ALLAN MONKHOUSE–AU REVOIR

THE manuscript of *The Wallet of Kai Lung* arrived out of the blue in July 1899. I was living then at Bisham Park Farm, a house that I had taken for six months. To it came a number of my literary friends, and among them E. V. Lucas, who was, as I have written, at that time my reader. On one such visit he brought with him the Ernest Bramah manuscript. Elsewhere[1] I have said that I cannot recall whether I looked at it first and then sent it to him for his opinion, or whether he looked at it and brought it to Bisham for my support, but I do remember that it was a careful typescript, sewn bookwise into a brown-paper wrapper, and that every manuscript of Ernest Bramah's that I have since seen has looked exactly like it. At that time the book was made up of only three tales, *The Transmutation of Ling* (much later to be published separately with illustration-decorations by Ilbery Lynch, a young artist whom Robert Ross had discovered and had sent to me) and the stories of Yung Chang and Kin Yen; presumably the rest of the book was added before the manuscript went to the printer. The first edition consisted of a thousand copies, in addition to which five hundred were printed for a special Colonial Edition; and a little later, old Dana Estes of Boston, attracted more by F. R. Kimborough's cover-design than by the contents, had me print for him an edition of seven hundred and fifty copies. These printings satisfied the

[1] My introduction to the edition of *The Wallet* published in 1923.

demand, I believe, for some seven years. The Kimborough design, by the way, was Japanese and not Chinese, an error that makes me hot under the collar when I think of it. The little design that appears on the cover of the 1923 edition is by Lynch.

Before the 1923 reprint appeared with my name on the title-page in the double capacity of publisher and introducer, Methuen's, moved no doubt by Lucas's belief in the book's quality, issued it in one of their cheap libraries. But no great number of people became its admirers. And that was odd, for the right men knew and talked of it—Sir Arthur Quiller Couch (who had read it in manuscript for Cassell before I had seen it myself and had urged it for acceptance), Hilaire Belloc, J. C. Squire and A. B. Walkley. Smith, Elder were the first publishers to refuse it; Chatto followed and then Cassell; William Heinemann (of all men!) saw nothing in it; and it went to Constable and to Lawrence and Bullen (where it cannot have fallen under the eye of A. H. Bullen) and Macmillan and Fisher Unwin (but not surely in Edward Garnett's day!). In America, at the time of the appearance of its successor, *Kai Lung's Golden Hours*, I was able to get it on to George Doran's list. Eugene Saxton came over to see what he could find for Doran and fell for Kai Lung with that leisurely precipitation which is one of his charms. Doran brought out the two Kai Lung books in a rather large format of their own choosing, in a set of two volumes, and had a considerable success with it.

And Ernest Bramah himself? I found him one of the kindest and the most amiable of men. And extraordinarily appreciative of anything I could do on his behalf. For instance, I never lost faith in *The Wallet* and, discussing its fate, he wrote: "In the meanwhile, with his interest in Kai Lung unshaken, in spite of the unsatisfactory result of that wandering minstrel's first appearance, Mr. Richards never ceased to press me for a successor. On an average he wrote to me twice a year on the subject. But it was not until last year [1921] that I began to see before me something like

273

sufficient material for a second volume." Bramah is small and—may I say?—he does not look ferocious; I believe him to be uncarnivorous, and indeed I think that he eschews the pleasures of the table—whether from compulsion or inclination I cannot say. When in 1912 I published my own first novel, *Caviare*, he delighted me with a letter in its praise:

DEAR MR. RICHARDS,

Permit me to add my tribute of congratulation to the stream.

I got your book (I don't have to do with a library) the other day and without saying in the language of the facile reviewer that I found it literally impossible to tear myself away until the last page was reached, I certainly found it too easy to neglect other things once I had got into it. At first, I confess, the epicureanism of your amiable Charles put me off a little ("I shall have steak-and-kidney pudding" fits me) but—if criticism is not an impertinence— I found the pages become better and better, and the last half of the book—all the American portion and the end— is quite irresistible. The climax of Ch. IX Book II struck me as one of the drollest and happiest touches I have ever roared over. The literary success being assured I will wish you a big financial one also; I think it ought to come off.

Yours sincerely

ERNEST B. SMITH

There is one thing that I think few Bramah admirers know. On 21 February 1931 at 2.30 the Men Students of the Old Vic Shakespeare Company presented *Kai Lung's Golden Hours*, "a Chinese Comedy, adapted for the stage by Allan D. Mainds, A.R.S.A." The programme is before me, as is Miss Lilian Baylis's card of invitation to the Old Vic, an announcement thereon indicating that there would be a "silver collection in aid of Vic and Wells building debts."

In sending me the invitation Bramah refers to my "continuous interest in Kai Lung" and expresses a doubt as to whether that interest would tempt me over Waterloo Bridge. Of course it did! But I prefer my Kai Lung within the pages of a book.

In the Winter of 1915-1916 my then manager, George Harrison Wiggins, who later went for a soldier and obtained a commission, was at his mother's house. His was a military family in those days: he had four brothers, all of them in the army; a fifth, a sailor, had given his life to his country. One of the soldiers had sent to his mother a little paper-covered book, *Fragments from France*, and Wiggins, finding it on his mother's table, and never having seen or heard of it or its author before, thought it would amuse me. Nor had I ever seen it. It did amuse me immensely, and I was as much interested in the legends beneath the pictures as in the pictures themselves. This Bairnsfather must be a clever fellow. Slowly it came into my head that the man who could have such ideas and could invent such legends could write a book, ought to write a book. So I wrote to him, either care of the Editor of the *Bystander*, in which the pictures originally appeared and in which his work was still appearing, or care of the War Office. My letter was brief. Of course, I said, I had no idea where he was or what he was doing, but if he was in Great Britain I would keep any appointment he cared to give me, and if he was abroad then I would come as near to the actual position as the military regulations would allow. . . . After a few days I received a letter from the Isle of Wight where, it appeared, he was enjoying a brief period of convalescence and was also busy training young troops. I could come down to see him if I chose. Of course I chose.

It was a particularly bleak, cold and unpleasant day when I arrived at the Solent shore; "the snow lay all about" and there was fog; it was doubtful if a boat would cross. There was a certain risk. However, the boat did cross and I set

my foot on the Isle for the first time, found Captain Bruce
Bairnsfather, trudged with him through the snow from the
pier into the town and found an inn where we could talk
without being frozen and without being interrupted. I set
forth my ideas. Bairnsfather was to write a book, a book
about the Front in which the letter press would have an
equal importance with the illustrations. There were to be
lots of illustrations, some full pages, some in the text. All
were to be new. He liked the idea. Yes, he would try his
hand at it. He saw no reason why he should not succeed.
Myself, I was sure there was no reason. Yes, he had no objection to entering into an agreement on the spot. One was
forthwith drawn up and signed. It provided for the payment of a hundred pounds on account of a royalty that
began at ten per cent. We drank to the success of our project, and we walked together down to the pier and Bairnsfather returned to his duty.

In the meantime the fog had thickened. The Solent on
such a night and in time of war was no water on which to
venture without precaution. It was very doubtful if the boat
would make the passage. It still snowed. A tiny handful of
passengers. One of them stood about discussing books with
a friend who had come to see him off. I "tumbled" to the
fact that he was one of W. H. Smith and Son's visiting
superintendents and that he was being seen off by a local
manager. When at length the boat did put out into the
murk I fell into conversation with him, told him who I was,
and we sat in the tiny saloon and talked about the state of
the book trade. No, he had not come across *Fragments from
France* in the course of his inspections. I told him about it
and of the book for which I had arranged and of my great
hopes for its success. He said he would make enquiries. And
not only did he make that promise but he kept it, writing
to tell me that observation at various stalls convinced him
that I was on a winner.

But there were difficulties to overcome. Naturally Bairnsfather told the *Bystander* people of his intention and the

Bystander people vigorously protested. By now Bairnsfather had become very much more of a property than I had realised; they had discovered him; they thought they should have a monopoly of his work, claimed in fact that by agreement they had secured such a monopoly. We—the *Bystander* people and I—had meetings. Bairnsfather, of course, was not free to attend them, nor did he in the circumstances wish to take any strong place on either side. He did not want to quarrel with people who had done so much to make him a success; on the other hand, he had signed an agreement with me. . . . He would do what was right. There were all the makings of a pretty lawsuit. Ultimately, however, the *Bystander* people came to realise that as a publisher wishing to produce a book I had not set out to snatch their darling from them, that indeed my book should have the effect of sending people to their paper, that the more successful the book was, the more valuable would their artist become. And so it was left. They withdrew their objections and I was free to have my book. And Bairnsfather set to work and delivered it punctually and in full measure.

Then I began to discover how promising was the venture. People who had pooh-poohed it and said that the public would be sick of the Bairnsfather type of humour long before I could produce his book began to be quite enthusiastic about my chances—but still they laughed at me when I said that I intended to produce an edition of at least fifty thousand copies. They said it was absurd to print such a number of a book by an unknown author (unknown in the *book*-shops, that is to say) and so on. It was not, in those days of shortage and restriction, so very easy to get the paper on which to print. However, that was achieved. I was, owing to the fact that my bank's manager, J. D. Wightman of the Westminster Bank—that same man who had believed in *Limehouse Nights*—believed in the book, able to pay cash for the large quantity that I required—and money talks.

Of course there was some risk of our all proving too optimistic. In the late Autumn of 1916 to test the matter and to distract my mind—for I had a couple of months before lost my eldest son, Gerard, in very unhappy circumstances—I set out with my wife on a tour in the North of England and in Scotland. I wanted—without interfering with my traveller, Ernest Dracott—to see for myself what the booksellers thought about the prospects of *Bullets and Billets*—the title we had chosen for the Bairnsfather—and about trade in general. We visited Cambridge, Peterborough, Leeds, York, Edinburgh, Glasgow, Manchester and Birmingham. At Edinburgh we found on arrival at the Caledonian Station that we had to go through a sieve of enquiry. Strangers had to explain their wish to travel in Scotland before being allowed to proceed, and the inquisition was perhaps a little more difficult in our case as my wife had been born Hungarian. It was a strange journey. We travelled much in the late hours of the day; the windows of the railway carriages were all obscured so that no light might escape to betray the passage of a train, and the stations were inconveniently dark. Altogether conditions were miserable and sombre in hue but, now and again, when our arrival at a station coincided with the presence of a troop train, fraught with both humour and tragedy. The booksellers, however, were encouraging. *Bullets and Billets*, about to appear, would be a success. I was amused in the case of one call I paid —on Richard Jackson Ltd. of Leeds. My wife, for want of something better to do, followed me into the shop and stayed, as if a customer, examining the various objects of art disposed in one of its rooms,—for Jackson was an art dealer as well as a bookseller. . . . Mr. Jackson was amiability itself to me and we talked for a long time. He would not however come down to real business. His buyer was away; he really didn't know at the moment much about that side of the work. Ultimately I left him. Picking up my wife as I went through to the street, I found that she had fallen victim to the salesman's wiles and had bought old ivory to a value which would certainly much exceed the total of Jackson's quarterly account! At Birmingham I received not only the welcome of that old-world book-man Charles Linnell, but a letter from London enclosing one from Frank Dodd in America, saying that he had been reading and enjoying the proofs of my third novel, *Bittersweet,* for which Houghton, Mifflin had not cared to make an offer owing to the fact that its contents were likely to shock the Bostonian moral conscience, and that he would like to publish it. Such a communication always makes grateful reading to an author, and I was delighted with what Dodd had to say. To this date I believe he maintains that had it not been that the book was published just as the United States went into War, it would have been a "best-seller". I am not at all sure that that view is not correct.

Bullets and Billets appeared and was all the success I hoped for. As I remember it, we practically sold out the first edition in the week of publication. I made a lot of money. I needed it. It had all been very simple. Rather like winning the Irish Sweep. That success, that money, came from the chance that one of her soldier sons sent the older Mrs. Wiggins a copy of *Fragments from France,* that it happened to be on her table when my George Harrison Wiggins visited her, and that he was sufficiently amused by it to take the trouble to bring it up from Kingston to show me, although, I think I am right in saying, he had no idea in his mind that I should see in it the possibilities of a book.

The more people a publisher knows, the more circles in which he mixes freely, and specially the more friends he has, the greater will be his chance of finding the books that will do him good, both commercially as a publisher and, from the point of view of his reputation, as a judge of what is good. And good books and successful books have a snowball effect. Once a publisher has any reputation at all, books, or ideas for books, will come to him from all quarters, from the most unexpected quarters. It was from a friend that I heard of and ultimately published Edward Ingram Watkin's *The Philosophy of Mysticism*; it was from the happy fact that my wife is Hungarian that came my publication of several books of Hungary, its history and its post-war problems; it was from a friend that I heard of that mountainous manuscript, *The Ragged Trousered Philanthropists*. It happened in this way: my secretary, Miss Hemmerde, had a cousin, Miss Jessie Pope. Miss Pope, as will be seen by anyone who looks through the index to *Punch*, was one of that paper's most industrious, and ingenious, contributors. I published several of her books: *The Shy Age*, a light study of adolescence; two books of War Poems and *Hits and Misses*. One day I heard that Miss Pope had learned from a neighbour that her children's nurse, knowing that Miss Pope was a writer of books, had confessed that her own father had written one—well, not exactly a book since it wasn't in print, but a story in the sense that it was a novel, the novel of his own life that wanted to get itself into print and to be a book. Politeness and curiosity made Miss Pope promise to read the manuscript, and it was brought to her. It *was* a manuscript! It must have been as long as *A Traveller at Forty* in its original form. Miss Pope told me of it. "Bring it along," I said: "Have you read it?" Miss Pope had read it. She thought it was ever and ever so much too long; full of repetition. It would have to be cut down. Ultimately she did bring it along. "I'll publish this", I told her, after examination, "if you will cut it down, say, to a hundred thousand words." She discussed the matter with its owner. She told her, what she and I must have sincerely believed, that its chances of success were very slight. But the opportunity of publication appealed to Miss Tressall—I will call her so for her father had taken "Robert Tressall" as his pen-name. The book was damnably subversive, but it was extraordinarily real, and rather than let it go I was quite willing to drop a few score of pounds on it. The date of publication was April 23, 1914.

Then Maynard Dominick appeared on the scene from

New York. Dominick had a nose. He read the subversive story, and, in spite of the fact that the conditions with which it dealt were English and had not even a superficial likeness to the conditions then obtaining in America, he arranged to publish it.

The book came out in London and in its first three months it sold in England one thousand seven hundred and fifty-two copies; it sold fourteen hundred copies to the Colonies apart from Canada, where the sale amounted to two hundred and fifty. Then it died. In America it had the same fate.

There came the War. A year or two later my friend, Clifford, was in Glasgow. Business brought him into connection with the Reformers' Bookstall. Its manager, Mr. Hardie, mentioned *The Ragged Trousered Philanthropists.* "Now there's a book of which I could sell any number you like." Clifford reported the remark to me and, knowing that my Mr. Dracott, in the course of his journey, would arrive at Glasgow, I said nothing and awaited events. Mr. Dracott sent me an order for a very large number of copies if only the book could be done at a lower price. So I set Miss Pope to work. We reduced what had already been cut down from, say, a million words to about sixty thousand, and a cheap edition duly appeared and sold in scores of thousands at the various branches of the Reformers' Bookstall and in such establishments as Henderson's Bomb Shop in the Charing Cross Road. Did I do harm by spreading such a book broadcast? I do not think so. It was a singularly sincere and moving story; it put a point of view very clearly and definitely before its readers; it was the truth as Robert Tressall saw it. If one wishes now to read it let him do his best to procure a copy of its first issue. The *Daily Herald* (before the Odhams-Elias regime) assisted its sale to the best of its ability. In fact a book which, on its first appearance and for several years after, had hardly done more than pay the expenses of its production and its share of establishment charges, became suddenly a great success and perhaps did something to alter the nation's history. Ordinary bookshops sold it scarcely at all, and in America there was no parallel revival.

I have told how the manuscript of *Limehouse Nights* remained for long on the shelf behind my desk. A like fate awaited a later book—Neville Cardus's *A Cricketer's Book*. He sent it to me in rather a dishevelled state in 1922. It was one of those offers that do not immediately attract the publisher. The packet was made up of newspaper cuttings and why, I asked myself, should I be expected to interest myself in a book which was to be made up of articles that had appeared in a daily paper, even though that daily paper was the *Manchester Guardian?* However, I had published P. F. Warner's *Cricket Reminiscences*, and I knew that Cricket had some devotees who read books even though their number was not as great as one would expect; and anyhow, whatever came out of the *Guardian* stable was worth backing on general principles. After a time, therefore, I brought myself down to a consideration of Neville Cardus's proposal, and, although I knew nothing about Cricket, and although the names of its most celebrated players were unknown to me, I said I would publish. However, I would have nothing to do with a cheap publication. Cardus had thought of a shilling or half a crown. I am by no means sure he was not right. The price I set on *A Cricketer's Book* was six shillings; thereafter I gave the same price to *Days in the Sun* and *The Summer Game*.

Cricketers do not frequent bookshops, I fancy, and neither Cardus nor I made a fortune. Nevertheless I was proud of my share in the production of these three books. Let me add that Neville Cardus, my friend, is a most difficult author to handle. In spite of the fact that the first proposal came from him—the result, I suppose, of some friend's urging—he will not believe that his stuff is worth reprinting, and the getting of a second and a third book out of him was as difficult as anything I have ever experienced. . . . But what a writer! I went to Manchester once and ordered a luncheon in his honour. *Homard à l'Armoricaine* figured in it. He told me that he did not, generally, care for eating, but that he did care for lobster. I do not think he thought better of me for offering him such a meal. I like him none the less. An austere, sensitive figure.

The importance of the *Manchester Guardian* in London's intellectual life was not, I fancy, nearly as marked in the 'nineties as it became with the growing years of the new century. In W. T. Stead's office, as I remember it, we knew of its existence and thought of it with respect, but I cannot remember either W. T. S. or anyone connected with him adopting the attitude that it was a paper one could not afford to miss. "What Manchester thinks to-day England will think to-morrow" was a phrase constantly on the lips of men of affairs, but it was used rather in connection with politics than with the intellectual tendencies of the time. No C. B. Cochran of those last decades had discovered the importance of Manchester's theatrical opinion. When I broke into publishing in 1897 the *Manchester Guardian* was one of the provincial papers in which one had to advertise if one advertised at all seriously, but I doubt if it counted as more important than half a dozen other papers published north of Oxford. I myself first became a *Guardian* addict when I discovered Masefield in its pages and after a time I did not allow a day to pass without reading its London letter and looking to see what new discovery had been made on the page on which most of *A Tarpaulin Muster* appeared.

In 1897 too I found out for myself how many books were sold in Manchester. J. D. Hughes, of Sherratt and Hughes, and others showed me. And when in 1905 I had to give up my offices in Leicester Square and attempt to restore my shattered fortunes at 7 Carlton Street off the lower end of Regent Street—a curious old corner which is now only half as attractive as it was when Miss Hester Frood painted it for me—I had a Manchester man, Filson Young, as my first reader. He had the *Guardian* in his blood, although more

than a year before he had come to London at Alfred Harmsworth's invitation to edit that famous centre page of the
Daily Mail. Filson Young not only read for me but he wrote
books for my list, and as they were good books they helped
those early Carlton Street lists of mine greatly. The first,
The Sands of Pleasure, was a novel; the first novel of its kind
to appear in England. It was so successful that I saw myself
regaining my old position and dared to launch out into unusual advertisement. Indeed I took a whole top half-page
to advertise its qualities in the *Standard*, the morning paper
which C. Arthur Pearson was to see fade away beneath him.
It was hardly a new thing for me to do, however, for in 1903
I had taken the whole of the front page of the *Daily Mail* to
proclaim the excellence of my authors' wares. Another thing
assisted *The Sands of Pleasure* to success: the kindness and
interest of the booksellers. But there was one man who
would not sell it—David Knox of John Smith and Son of
Glasgow. His interest in me made him read in it, and when
he had got well into the Paris chapters he set to work to burn
it. It must have been a laborious process but he persisted.
And, having succeeded in destroying the accursed thing to
the last page (he sat down and gave me his opinion of me
and my publication. A year or two before he and I had provisionally arranged to spend a few days together in Paris. He
had never been abroad and he felt that I should be a good
courier. Dear fellow, he told me that he knelt down at the
side of his bed that night and thanked God that he had been
spared a visit to so scarlet a city! Our friendship outlived
the incident.

When *The Sands of Pleasure* was well away and climbing
into big figures Filson Young would have it that I should
go to Manchester under the plea that I could see its booksellers—always a pleasant job—and that I should attend a
dinner that he was proposing to give to his old *Guardian*
colleagues. Then, but not till then, I became aware of the
intellect and the literary talent that C. P. Scott had at his
disposal. All the same, I forget what we talked of. Perhaps

that was the chef's fault: the Midland Grand Hotel did its best and readers of the novel whose success the dinner was to celebrate would recognise in the names of its dishes the names of the characters.

I did so well with *The Sands of Pleasure* that I commissioned its author to embark on a serious attempt to rediscover and retell the story of Columbus, a biography whose sea subject peculiarly fitted it to his pen. There are books that do not get their deserts. *Christopher Columbus and the New World of his Discovery* is, I think, one of them. And no critic has ever done justice to Filson Young as a writer of English.

At that agreeable banquet Allan Monkhouse was one of the guests. How much Manchester owes to Monkhouse for his critical perception, the steadiness and sobriety of his literary judgments, through these many years of violent change and revolt! I had an ambition—to induce Monkhouse to write, not exactly his biography and assuredly not his reminiscences, but, in a sense, his *apologia*, a declaration of his faith seen in terms of his own experience. Reared in commerce, he had, I believe, drifted into the practice and criticism of literature and into literary journalism. Always he brought his subjects to the bar of no sectarian or provincial or fashionable prejudice but to that of the truth in which he believed. Such a book, as I saw it, might have been an explanation of Manchester life and of the Manchester point of view, of all provincial life and thought indeed, as contrasted with those of the centre. Monkhouse through his years has resisted the temptation to bring his wares to the capital. There must be a policy, a philosophy, behind his persistent preference for the North.

And now I come to the end of my allotted tale of words. So much unsaid; so much undone. A brave business, publishing, but often a bitter one. Success comes now and again so easily and so little deserved; in how many cases does it seem to be withheld until too late from the very books which deserve it most? Not that I can complain on that score. I have had as many successes as are good for me; I have made as many discoveries as I could have hoped for even in my most sanguine eighteen-ninety mood. There are still intelligent people who believe that publishers can forecast the success of a book, and that, by some cunning of their own, they can avoid losses on any book. Then should we of the trade all be millionaires! It is now more difficult to judge beforehand than ever it was, and, now more than ever, even when a book has seemed to have scored a success, it brings to its author but a trumpery wage. Personally, I see danger in the herd instinct as applied to literary supply and demand. Lined up by book societies, martialled by literary journalists, brought to obedience by excessive advertisement, the members of the reading public have now all to read the same books in the same seasons or they will be out of the fashion, they will miss their conversational cues. . . . There are more books than there ever were; the skill with which they are written is greatly superior to that shown in the books of a generation or so ago; the number of readers has immeasurably increased. And yet fewer authors are being kept pleasantly alive by the labour of their pens. In fact the tendency is for the herd instinct to make a few writers greatly popular and to leave the greater number to neglect. Let me hope that this is but a phase. . . .

THE END

ILLUSTRATIONS

THE AUTHOR IN 1909
From a pencil drawing by Henry Lamb

290

GRANT ALLEN
From a photograph

THOMAS RICHARDS, THE YOUNGER, WITH FRANKLIN RICHARDS:
the Author's Grandfather and Father

292

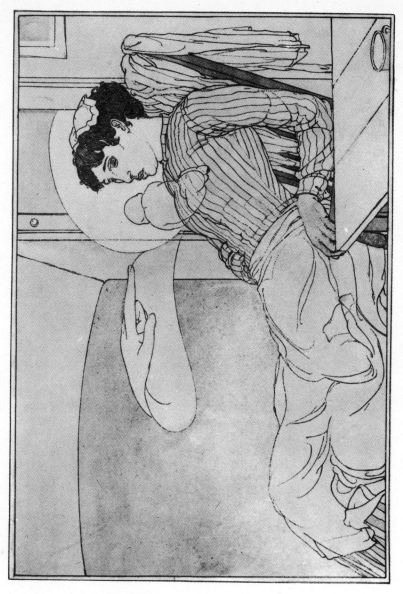

THE ANNUNCIATION OF ESTHER WATERS
From an unpublished water colour drawing by Ilbery Lynch

THOMAS HARDY IN THE 'NINETIES
From a photograph

BERNARD SHAW
From a photograph by Frederick H. Evans

19th June 1898.

Until the end of October Mr. and Mrs. Bernard Shaw's address will be Pitfold, Haslemere, Surrey. Telegraph office: Shottermill. Railway station: Haslemere (Waterloo line), 1½ miles. Permanent London addresses as usual: Mrs. Shaw at 10 Adelphi Terrace, W.C.; and Mr. Shaw at 29 Fitzroy Square, W. (Telegrams: "Socialist, London.")

My wife has been having _such_ a delightful honeymoon! First my foot had to be nursed; and the day before yesterday, just as it was getting pretty well, I fell downstairs & broke my left arm close to the wrist. I am afraid this will make a hopeless mess of the Wagner book. I had got to work fiercely again when it occurred, and had actually carried the exposition to within one act of the end of The Ring; but in my present smashed condition I daren't attempt to work against time. I am very sorry, as I had hoped to complete the MS next week.

A BERNARD SHAW *postcard, much enlarged*

296

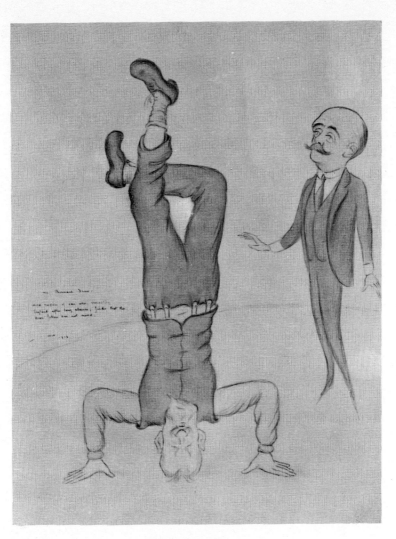

Mr. Bernard Shaw
Mild surprise of one who, revisiting England after long absence, finds that the dear fellow has not moved.
Max

1913

January 31, 1912
Cap Martin

THEODORE DREISER, GRANT RICHARDS AND SIR HUGH LANE
on the Riviera, 1912

298

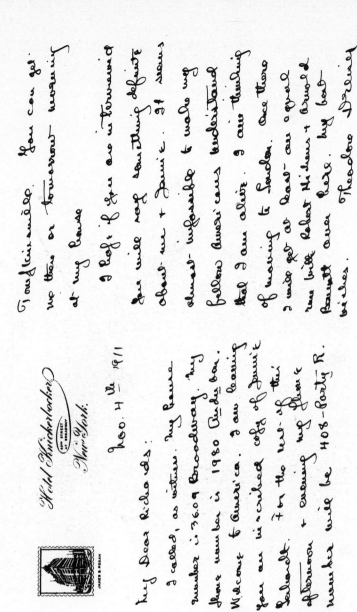

Facsimile of DREISER LETTER, *much reduced*

299

ARNOLD BENNETT
By Sir William Orpen
"Orp's Little Joke"

300

MAX BEERBOHM, 1905
From a painting by William Nicholson

301

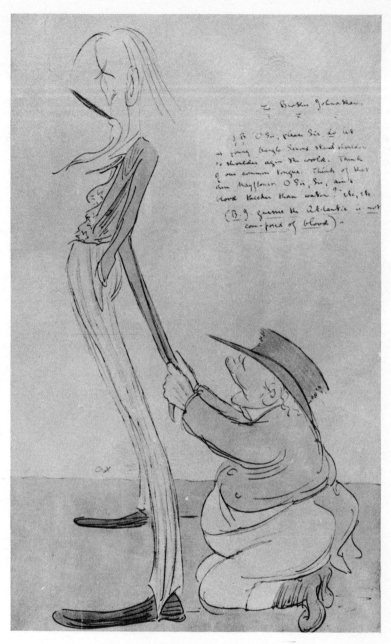

THE SECOND CHILDHOOD OF JOHN BULL
by Max Beerbohm, 1901
To Brother Jonathan
*J. B. "O Sir, please Sir, do let us young Hanglo-Saxons stand shoulder
to shoulder agin the world. Think of our common tongue. Think
of that there Mayflower. O Sir, Sir, ain't blood thicker than water?"
etc., etc.*
(B. J. guesses the At-lantic is not com-posed of blood.)

THOMAS BURKE

RONALD FIRBANK
From a photograph

ERNEST BRAMAH
From a photograph

7 CARLTON STREET, REGENT STREET
From a sepia painting by Hester Frood

FRANK NORRIS

To Grant Richards Eagre from F. P. Dunne June 1899

FINLEY PETER DUNNE

Caricature of KING EDWARD VII *by Max Beerbohm*

INDEX

INDEX

INDEX

INDEX

Hamilton, Adams and Co., 4
Hanson, Edward, 35
Hardy, Thomas, 53, 207
Harmsworth, Alfred (Lord North-cliffe), 46, 56, 103, 116, 215
Harper and Brothers, 174, 177-80, 203
Harris, Sir Augustus, 31, 165
Harris, Frank, 1, 89, 165-6, 173
Hartrick, A. S., 31
Harvey, Len, 124
Haynes, E. S. P., xiii, 245
"Hearsay, Terence", see A. E. Housman
Heinemann, William, 10, 12, 30, 33, 35, 37, 67, 88, 104, 173, 213, 229, 240, 245, 257, 273
Helmet of Navarre, The, 178
Henley, W. E., 34, 65, 165, 210, 214
Henry and Co., see J. T. Grein
Heron-Allen, E., 48
Herrnskretchen, 7
Heslewood, Tom, 84
Hichens, Robert, 176
Hill, Raven, 31
Hind, Lewis, 9, 10, 207
Historical Guides, The Grant Allen, 12, 39, 104
Hobbes, John Oliver, 9
Hogarth Club, 9
Hogg, Mr., see Samuel French
Holdsworth, Annie, 104
Holiday and Other Poems, 219
Holt, Elliot, 127
Holt, Henry, 88, 98
Hooligan Nights, 123
Hope, Anthony, 76
Hospital Sketches, 105
Houghton Mifflin Company, 279
Housman, A. E., 29, 86-7, 91 *et seq.*, 124, 201, 228, 267-71
Housman, Clemence, 91
Housman, Laurence, 72, 91, 103, 217
Howells, W. D., 171
Hudson, Miss A. H., 3
Hudson, Frederic, 114
Hughes, J. D., 283
Huneker, James, 173
Hunt, Violet, 212
Huxley, Professor, 12
Hyde, William, 96, 98
Hydriotaphia, 36

Ibsen, Hendrik, 85, 125, 131
Idylls of the Poor, 202

Illumination, 9
Impressions and Opinions, 34, 56
In Court and Kampong, 33, 40
Isaacs, I. H. S., *see* Temple Scott
Island of Doctor Moreau, The, 213
Iwan-Müller, E. B., 214, 216

Jacobi, C. T., 32, 35-6
Jackson, Richard, 278
Janvier, Thomas A., 145
Jennie Gerhardt, 171, 175, 189, 191, 203, 204
Jepson, Edgar, 19
Jerrard, T. W., 4
Jésus-la-Caille, 197
John, Augustus, 106, 252, 257
Johnson, Lionel, 9, 85
Johnson, R. Brimley, 73
Johnson, Dr. Samuel, 265
Jones, Sir Henry Arthur, 148, 189
Jones, Kennedy, 119
Joubert, 151
Jude the Obscure, 9

Kai Lung's Golden Hours, 273
Keats, John, 22 *et seq.*, 105
Kelmscott Press, The, 30-2, 128
Kennard, Sir Coleridge, 258, 262
Kennerley, Mitchell, 96, 97, 98, 121
Kernahan, Coulson, 111
Kimborough, F. R., 272
King, George, 115
Kipling, Rudyard, 54, 85, 170
Kirk, Eve, 3
Knopf, Alfred, 261
Knox, David, 62-3, 284
Kruger, Paul, 151

Lambert, George, 110
Lankester, Professor Ray, 12
Lane, Sir Hugh, 106, 107, 183, 202
Lane, John, 4-5, 9, 12, 19 *et seq.*, 30, 35, 59, 67, 218, 222
Lang, Andrew, 89, 207
Lanier, H. W., 169
Lanier, Sidney, 169
Last Poems, 92, 267
Latour, Fantin, 108
Laurie, T. Werner, 186
Lawrence and Bullen, 82, 273
Lawrence, D. H., 237
Leaf, Walter, 36, 217
Leather, Robinson K., 78
Lee, Vernon, 103
Lee-Hamilton, Eugene, 104

314

INDEX

INDEX

316

INDEX

INDEX

INDEX